"The most important book on the psychology of women in this century. Reading this book is both a personal and intellectual journey. *Loving to Survive* is an illumination both of abused women and every woman's experience."
— June Peters*
Author of *The Phoenix Program*

"*Loving to Survive* may be the most controversial— and most important—book written during the past two decades. In asserting their theory, the authors ask readers to re-consider virtually all that has been deemed 'true' about relationships between men and women. Such a dramatic paradigm shift will challenge most readers. Whether the reader likes or dislikes this book, one thing seems certain: it will generate dialogue that will surely engage people both intellectually and emotionally."
— Donna M. Stringer
President, Executive Diversity Services, Inc.

Feminist Crosscurrents
EDITED BY Kathleen Barry

American Feminism: A Contemporary History
Ginette Castro
TRANSLATED FROM THE FRENCH BY
Elizabeth Loverde-Bagwell

Lesbian Texts and Contexts: Radical Revisions
EDITED BY Karla Jay and Joanne Glasgow

*Fraternity Gang Rape: Sex, Brotherhood,
and Privilege on Campus*
Peggy Reeves Sanday

Sexuality and War: Literary Masks of the Middle East
Evelyne Accad

Law, Gender, and Injustice: A Legal History of U.S. Women
Joan Hoff

*Loving to Survive: Sexual Terror, Men's Violence,
and Women's Lives*
Dee L. R. Graham with Edna I. Rawlings and Roberta K. Rigsby

Loving to Survive

Sexual Terror, Men's Violence, and Women's Lives

Dee L. R. Graham

with Edna I. Rawlings and
Roberta K. Rigsby

New York University Press

New York and London

New York University Press
New York and London

Copyright © 1994 by New York University

Library of Congress Cataloging-in-Publication Data
Graham, Dee L. R., 1948–
Loving to survive : sexual terror, men's violence, and women's
lives / Dee L.R. Graham with Edna I. Rawlings and Roberta K. Rigsby.
p. cm.—(Feminist crosscurrents)
Includes bibliographical references and index.
ISBN 0-8147-3058-2:—ISBN 0-8147-3059-0 (pbk.) :
1. Women—Crimes against—United States. 2. Abusive men—United
States. 3. Women—United States—Psychology. I. Rawlings, Edna I.
II. Rigsby, Roberta K. III. Title. IV. Series.
HV6250.4.W65G73 1994
362.82'92'0973—dc20
94-3057
CIP

New York University Press books are printed on acid-free paper,
and their binding materials are chosen for strength and durability.

Manufactured in the United States of America

10   9   8   7   6   5   4   3   2   1

Book design by Kathleen Szawiola

This book is lovingly dedicated to
the late Mrs. Georgia Faye Smith Fought
and to the late Ruth McCrary Dew.

Contents

Tables

Foreword

The current women's movement of the 1990s is more vigorous than ever. But despite all of its creative energy and political determination, for the last twenty years the "prophets of doom" in the media have continually proclaimed it dead while academicians designate our demise in terms such as *postfeminism*. Yet feminism has expanded to encompass the global dimensions of patriarchal oppression with theories and actions that reveal a sharpened politics and deeper analysis of sex class conditions. The racial, cultural, and national diversities among women make the work of international feminism all the more profound as it carves out and celebrates that which women share in common and politically unifies us against patriarchal domination.

Since the late 1960s, the women's movement has proven itself to be the most viable social movement of those years and the 1970s, the most urgently necessary of the 1980s, and now is one of our strongest hopes in the 1990s. Feminism has refused the conservative and Fundamentalist efforts to reduce women to their reproductive functions and has contested the liberal idea of women as pornographic sexual objects. Feminist scholarship, at its best, is charting its own course and emerging from women's lives to define theory and shape research around the globe.

The Feminist Crosscurrents Series is committed to emphasizing the critical links between scholarly research and theory and feminist politics and practice. This series recognizes that radicalism is critical to any movement of feminist thought and that women's oppression constitutes a class condition. We are concerned with theory and analysis that enlightens research and activism on how sex, class, gender stratification, and race interface in the lives of women; yet, we do not invalidate white, middle-class women's experience by reducing it, as many have tried, to "privileged" or "bourgeois." And we do not avoid works that may be considered "too hostile" because they expose systems of male privileges and awards as class conditions of domination over women. We seek to present works from a diverse, international community of feminist scholars in a broad range of academic disciplines that speak to the fullest dimensions of the condition of women. Our series has been launched with a range of works that reflect this goal and includes works on women, sexuality, war in the Middle East, an anthology of lesbian literary criticism, a French study of the women's movement in the United States, and an anthropology of fraternity gang rape.

The work of Dee Graham and her colleagues expands and extends the range of this series by contributing significantly to deepening the study of sexual colonization of women by men in private life. *Loving to Survive* represents the best of feminist research approaches to exploring the anomaly—those unexplained inconsistencies that often are treated simply as "the way things are." Graham, through the unique and highly creative development of the Societal Stockholm Syndrome, brings a critical feminist lens to the treatment of women in male-female relationships and finds hostage conditions to present the most immediately relevant and parallel condition. Importantly, Graham does not fall in line with syndrome psychology, merely adding to the psychological indexes one more "syndrome" which leads to a new version of blaming the victim. Instead of probing *intra-individual* explanations for the abuse women take and expect in order to love to survive, Graham turns to male-dominated society and the power relations of patriarchy. Graham's deep respect for and commitment to women who are loving to survive is lodged in her connection to and high regard for the feminist activism, research, and literature, for it is there that other alternatives, yet another world, is made possible. This work is among the best examples of how, in exposing the worst of male domination, women are able to aspire to and create the best of possibilities.

Kathleen Barry
Pennsylvania State University

Preface

My colleagues and I, as authors of these chapters, make two promises to our readers. Our first promise is that the new way of looking at male-female relationships that we present here will forever change the way you look at women, at men, and at male-female relationships. Our second promise is that the journey on which this book seeks to take you will be emotionally challenging.

Most women who have read sections of the book in manuscript form tell us it was painful for them to read the ideas we present. (Strangely, men have had more positive reactions to the ideas.) However, many of the women who at first respond negatively later become excited about the ideas we propose—after they have had the opportunity to work through their initial shock and resistance. In other words, it is difficult even to consider our ideas, much less accept them.

And here is where we return to our first promise. Significantly altering one's worldview is a difficult task—one that people fight and one that arouses strong feelings. It is because this book is likely to seriously alter your worldview that we say it will take you on a journey. While we don't expect everyone to accept all of our arguments, we anticipate that even those who disagree will be deeply impacted by the new perspective we offer them. Our hope is that you will observe male-female interactions in your own life and in the lives of those around you and that the picture we present helps you understand women, men, and their relationships.

And where are we going on this journey? We regard the effects of men's violence against women as crucial in understanding women's current psychology. Men's violence creates ever-present—and therefore often unrecognized—terror in women. For instance, this terror is experienced as a fear, by *any* woman, of rape by *any* man or as a fear of making a man—*any* man—angry. We propose that women's current psychology is actually a psychology of women under conditions of captivity—that is, under conditions of terror caused by male violence against women. (In fact, the conditions of women are conditions of slavery.) We also propose that no one has any idea what women's psychology under conditions of safety and freedom would be like. We propose that a psychology of women under conditions of captivity (and slavery) is no more "natural" for or intrinsic to women, in a genetic or biological sense, than a psychology of wild animals in captivity is natural for them.

We set forth the idea that women's responses to men, and to male violence, resemble hostages' responses to captors. More specifically, we propose that a construct recognized in hostage-taking events, known as Stockholm Syndrome, wherein hostages and captors mutually bond to one another, can help us understand female psychology and male-female relations.

We propose that women's bonding to men, as well as women's femininity and heterosexuality, are paradoxical responses to men's violence against women. Like captors who need to kill or at least wound a few hostages in order to get what they want, men terrorize women in order to get what they want: women's continued sexual, emotional, domestic, and reproductive services. Like hostages who work to placate their captors lest those captors kill them, women work to please men, and from this response springs women's femininity. Femininity describes a set of behaviors that please men (dominants) because they communicate a woman's acceptance of her subordinate status. Thus, feminine behaviors are survival strategies. Like hostages who bond to their captors, women bond to men in an effort to survive, and this is the source of women's strong need for connection with men and of women's love of men. We believe that until men stop terrorizing women—even in women's memories—we cannot know if women's love of men and women's heterosexuality are anything other than Stockholm Syndrome survival strategies. We refer to this theory of women's current psychology as Societal Stockholm Syndrome theory.

While the theory proposed here is emotionally challenging, it can make the world more understandable by exposing the relationship between seemingly disparate phenomena. For example, Societal Stockholm Syndrome theory explains why many women oppose the Equal Rights Amendment, why most women reject the very theory—feminism—

which espouses women's point of view and seeks to increase women's rights, why women work so hard to connect to men when it would be so much easier to get our needs for connection met by other women, why many women have a "love addiction," and why women love men in the face of men's violence against us. Societal Stockholm Syndrome theory shows that these paradoxical behaviors and beliefs of women are survival strategies in a culture marked by male violence. Thus, unlike theories of female masochism or of codependence, this theory blames male violence against women, not women, for the occurrence of women's seemingly irrational behaviors.

This book describes what we believe to be a universal law of behavior, which operates when a person existing under conditions of isolation and inescapable violence perceives some kindness on the part of the captor. The influence of this law usually is outside the awareness of those whose behavior and emotions it drives. But this book does more than describe women's current psychology as that of a hostage or captive. It also identifies the conditions that produce that psychology and in a broad sense suggests some strategies women may take to create a new world in which we will be both safe and free.

In developing Societal Stockholm Syndrome theory, I am clearly indebted to the previous literatures on "hostage" groups. My intellectual debts also extend back to Freud, who identified and developed psychological explanations for key issues in women's psychology: femininity, women's love of men, and heterosexuality. However, Freud's psychoanalytic theory, as well as current theories of women's psychology (e.g., codependence or love addiction theory and self-in-relation theory), are incomplete in that they do not fully deal with the cultural context within which female psychology emerges. Only radical feminist theorists have recognized the centrality of men's violence to women's lives. This book therefore builds upon and extends the ideas of such feminist social critics and theorists as Kathleen Barry, Susan Brownmiller, Andrea Dworkin, Catherine MacKinnon, Jean Baker Miller, and Adrienne Rich.

Overview of the Book

In chapter 1 we discuss several hostage-taking events, including the 1973 event that led to the coining of the term "Stockholm Syndrome," which refers to the bidirectional bonding of hostages and captors. Discussion of several hostage-taking events allows us to begin to assess the extent to which hostages bond with their captors, the conditions conducive to captor-captive bonding, the nature of the bond, and the psychodynamics underlying bonding to a captor/abuser/oppressor.

Chapter 2 describes both Graham's Stockholm Syndrome theory (an extension of the "classic" Stockholm Syndrome concept presented in chapter 1) and the outgrowth of Graham's Stockholm Syndrome theory referred to as Societal Stockholm Syndrome theory. Graham's theory emerged from analysis of nine different "hostage" groups (hostages, concentration camp prisoners, cult members, prisoners of war, civilians in Communist China who were subjected to thought reform, battered women, abused children, victims of father-daughter incest, and prostitutes procured by pimps) in which bonding to an abuser/captor occurred. Graham's Stockholm Syndrome theory identifies four hypothesized *precursors* of Stockholm Syndrome (perceived threat to survival, perceived inability to escape, perceived kindness from captor, and isolation) and nine *major indicators* of the presence of Stockholm Syndrome in victims, and describes the *psychodynamics* underlying Stockholm Syndrome as they are manifested by members of numerous hostagelike groups. This chapter also explains the process by which victims generalize Stockholm Syndrome psychodynamics to relationships with persons other than their captors. A special case of this process of generalization is Societal Stockholm Syndrome. It involves the bonding of an oppressed group to an oppressor group, for example, the bonding of women as a group to men as a group.

Chapter 3 takes up the idea that Societal Stockholm Syndrome is present in all oppressor-oppressed group relations. We show how one might assess the relevance of Societal Stockholm Syndrome to any particular set of unequal group-group relations. In particular, we address two questions: whether the four hypothesized precursor conditions for the development of Stockholm Syndrome (perceived threat to survival, perceived inability to escape, isolation, and perceived kindness) are present in male-female relationships, and if so, to what extent.

In chapter 4 Graham's nine indicators of Stockholm Syndrome are shown to characterize women's current psychology. Chapter 5 confronts the possibility that women's femininity, love of men, and heterosexuality are expressions of Societal Stockholm Syndrome. We argue that, as long as the four Stockholm Syndrome-conducive conditions are present in male-female relations and as long as most women are feminine, love men, and are heterosexual, we cannot know if these qualities of women are anything other than Societal Stockholm Syndrome responses.

Chapter 6 asks how women can transform our hostage psychology (Societal Stockholm Syndrome) while still experiencing male violence, ideological and physical isolation from one another, inability to escape, and dependence on small male kindnesses. To develop a world in which relationships are based on mutuality rather than dominance and subordination, we need to be able to imagine such a world. For the captive or slave, imagining is a subversive and revolutionary act. To help us develop new visions and move out of slavery, the chapter draws on four themes from feminist science fiction: empathy and women's power of connection, language that articulates women's perspectives, distrusting men/holding them accountable for their violence, and women as warriors/honoring our anger. Four methods of resistance are also described: claiming space, keeping track, looking out for one's own, and getting savvy. The authors do not present these themes and methods as *the answers* to transforming our slave psychology; our concern here is with *the process* (imagining new ideas) apparent in women's science fiction rather than the actual societies presented in such writing. We emphasize process because we recognize that the particular paths of action chosen by different women will differ and that there is room for many approaches to a shared goal. Our goal is to inspire women to redirect our (women's) courage and resourcefulness from surviving by loving our captors to thriving by loving ourselves, other women, and those men who will return empowering, healthy love.

Some Comments about Purpose and Style

The reader should realize that the theory presented here is that, a theory. Theory has the following functions: it helps make sense of facts (for example, behaviors) not previously understood by hypothesizing certain relationships between those facts; it encourages research designed to test that theory, thereby leading to the generation of new information; and, if accurate, it helps predict future behavior. Societal Stockholm Syndrome theory is presented for these three reasons and because, if found to be accurate, it has the potential to help women uncover ways of improving our situation. However, because this theory is being presented for the first time and despite the fact that an enormous amount of research in the literature supports it, it is an empirically untested theory. Further, because this research was conducted on predominantly white, college student samples, it is unclear to what extent the findings generalize to other groups. The reader is therefore encouraged to approach the topic with the skepticism and open mind of an objective researcher. The life experiences of each reader will provide tests of this theory. Rather than accepting or rejecting the theory outright, the reader is encouraged to test for herself the utility of Societal Stockholm Syndrome in making sense of her own and other's behavior on the basis of Societal Stockholm Syndrome theory and to see whether those predictions are born out. If the theory is valid, they will be.

The author breaks with stylistic convention and uses the words "we," "us," and "our" as opposed to "they," "them," and "their" when referring to women as a group. There are numerous reasons for this. All too often women are left to wonder whether writers and speakers intended to include females when so-called generic terms such as "man" and "he" are used. The language used here is employed to help ensure that every reader knows that this book was written *to* women *by* women *for* women *about* women. It seems grossly unfitting to be a woman writing to women about women's lives and women's perspectives and to use words that imply that "women" refers to people other than the intended audience and the author.

Use of the terms "they," "them," and "their" when referring to women discourages women from thinking of ourselves as members of a group with a unique set of perspectives. While the author realizes that within the group women there are many different perspectives and many sub-groups, still, there exist experiences that we all have *because we are female*. The issues raised by those common experiences are the topic of this book. Use of the terms "we," "us," and "our" encourages exactly the sort of group consciousness that is needed to tackle those issues. The more conventional style also prevents us from experiencing ourselves as both the object of focus and the locus of decision-making. In other words, this author believes that use of the terms "we," "us," and "our" will encourage women to see ourselves as persons capable of changing the world so as to make it a safer, healthier place for ourselves and one another.

Acknowledgments

As author of this book, I wish to thank Dr. Robert Stutz for giving me release time from teaching, the Center for Women's Studies at the University of Cincinnati for giving me a summer grant so that I could work on this manuscript, and Drs. Roberta Rigsby and Edna Rawlings for writing chapter 6. Numerous people have given me the intellectual and emotional support to make this book become a reality: Dr. Edna Rawlings, Sue Hull, Barbara Breckel, Dr. June Peters, Andrew Bambic, my family members—Margaretta B. Graham, Rudolph S. Graham, Lee G. Covington, and Brent S. Covington—and other friends (you know who you are). Dr. Edna Rawlings has enthusiastically encouraged the development of Stockholm Syndrome theory as it applies to women and contributed to several of the chapters here (chapters 1, 4, 5, and 6). I am particularly appreciative of the help she provided with regard to the manuscript during the month before it was sent to the publisher, as well as for the day-to-day help she provided that enabled me to spend time working on this project. Dr. Roberta Rigsby, in addition to being a primary author of chapter 6, has provided editorial support throughout the writing of the book. In addition, Barbara Breckel, Dr. June Peters, Dr. Maria Blake, Dr. Sarah Hoagland, and Dr. Donna Stringer generously provided feedback to various drafts of the manuscript; I also want to thank the many graduate and undergraduate students who read early drafts of various chapters and provided feedback and Alice Calaprice who copyedited the manuscript. Dr. Kathleen Barry, editor of this series, Niko Pfund, editor in chief of New York University Press, and Despina Papazoglou Gimbel, managing editor of New York University Press, helped move the project along by providing immediate feedback and support; working with them has been a real pleasure. I thank Dr. Edna Rawlings, Patty Callaghan, and Joan Shell for their help in finding a suitable title for this book, Niko

Pfund for the subtitle, and Shirley Doxsey for typing six of the tables. I also want to thank Dr. Sonia Johnson for providing an encouraging response to early drafts of two chapters. It has been a joy sharing this project with so many others, and I'm enormously appreciative of the support I've received.

Finally, the authors wish to acknowledge the following for granting permission to reprint from copyrighted material:

John Carta-Falsa (October 31, 1992, personal communication). Printed with permission.

Ellen Goodman (January 26, 1993). Gays and the military: What men fear. *The Cincinnati Enquirer,* p. 7A. © 1993, The Boston Globe Newspaper Company. Reprinted with permission.

Margaret T. Gordon and Stephanie Riger (1989). Table 2.4 from *The female fear,* pp. 16–18. © Margaret T. Gordon and Stephanie Riger. Reprinted with permission.

Helen M. Hacker (October 30, 1951). Women as a minority group. *Social Forces,* chart 1, p. 65. Copyright © The University of North Carolina Press.

Carolyn Kowatsch (March 20, 1993, personal communication). Printed with permission.

Extracts from Daniel Lang's "The bank drama" are reprinted by permission of Harold Ober Associates Incorporated. The material first appeared in the *New Yorker* issue of November 25, 1974. Copyright © 1974 by New Yorker Magazine, Inc.

Marjorie W. Leidig (1981). Violence against women: A feminist-psychological analysis. In S. Cox, ed., *Female psychology: The emerging self.* 2d ed. Selected quotes from pp. 190–205. © Marjorie Leidig, 1981. Reprinted with permission.

B. McClure (1978). Selected quotes from "Hostage survival." *Conflict 1*(1 & 2), 21–48. © Taylor and Francis. Reprinted with permission.

Robin Morgan (1989). The demon lover. *Ms.* 17 (9). Copyright © Robin Morgan, 1989. Reprinted with permission.

June Peters (forthcoming). *Treatment for abused women.* Columbus, Ind.: Quinco Behavioral Health Systems. Reprinted with permission.

E. I. Rawlings and Dianne K. Carter (1977). Table titled "Types of Ego Defenses among Victims of Discrimination" from *Psychotherapy for Women: Treatment toward Equality*. Copyright © Charles C. Thomas. Reprinted with permission.

Laurel Richardson (1983). Selected quotes from "No, thank you! A discourse on etiquette." In L. Richardson and V. Taylor, eds., *Feminist frontiers: Rethinking sex, gender, and society*. Copyright © Laurel Richardson. Reprinted with permission.

Donna Stringer (March 9, 1986). Table titled "Male and Female Rights and Responsibilities Regarding One Another" from "The Brownmiller legacy: A 10-year evaluation of unexplored issues in women and violence. A model for understanding male response to female efforts to change violence against women." Paper presented at the Annual Conference of the Association for Women in Psychology, Oakland, Calif. Copyright © Donna Stringer. Reprinted with permission.

Carolyn Swift (1987). Selected quotes from "Women and violence: Breaking the connection." *Work in Progress No. 27,* Stone Center Working Papers Series, Wellesley College, Wellesley, Mass. Copyright © Carolyn Swift. Reprinted with permission.

Carolyn Wesselius and James V. DeSarno. Selected quotes from "The anatomy of a hostage situation." *Behavioral Sciences and the Law, 1(2),* 33–45. Copyright © John Wiley and Sons, 1983. Reprinted with permission.

Dee L. R. Graham
Department of Psychology
University of Cincinnati

Love Thine Enemy: Hostages and Classic Stockholm Syndrome

> The true nature of the Stockholm Syndrome is far from completely understood, although many attempts have been offered to explain it.
>
> (Soskis and Ochberg 1982, p. 124)

The term "Stockholm Syndrome" was coined in 1973 to describe the puzzling reactions of four bank employees to their captor. Three women (Birgitta Lundblad, Elisabeth Oldgren, and Kristin Ehnmark) and one man (Sven Safstrom), taken hostage in one of the largest banks in Stockholm, were held for six days by two ex-convicts, Jan-Erik Olsson and Clark Olofsson, who threatened their lives but also showed them kindness. Reporter Daniel Lang, curious about the "sort of community" that developed between the captors and captives, interviewed the major parties involved in the ordeal. The following description is based on Lang's (1974) thorough and thoughtful examination of the events of the six days and of their effects on the captors and captives. Because this case illustrates many important elements and paradoxes found in captor-captive bonding, we will describe it in detail.

On August 23, 1973, Olsson, an expert on the use of explosives, entered one of the largest banks in Stockholm, Sweden, carrying, among other things, a loaded submachine gun, reserve ammunition, plastic explosives, blasting caps, a knife, and a radio. When, immediately upon entering the bank, he fired his submachine gun into the ceiling, the bank's customers and forty employees instinctively dropped to the floor, rushed to hide, or ran out of the bank. He ordered a male bookkeeper to bind the hands and ankles of Lundblad, Ehnmark, and Oldgren, three female employees of the bank, as they lay on the floor. He then demanded to talk to the police. Morgan Rylander, a police sergeant, was the first to appear on the scene. Olsson told him to get a high-ranking police officer, and Rylander complied. While Rylander was gone, a second police officer appeared, holding a revolver. Olsson didn't see him, but hostage Lundblad did and screamed at the policeman, "Don't shoot!" When the policeman called out to Olsson, "Drop your gun," Olsson shot him in the hand, permanently damaging it.

Rylander returned, reporting that a high-ranking officer was en route. Olsson ordered Rylander to get everyone out of the bank except for the three bound hostages. Rylander did so, removing even two armed policemen.

Negotiations began when Sven Thorander, the high-ranking officer, arrived. Olsson's first demand was that the police bring him Clark Olofsson, a prisoner who was serving a six-year term for armed robbery and as an accessory in the murder of a policeman. He also demanded money, two pistols, helmets, bullet-proof jackets, and a fast getaway car. Olsson's plan was to take the hostages with him in his escape. Lang reports: "For emphasis, he pointed the submachine gun at his three captives. 'If anything happens to them, the police will be to blame,' he told Thorander" (Lang 1974, p. 58). Thorander was not empowered to accept or reject these terms, so he relayed them to the Minister of Justice, Lennart Geijer. Geijer took the "unalterable position" that "under no circumstances" would Olsson "be permitted to leave the bank with the hostages" (p. 58). Prime Minister Olof Palme concurred. "When Thorander, in disclosing the government's position, asked Olsson if he would consider trading the hostages for Olofsson's company, the convict [Olsson] simply seized Elisabeth Oldgren by the throat and jammed his submachine gun against her ribs" (p. 59).

As Olsson was waiting for the police to round up the money he was demanding, he let the women use the phones. Lundblad made her call, but only a "day mother" for her children was at home to receive it. "When she hung up, Birgitta's eyes were wet. Lightly, consolingly, Olsson touched her cheek. 'Try again; don't give up,' he said" (Lang, p. 64).

As Olsson surveyed the bank building, he kept his hostages "clustered close to him." This was smart, for sharpshooters were stationed around the perimeter of the bank, watching the windows and doors, waiting for an opportune moment when they might kill him with a single shot. On one occasion, after sighting one of the sharpshooters, Olsson fired at them. Through the bank's windows, Olsson could see a blue Mustang that the police made available to him as a getaway car. But Olsson knew that without the hostages the car was only a trap. So the car continued to sit there throughout the remainder of the ordeal.

Olsson calmed down when Clark Olofsson arrived and, for the first time, unbound the hostages. Olofsson assisted Olsson by acting as an intermediary with police, using explosives to open a cashier's drawer and empty it of its money, taking the film from security cameras, and surveying the bank for "infiltrating" police. It was in the latter role that he discovered Sven Safstrom, a bank employee who had hidden in a stockroom after Olsson fired into the ceiling upon entering the bank. Safstrom thus became the fourth hostage of Olsson and his newly arrived accomplice.

At 11 P.M. on the first day of the takeover of the bank, Olsson called Prime Minister Palme. By this time, Olsson had the money and car he had demanded, and Olofsson was already present. The only demand not granted was the police's permission to take the hostages with him. Olsson

> told Mr. Palme he wanted orders issued for his immediate departure from the bank with the hostages; failing that, he said, there would be no more hostages. . . . [T]he next sounds that Mr. Palme heard were frightened gasps from one of the captives. Olsson had seized Elisabeth by the throat and was telling the Prime Minister that he had one minute in which to change his mind, or the young woman would die. Mr. Palme told [Lang], 'He began a countdown, but when fifteen seconds were left he stopped, and I heard the phone go dead.' (Lang, p. 66)

After the phone call to Palme, Olsson, Clark, and the four hostages "turned in." Olsson had Elisabeth Oldgren sit in a chair facing the doorway of the vault. At her feet was an explosive charge in the event the police stormed the vault that night. Oldgren fell asleep quickly but awoke after midnight due to the chill in the vault. "Just as she opened her eyes, shivering, . . . [Olsson] draped his gray wool jacket around her shoulders.

Recalling his action when she and [Lang] talked, Elisabeth said, 'Jan was a mixture of brutality and tenderness'" (Lang, p. 66).

The next morning, Friday, began with Olsson firing two rounds from his submachine gun at a civilian and a policeman on the stairway of the building. Later that day, Commissioner Lindroth asked to inspect the hostages. This request was granted by Olsson. By this time Lindroth had determined who the hostages were and investigated their backgrounds. He had found nothing "that impugned their characters in the slightest" (Lang, p. 71). However,

> he told associates immediately afterward, the inspection was charged with a strange atmosphere. The hostages, he reported, showed hostility toward him, their mien sullen and withdrawn. Kristin, he recall[ed], practically curled her lip at him. No one had any requests to make of him; he could detect no imploring looks. On the other hand, a peculiar amity prevailed between the hostages and Clark, and presumably, by extension, between the hostages and the robber [Olsson], waiting in the wings. . . . [T]heir manner with Clark was entirely relaxed, and at moments even convivial; nor was the hostages' attitude unreciprocated. . . . Clark had an arm around the shoulders of [Kristin and Elisabeth] in a display of easy camaraderie. As the Commissioner subsequently told aides, there was nothing for him to do but conclude that he was up against a mystery whose clues, if any existed, were like none to which he had ever been exposed. . . . The Commissioner made the following terse, factual entry in his account of the bank drama: "All the hostages seemed physically fit, and they all entreated me to let them leave the bank premises together with Olsson and Olofsson." (Lang, pp. 71–72)

After the inspection, Lindroth told reporters what had transpired. The reporters' response was to call the hostages to question whether they were indeed "prepared to entrust themselves to Olsson's ministrations wherever he went" (Lang, p. 72). Many of these phone calls were broadcast. They "baffled the Swedish public, setting off a wave of theorizing about the captives' odd pliancy" (p. 72).

At one point, Olsson pulled Sven Safstrom aside and,

> as though indulging in shoptalk, said he was going to shoot him. However, Olsson had added quickly, he wouldn't kill Sven, as he had originally planned, but would merely hit him in a leg; he would aim carefully, he promised. He explained the rationale of his decision: he had to shake up

the police or see his chances for escape go glimmering. Surely, the robber said, Sven could understand that. In any event, he concluded, Sven was to stand by until he received a signal, and then was to proceed to the foot of the staircase, where the police could see his body fall; in the meantime, Sven could avail himself of all the beer on hand in order to buoy his courage. (Lang, pp. 77–78)

Safstrom later told Lang, "I still don't know why the signal never came. All that comes back to me is how kind I thought he was for saying it was just my leg he would shoot. . . . But the robber was *not* kind. . . . He was an outlaw who dared to take over our lives, who could have killed us. I have to force myself to remember that fact" (p. 78).

That same day, the second day of the ordeal, Kristin Ehnmark called Prime Minister Palme, whom she did not know personally. In this forty-two-minute phone call, for which the police have a full transcription, Ehnmark implored Palme to let her and the other hostages go with Olsson:

> *Kristin:* I am very disappointed. I think you are sitting there playing checkers with our lives. I fully trust Clark and the robber [Olsson]. I am not desperate. They haven't done a thing to us. On the contrary, they have been very nice. But, you know, Olof, what I am scared of is that the police will attack and cause us to die.
>   . . .
> *Prime Minister:* . . . The police will not harm you. Can you believe that?
> *Kristin:* You must forgive me, but in this situation, I do not believe it.
> *Prime Minister:* I think that's terribly unfair. Here are a great many policemen risking their lives, who have not moved aggressively in all this time. The purpose, of course, is to protect you.
> *Kristin:* Of course, they can't attack us. . . . [Olsson] is sitting in here and he is protecting us from the police.
>   . . .
> *Prime Minister:* Can't you get the guy to put down his gun? Can't you explain that the whole thing is hopeless?
> *Kristin:* No, no, it won't work.

Prime Minister: Why not? Isn't he a human being?

Kristin: No, no, he's made up his mind.

. . .

Kristin: . . . Now, I tell you, I'm beginning to get angry. Call Norrmalmstorg and tell them every thing is straightened out. Let us go with Clark and the robber. (Lang, pp. 72–74)

The phone call ended with Kristin Ehnmark sarcastically telling Prime Minister Palme, "Thanks for the help" (p. 74).

In another call, Birgitta Lundblad finally reached her mother. When she hung up, Lang reports, "her tears were more copious than they had been on the previous day. . . . Olsson, sitting in an easy chair, drew her to his knees and consoled her. When [Lang later] interviewed Birgitta . . . , she said, 'The robber told me that every thing would be all right if only the police would go away. I agreed with him then. Yes, I thought, it is the police who are keeping me from my children'" (Lang, p. 77).

Waiting for the government to break in their commitment not to let him take the hostages with him, Olsson set up his "headquarters" in the bank's ground-floor safe-deposit vault. The police had set their headquarters up on the floor above. The vault had an oppressive quality to it, being only eleven feet wide and seven and a half feet high, though forty-seven feet long. When Elisabeth Oldgren complained of claustrophobia, Olsson "put a length of rope, perhaps thirty feet, around her neck and let her out for a walk" (Lang, p. 63). Oldgren later reported to Lang, "I remember thinking he was very kind to allow me to leave the vault" (Lang, p. 63). Later that same day, Olsson permitted Ehnmark and Lundblad, unleashed, to leave the vault to go to the lavatory. "Out of Olsson's sight, both saw police. . . . One of the officers asked Kristin in a whisper how many hostages the robber had taken. 'I showed them with my fingers,' Kristin said. 'I felt like a traitor. I didn't know why'" (Lang, p. 64). Lundblad also suffered conflict: "All I had to do was take a few steps toward them. . . . I was afraid I might endanger [the other hostages] if I didn't go back" (Lang, p. 64).

One of the female hostages was approached by Olsson on Friday evening after the group had lain on the floor to sleep. He asked if he could lie beside her and she consented. When he asked if he could caress her, she again consented. In giving testimony, she later explained her behavior: "I thought that if I could get on an intimate footing with him, I might be able to persuade him to give up his whole enterprise, or maybe if some of the anxieties he surely had pent up within himself were relieved he would not want to go on with this whole thing" (Lang, p. 92). She had allowed him to touch her breasts and hips. When upon getting excited, he asked her if he could continue, that is, have intercourse, she refused, "taking care . . . to do so in a light tone, 'because I was afraid he would take over and be in charge' " (p. 92). Olsson acceded but was still excited and so turned away from her and masturbated himself to orgasm.

On the morning of the third day of the takeover, Saturday, a policeman stealthily approached the bank vault in which the captors and their hostages had just awakened and thrust shut the vault's door, after which he locked it shut from the outside. Olsson soon afterward realized that the police might use tear gas. Tear gas was important to Olsson because he believed that after fifteen minutes' exposure, a person becomes permanently retarded. Safstrom later reported to Lang: "He had told us that he would kill us all as well as himself rather than let us become that way. Hearing him say that, I remember, was another time when I thought of him as a very kind man" (Lang, p. 82).

This same Saturday morning, Olofsson asked the police to unlock the door long enough for one of the hostages to get some supplies. These had been voted on by the group and included such things as food, a chemical toilet, toilet tissue, and a hot plate. The police vetoed this request, after hours of consideration. The entire group was frustrated and angered by this. Olofsson scribbled on a blank bank form: "The girls [sic] have begun to believe that the police intend to sacrifice them and are only looking for an excuse to justify the massacre later on. The girls [sic] believe that the police will make sure that it was we who started it and that the police simply defended themselves, so that they can afterward regret that everyone was killed" (Lang, p. 94). Lang asked Lundblad after the ordeal whether she agreed with Olofsson's words. She nodded yes and said, "We were facing two threats, and one was all we could possibly handle. About the robber's threat we could do nothing—he was armed and we were with him. But we weren't with the police. We imagined we could protect ourselves against them. To imagine that, of course, meant believing in Jan" (Lang, pp. 94, 96).

Suspicious of Safstrom, Olsson tested him on Saturday. Olsson acted as though asleep and "let the submachine gun dangle from his lap, inches from [Safstrom's] grasp" (Lang, p. 63). Safstrom made no move for the gun. Olsson later reported to Lang, "I was glad for his sake he didn't" (p. 63).

At one point one of the hostages began to menstruate, and the group in the vault did not have any tampons or sanitary pads. Lang reports: "The convicts had been adamant in insisting that the police must fill this lack forthwith if negotiations were to proceed. [Lindroth stated,] 'The criminals could talk of nothing else'" (Lang, p. 84). Realizing the concern that the captors had shown for their captives, police at this time determined that the captors might not be able to kill their hostages.

Once the vault door was shut, tear gas became the police's tactic of choice for ending the ordeal. Toward this end they began drilling holes in the ceiling of the vault so that the gas could be directly sprayed into it. Timing was crucial. If Olsson was not immediately rendered unconscious by the gas, he might murder one or more of the hostages. To prevent this, the police attempted to exhaust the captors, and thus the captives, in the hopes Olsson would realize that, short of dying, he had no alternative but to surrender.

Olsson later reported to Lang that it was never far from his mind that murdering one or more of the hostages would help him convince the police that they should allow him to escape with the remaining hostages. Meanwhile, he "catered to the needs of his possible victims," wiping away Oldgren's tears, giving Ehnmark a bullet from his submachine gun as a keepsake, and apologizing to Lundblad for having made her nervous enough to resume smoking. Safstrom reported: "When he treated us well, we could think of him as an emergency God" (Lang, p. 96).

By late Saturday afternoon, the group did not know if more food would be sent in, and everyone was hungry. Olsson, however, had saved three pears in his pocket from a previous meal. Yet, under these conditions, he carefully cut each of the three pears in half and gave a piece to each of the "inmates." Lang points out that it was at this time that "the faintest outlines of a community" were detectable (p. 97). Hostages did chores such as moving furniture and emptying the wastebaskets that had served as toilets. Lang reports: "Instinctively, the hostages aimed at pleasing the criminals. Referring to this, Kristin said to me later, 'If someone likes you, he won't kill you.' Elisabeth felt the same way. 'I couldn't have stayed normal if I had opposed the robber,' she told me" (p. 97). Ehnmark said that "whoever threatened [our] world was our enemy" (p. 100). Olsson and Olofsson talked of prison life with the hostages. Lang reports that Safstrom said, "We were all sympathy, taking in everything they told us. We acted as though they were our victims, not the other way around" (p. 102). Hearing newscasts of themselves, letting them know they weren't forgotten, helped the hostages keep up their morale.

On Sunday afternoon, Kristin Ehnmark had a nightmare. She awoke screaming "Don't! Don't!" Lang reports, "Clark was instantly at her side, soothing her until she was herself again" (p. 90).

Subsequent to the ordeal, Ehnmark reported to the police that she at times held hands with Olofsson: "Perhaps it sounds a little like a cliche, but Clark gave me tenderness. . . . It made me feel enormously secure. It was what I needed" (p. 92).

The police began drilling holes into the vault ceiling Sunday evening. Olsson's response was to plant an explosive in a vent.

> In putting distance between himself and the charge, the robber came upon Kristin and Elisabeth huddled together on the floor, hands clapped to their ears, a blanket over their heads. Patiently, he advised them to do as he was doing—move farther away, beyond the small alcove. He told them, too, to forget about holding their ears but to keep their mouths open. Elisabeth said to me, "I remember thinking, Why can't the police be considerate like that?" (Lang, p. 102)

When the explosive went off, the drilling stopped. This made Olsson feel victorious. "Strutting and victorious in manner, he shouted imprecations through the damaged vent. His ranting bothered Sven, who told me, 'I felt unsafe, seeing Jan act that way. I wanted to think of him as our protector'" (Lang, p. 102). When the drilling resumed, Olsson ordered the hostages to lie under it and informed them that, if the drilling continued, the ceiling might collapse on them.

By 3 A.M. holes were cut through the vault ceiling, and water that was being used to cool the drill was trickling into the vault. Fearful that tear gas would soon be pumped in, Olsson tied nooses to upper cabinet drawers of the vault and had all the hostages stand with them around their necks. Upon realizing this, the police temporarily discontinued their operations and, because the inmates had eaten nothing except for the pears for over fifty hours, food and beer were lowered into the vault. It was now about five in the morning and these were the last rations they would receive. Olsson permitted the hostages to loosen their nooses enough to test the food and beer. None would touch the tampered-with beer bottles. Thirty minutes afterward, seeing no ill effects in the hostages, the captors ate their share of the food. But it was hours later before Olsson permitted the hostages to stop standing with the nooses around their necks. Even then he demanded that they keep them tucked in their clothes, ready to be put on again at a moment's notice.

By Monday, the fifth day of the takeover, the six "inmates" realized that the end of the ordeal was close. Olsson was "mercurial" in his moods, "alternating between a tenderness and a brutality that had both become heightened," according to Oldgren. Ehnmark reported: "From the moment Jan made me his hostage, I was afraid he would suddenly kill me, but now [with the closing of the vault door] it was the police I was afraid of—even more so than when I had talked with the Prime Minister" (p. 88). Safstrom reported that the hostages, while together, felt "very much alone" (p. 90).

The drilling continued. As a hole was being finished and a shield put over it by a policeman above the vault, Olsson fired at him. Tuesday morning, at 8:35, during a similar maneuver, Olsson fired at another policeman and wounded him in his hand and cheek. Minutes after 9 A.M., police sprayed tear gas into the vault. "Too late, Olsson . . . ordered the hostages to put on the nooses. But there was no chance either to obey or disobey his last command" (p. 112). A foulup by the police ensured that the fumes did not cause unconsciousness but rather choking and vomiting in its victims. At this point, Olsson yelled, "We give up, let us out!"

A policeman shouted, "Hostages first!" Lang reports:

> But there was no movement in the vault. The hostages kept their ground, rejecting rescue. Defiantly, Kristin shouted back, "No, Jan and Clark go first—you'll gun them down if we do!" Startled, the would-be liberators

hesitated, then finally opened wide the outer door and made way for Olsson and Clark. As they stood framed in the doorway, the convicts and hostages quickly, abruptly embraced each other, the women kissing their captors, Sven shaking hands with them. Their farewells over, all six walked out of the vault, Olsson and Clark in the lead. (Lang, p. 114)

Taken on stretchers and put in ambulances, the hostages continued to be concerned about their former captors. Oldgren wondered what was happening to them and expressed the wish that "whatever was being done for us should be done for them" (Lang, p. 114). Ehnmark refused to lie down on her stretcher. Rather, she sat up, searching for Olsson and Olofsson. Seeing Olofsson being worked over by the police, she yelled to him, "Clark, I'll see you again!" (p. 114).

Following their release, the hostages continued to see the police as "the enemy" and their captors as their protectors who gave them life. One hostage accused psychiatrists of trying to "brainwash" her so as to turn her against her captors. Safstrom tried to find hatred for the captors but couldn't; he instead began being concerned about the prison life for inmates. In police custody, Olsson told police to give Lundblad the radio he used throughout the takeover. Six months later all four former hostages testified against the captors. Olofsson was returned to prison to finish his prior terms and would not get out for almost six years. Olsson was sentenced to ten years. Approximately one year after the ordeal, one of the hostages visited a captor after having experienced a "powerful impulse" to do so. She refused to tell anyone what they had discussed. According to *U.S. News and World Report* reporter Peter Annin (1985), two of the women hostages became engaged to the two captors.

Stockholm Syndrome as Paradox

If the reader will consider how she or he would expect hostages to feel toward their captors, before and after release, the paradoxes that are Stockholm Syndrome become evident. A number of these paradoxes are listed in table 1.1, where the perspective of hostages who have developed Stockholm Syndrome are contrasted with the perspective of outsiders.

The Stockholm bank siege has many of the apparently inexplicable components of Stockholm Syndrome:

TABLE I.I
Paradoxes That Are Stockholm Syndrome

Hostages' Perspective	Outsiders' Perspective
1. Feel gratitude toward captor for permitting them to live (or giving them their lives back).	1. Believe no one has right to willfully threaten or take another's life.
2. Find it difficult to feel anger toward captors; instead feel gratitude.	2. Expect hostages to feel rage at captors for jeopardizing hostages' lives and subjecting them to terror.
3. See captors as kind. Psychological impact of captors' small kindnesses supersedes psychological impact of terror.	3. See captors as indifferent to hostages' and others' suffering.
4. An open door does not look like an open door.[a]	4. Find it difficult to comprehend why hostages don't escape when apparently have opportunity to do so.
5. Won't try to escape, if given opportunity, if captor might be killed in the escape attempt.	5. Don't understand why hostage would be concerned about whether a captor is killed during an escape attempt; wouldn't death be a just punishment for captor?
6. See captors as "good guys" who are protecting them and police as "bad guys" who are trying to kill them.	6. See captors as "bad guys" and police as "good guys."
7. Are sympathetic to the politics of their captors.	7. Think hostages should be politically polarized against their captors.
8. May refuse to testify against captors; seek leniency and may develop defense funds to help get captors off.	8. Expect hostages to want their captors to receive maximum prison sentence possible for hostage taking.
9. Remain loyal to captors following release, not feeling safe enough to be disloyal without expecting retribution.	9. Don't understand why hostages remain loyal to their captors following release; feel the sympathy and loyalty hostages expressed while captives surely weren't real.
10. Don't feel safe following release. Fear captors coming back to hold them captive again.	10. Think former hostages are safe once released.

[a] This statement is credited to Martin Symonds (1982).

- Captors who showed their hostages kindness while they terrorized them with threats of physical violence and death
- Hostages who did not escape when they were apparently able to do so
- Development of an emotional closeness between the hostages and captors
- Hostages who identified with their captors, taking on the captors' attitudes and beliefs, whether about the police, tear gas, or the need for reform of the prison system
- More specifically, hostages who came to believe that those trying to win their release, not the captors, wanted to kill them
- Hostages who perceived those trying to win their release as enemies and captors as friends
- Hostages who were unable to acknowledge the full extent of their terror until the event was over
- Hostages who were grateful for, and won over by, small kindnesses shown by captors and were seemingly without anger at their captors for holding them hostage and for threatening them with physical violence and death
- Hostages who came to see their captors as a source of security and humaneness and the police as a source of terror
- Hostages who felt they owed their lives to their captors
- Hostages who maintained their loyalty to their captors long after their release had been won

Two additional elements present in the bank siege were that time became undifferentiated for the hostages and that, following release, the hostages feared their captors would return to terrorize them once again (Lang 1974).

Are the responses of the four hostages and two captors in the Stockholm bank robbery idiosyncratic, or might we expect virtually anyone to respond as they did under similar circumstances? Soskis and Ochberg (1982) reported that Stockholm Syndrome is thought to have developed in approximately one-half of all victims of recent terrorist hostage cases. However, the incidence may actually be much higher, as estimates are limited by the skill and knowledge of interviewers of former hostages. If some hostages do develop the syndrome and others do not, what determines who will? Answers to these questions would permit us to identify the conditions that give rise to the development of this syndrome. Below we will describe two additional hostage incidents which shed light on why bonding occurs between some hostages and captors but not others.

Siege of a Law-Enforcement Facility: A Case in Which Only One of Seven Hostages Developed Stockholm Syndrome

Psychiatrist Cassie Wesselius and FBI Special Agent James DeSarno (1983) describe a hostage-taking siege in which only one out of seven hostages showed Stockholm Syndrome symptoms. The siege lasted only three and a half hours and was ended by the killing of the captor with a sniper's bullet. Former hostages were interviewed by Wesselius and DeSarno four months after the event.

On a Saturday in 1981 a man carrying sacks filled with pistols, a sawed-off shotgun, ammunition, and an automatic machine gun, among other things, forced a security guard to allow him entry into a law-enforcement building. The alternative was to be killed with the automatic machine gun. By taking the security guard with him, the captor gained entry to the law-enforcement office. Disappointed that only clerical staff were present on this weekend day, he demanded to see five officers and a specific chaplain. If his demands were not met, he would kill all seven hostages present. Not only did they believe him, but they realized, from the way he spoke, that he probably was paranoid. Meanwhile, he ordered the staff to go about their usual business. One hostage's job was switch-board operator, and he dubbed her "my secretary."

The captor seesawed between calm and volatile behavior throughout the siege, at times holding the barrel of his automatic against the head of a hostage. From moment to moment the hostages did not know how he would react next. The constant crying of one hostage unnerved him, making him more violent, and he asked her to leave the area. When she did so, he and the remaining hostages were relieved. The authors note, "The release of the crying hostage was the first demonstration of the creation of a common goal between HT [the captor] and the hostage group" (Wesselius and DeSarno 1983, p. 35).

The policeman negotiating for the hostages' release asked the captor to release three of the seven hostages "to demonstrate that he was a humanitarian and working in good faith with the officials" (p. 35). This he did only after reassurances by the negotiator that it did not indicate weakness or loss of control on his part. He also required reassurances to assuage feelings of being trapped or out of control. Because an on-site psychiatrist deemed his behavior to be "erratic and homicidal," police decided that they should take him at the first opportune moment. This they did, ending the siege with his being shot and killed by a police sniper.

All hostages revealed symptoms of Post-Traumatic Stress Disorder, characterized by insomnia, nightmares, flashbacks, strong startle responses, distrust of others, irritability, anhedonia, jitteriness, etc. Many experienced the event as unreal when it was happening.

The security guard who let the captor into the facility, the first hostage, reported only negative feelings toward the captor and was glad that he was killed. The guard believed that, because of his uniform, he intimidated the captor. This security guard was also the most badly treated hostage: he was the most frequently threatened and was told he would be the first killed. Four months later, he still harbored negative feelings toward the other hostages, for he believed they kept the captor agitated. He also felt guilty for letting the captor into the building. He had "reservations" about being interviewed by the authors.

The second hostage, with whom the captor spent the most time and dubbed "my secretary," was the only one who expressed any positive feelings toward him. Her feelings ranged from sympathy and pity to friendliness and compassion, with diminishing dislike. Her predominant feelings toward the captor during the siege were anger and sometimes fear and hate. She described him as "clean cut, attractive, and well-dressed," while the others saw him as "dirty, malodorous, and carelessly dressed" (p. 37). In addition, while she saw him as highly agitated, hostile, and unpredictable, as well as paranoid, berserk, and suicidal, she also saw him as depressed and confused. This hostage expressed anger at the negotiator for not getting the chaplain as the captor demanded. Her feelings were that, if this demand had been met, the hostages would not have been in danger. She felt it was terrible that he had been shot and killed. She was the only one who seemed ashamed that she had been a hostage. Although she later had to deal with the paperwork regarding the siege, and repeatedly read the captor's name, she did not remember it at the time of the interview.

The third hostage was the one who had wept during the ordeal and who had been released after only forty-five minutes of captivity. She claimed that the captor released her only because he wanted her to report which authorities were outside. Fearing the captor and hating him, she believed that he would not have allowed the police to capture him alive. She saw him as hostile and unpredictable, among other things, as well as confused. Her feelings toward the authorities were also negative and included fear and anger.

A fourth hostage was wounded in the leg by a policeman's ricocheting bullet. At the time he thought that the captor had shot him, and that he was dying. Anger, hatred, and fear characterized his feelings toward the captor. A fifth hostage, who had had little contact with the captor, was also injured by a ricocheting bullet. He was the only one who did not perceive the captor as insane, and the only one not experiencing Post-Traumatic Stress Disorder symptoms. Although he felt threatened by the captor, he frequently also felt neutral toward him, and he had both positive and negative feelings for his rescuers.

The sixth hostage, released after only two hours, expressed positive feelings toward the other hostages, perhaps indicating "survivor guilt." Although denying that the hostages had been physically or psychologically abused by the captor, she nonetheless expressed "anger, dislike, hatred, and fear" toward him. She had had little contact with him.

The seventh and last hostage had little contact with the captor but still felt anger, hatred, and fear toward him; he had also felt threatened. He denied any positive feelings for the captor, but had both positive and negative feelings for his rescuers.

Wesselius and DeSarno's analysis is that only the second hostage evidenced Stockholm Syndrome. The reasons for this, they concluded, are that she spent the most time with him and had the most positive contact. She also was isolated from the other hostages, who were held captive together. Evidence that she did in fact develop Stockholm Syndrome, despite the "brevity of the situation," was that "she had positive feelings towards him, was angry with the outside authorities, and felt it was a shame that he was killed. She was the only hostage to describe [the captor] as clean cut and attractive, even though in reality he was malodorous and shabbily dressed" (pp. 44–45).

Comparison of this hostage's responses with those of the others raises two issues: the speed at which Stockholm Syndrome develops, and the question of whether some demonstration of kindness or loyalty on the part of the captor (e.g., calling a hostage one's secretary and thus implying that she is important to him or is his helper) is necessary to the development of Stockholm Syndrome in hostages. The fact that this hostage was the only one seeing the hostage as clean and well dressed raises the issue of whether a certain amount and type of perceptual distortion is necessary to the development of Stockholm Syndrome. At least two other cognitive distortions appear to have occurred. It is possible that feeling shame for being a hostage is a form of taking one's captor's perspective (a cognitive distortion); it suggests one believes one must have deserved the punishment of being held hostage, a belief presumably held by the captor. Particularly noteworthy is this woman's difficulty in remembering her captor's name—another cognitive distortion—but the basis for her memory lapse is unclear.

In this hostage-taking incident, only one of the hostages clearly evinced Stockholm Syndrome; by contrast, in the next incident we will discuss, only one hostage did *not* develop it. The differences between these two hostages and their fellow hostages, as well as the differences between the two of them, can help us delineate factors likely to encourage the development of Stockholm Syndrome.

TWA Flight 847: A Case in Which Only One of Thirty-Six Did Not Develop Stockholm Syndrome

On June 14, 1985, a TWA plane, flight 847, was hijacked by Lebanese Shi'ites as it took off from the Athens airport in Greece. Peter Hill, along with thirty-six other passengers on that flight, was held hostage for fourteen days. During his captivity, Hill remained hostile toward his captors and collected evidence, including glass fragments that are believed to have been part of the housing for the captors' weapons. While the captors slept, he also took photographs of the captors and of the hideout to which they were taken. He reports (Hill, with Friend, 1986) that the seven other hostages he was paired with did not show much enthusiasm for his picture taking, though none ever asked him not to do it. He also found a survey plot of the building in which they were hidden, a layout of the very apartment they were in, pictures of the hijackers, "travel documents, visas, wedding photos and other personal effects"—all of which he kept hidden on his body, along with his roll of film.

Like the other hostages, Hill's life was threatened. He remembered that four times during the ordeal he feared for his life. One of these times was when Robert Stethem was murdered by the hijackers.

Hill describes numerous examples in which the other hostages and the hijackers showed signs of having developed what he now recognizes as Stockholm Syndrome. One hostage, who was in marketing, offered to help the captives communicate their message to the American people. In other cases, hostages would light their captors' cigarettes. When the hostages were brought together in a Beirut schoolyard just prior to their release, Hill reports that hostages and guards rode motorcycles and played soccer together. And one of the hostages, carrying the Koran under his arm and Muslim prayer beads, just prior to release hugged his captors good-bye in the traditional Lebanese embrace.

Why was Peter Hill's response to his captors so different from that of the other hostages? Perhaps, by having begun his captivity collecting evidence so he could later piece together the how and why of the hijacking, Hill was predisposed to seeing his captors differently from the other hostages. However, Gerard Vaders (Ochberg 1977, 1982), a reporter and hostage who secretly kept notes on events transpiring when Moluccans hijacked the train he was on, nonetheless developed Stockholm Syndrome. Perhaps, again, the best cue comes from Hill's own answer to the same question, "Why was I different?" Hill reports that his father had been killed fighting in World War II. Having never served in battle himself, he saw this hostage-taking ordeal as his opportunity to help his country by "stand[ing] up and be[ing] counted" (Hill, with Friend, 1986,

p. 64). In particular, Hill saw his actions as an attempt to "prove something to myself about myself as a man" (Hill, with Friend, 1986, p. 64).

At least one of the other hostages, Victor Amburgy (1986), was angered by Peter Hill's behavior during their captivity, arguing that Hill's actions put all the other hostages' safety in jeopardy. What is immediately apparent is the different goals of these two hostages. One sought to be "a man" in spite of the added risk to his and others' lives. The other was willing to do what he had to do in order to survive.

This difference suggests that, in order for Stockholm Syndrome to develop, a hostage must have survival as his or her foremost goal. But other interpretations are also possible. It may be that strongly held beliefs or perspectives, such as seeing the captors as an enemy, which exist at the first moment of capture, block a hostage's willingness to accept kindness from the captors and therefore block his or her likelihood of identifying with the captors. Or it may be that activities that keep the mind off the captors, such as collecting evidence, serve to inoculate hostages from developing the syndrome. Or all of these factors may be at play. Later in this chapter we will discuss other circumstances as well.

Time Factors in the Development and Maintenance of Stockholm Syndrome

Besides the question of why some hostages develop Stockholm Syndrome and others don't, there are also questions concerning time: How long does it take the syndrome to develop, and how long does it last? These questions may need to be reframed. Although some experts, such as Frank Ochberg (1977), claim that it takes three to four days for Stockholm Syndrome to develop, time per se may not be the relevant variable; rather, it may be what events, including psychological processes, go on in time. As we saw in Wesselius and DeSarno's description of the siege of the law-enforcement facility, "the secretary" apparently developed Stockholm Syndrome in only three and a half hours of captivity. It may be that the development of Stockholm Syndrome in hostages is dependent upon, for example, hostages' perceptions of how long their captivity might continue, or whether they perceive escape as possible. Within the same hostage-taking situation, hostages who believe their captivity might end soon may be less likely to develop Stockholm Syndrome, or may develop it more slowly, than those who believe the ordeal may be lengthy.

Furthermore, there is no simple, obvious relationship between the persistence of Stockholm Syndrome after release and the time elapsed since release. Strentz (1980) notes: "To date, there is no evidence to indicate how long the syndrome lasts" (p. 138). Based on an interview with Lt. Robert Louden of the New York City Police Department, Kuleshnyk (1984) concluded that the time the syndrome lasts varies among hostages. Although in most cases it becomes weaker with time, there have been cases in which hostages visited their captors in jail up to two years after their release. Ochberg (1977) noted that at the time of the interview with Gerald Vaders, which was two years after the hijacking, Vaders, a hostage held for thirteen days by seven Moluccan gunmen, still showed signs of Stockholm Syndrome. Ronald Crelinsten (1977), however, reported that Vader's positive feelings toward the Moluccan captors disappeared when, eighteen months after the incident, a second hostage-taking occurred. If the latter is accurate, it suggests that "long term effects [of the syndrome] can occur and are susceptible to change when conditions pertaining to the original incident change" (Crelinsten 1977, p. 209). To the extent that perceptual distortions—as with the "secretary" in the law-enforcement holdup—are necessary to the maintenance of Stockholm Syndrome, challenging or breaking down those distortions may serve to disrupt the bond. Further observation and research are required before we can know what events can disrupt the positive bonds captives develop for their captors, and why.

The Roles of Sex and Age

Perhaps contrary to popular beliefs about the sexes, males and females appear equally likely to develop the syndrome. Furthermore, no age group is exempt from developing it (E. E. Flynn 1990).

Caroline Moorehead (1980, p. 215) has observed the following:

The form the affection takes, psychiatrists say, is determined by the age and sex of kidnapper and victim. [Hostages] Judge di Gennaro and Geoffrey

Jackson both spoke of their guards as if they were misguided friends of their own children, in an avuncular and somewhat patronizing way. In women, the affection has sometimes turned into romantic attachment, sexuality providing a primitive way of coping with the intense fear and uncertainty.

Moorehead cites Dr. Ferdinando Imposimato as noting that the decision of some women hostages "to make love to their jailers had come from a need for an ally, a protector in the midst of such horror and confusion" (p. 215). But why would the affection take a romantic and/or sexualized turn in female hostages of male captors?

Graham, Rawlings, and Rimini (1988) note that rape and the threat of rape, though uncommon among male hostages, are common among female hostages. (See, for example, Barthel 1981; Dortzbach and Dortzbach 1975; Hearst, with Moscow, 1982; Lang 1974; and W. E. Smith 1985.) Thus, being taken hostage involves an added element of terror for the female hostages. Is it possible that their participation in sexualizing the captor/hostage bond is a response to their captors' sexualizing the aggression and threats directed at them? Does their participation in romanticizing the interaction "normalize" that interaction, thereby reducing their terror?

Principles of Behavior for Hostage Survival

To the extent that Stockholm Syndrome is present, those trying to win the release of captives cannot count on the hostages being "truthful" or helpful. Nor can prosecutors count on hostages' cooperation in a courtroom (Kuleshnyk 1984).

In spite of these problems created by Stockholm Syndrome, law-enforcement personnel attempt to encourage the captive-captor bond since it is believed to improve the likelihood of the hostages' survival. In fact, officials who have studied Stockholm Syndrome have suggested rules or principles of hostage behavior vis-à-vis the captor to improve hostages' chances of surviving captivity.

Turner's (1990) recommendations to persons taken hostage include the following:

1. Maintain hope and do what you can to ensure that your captor maintains hope. A captor without hope may give up, killing himself or herself and all hostages.
2. Stay calm and encourage the captor to stay calm.
3. Blend in with the other hostages, keeping a low profile.
4. Rest early on so you won't become short-tempered with your captor, for your captor, who won't be able to rest, will become increasingly short-tempered as the ordeal continues.
5. Use "extreme caution" in evaluating escape opportunities, for a failed attempt can lead to reprisals against the attempted escapist, while a successful attempt can lead to reprisals against fellow hostages.

Turner is advising hostages to manage both their own affect and the affect of the captor in ways that will improve their chances of surviving.

It is important that hostages not express hostility and antipathy toward their captors, for such behaviors may intensify the captors' antagonism, relieving their guilt for making them hostages in the first place. Such behaviors also serve to relieve captors of guilt for any harm done to hostages in their efforts to get their demands met (Kuleshnyk 1984).

McClure (1978, pp. 36–37), himself a former hostage, offers the following additional suggestions for hostage survival in kidnap-imprisonment situations:

Perhaps the most important job of the hostages during a protracted imprisonment is to neutralize the hostility of these jailers and then win them over. . . .

Anything that will show [the hostages] as individual human beings, rather than symbols of a class or system, should be exploited. . . . [T]hey should take every opportunity to talk to [their captors]. Without any suggestion of Socratic nagging, prisoners should ask questions that draw the guards out about their family, cultural and personal interests, goals, and motivations. Where there are natural parallels in the hostages' own background, these should be noted. The unspoken message of the hostage's attitude should be this: I take you seriously and know you are capable of doing anything you say you'll do, or threaten to do. But I also know you are a decent, fair-minded person, and I want us to get to know each other better.

But McClure repeatedly warns that, while showing proper respect for the captor's power and humanity, "the answer for the hostages is not to be completely passive and compliant toward the captor; this can be almost as serious an error in some cases as being too belligerent" (p. 42). If the hostages appear fawning, obsequious, and sycophantic to their captors, they will only draw contempt. The prisoner is exhorted to walk a fine line with respect to her or his relationship with the captor, neither encouraging the captor's hostility nor fulfilling the captor's stereotype of the hostage by being obviously submissive for the sake of survival.

Further, McClure warns that hostages must control the extent of their identification with the captor, walking another fine line: "The problem with spontaneous identification under stress is that the hostages lose their sense of proportion and can become satellites of the person who threatens their life" (McClure 1978, p. 43). Once a satellite, a hostage can easily behave in self-defeating ways, such as warning a captor that the police can see and shoot him, when the police's fire could win the hostage's release.

Like Kuleshnyk, McClure warns against the development of negative transference, or "the development of antipathy and even aggressive hostility by the hostages toward their captors," noting that "the result has always meant hardship for the hostage" (McClure 1978, p. 42). The reasons are that "such hostility liberates the captors from any guilt they might have felt in seizing the victim, . . . [i]t justifies and intensifies any feeling of hate which the captors may attach to the hostage, . . . [and] [i]t may also wound the ego of a basically insecure captor, prompting direct retaliation" (p. 42).

Stockholm Syndrome in *captors* can be fostered during negotiations by, for example, asking them to check on the health of captives or discussing captives' family responsibilities with them. Any action by negotiators which encourages captors to see captives as humans promotes the syndrome in abductors, unless the captors are sociopaths (Strentz 1982). Also, any action that encourages captors and hostages to work together, for example, to prepare food, distribute blankets, and so on, nourishes the syndrome in captors (E. E. Flynn 1990).

In anticipation of our later application of Stockholm Syndrome to women's psychology, we suggest that the reader reflect on parallels between principles for hostage survival and lessons on femininity, which women are taught about how to get along with men.

Classic Stockholm Syndrome Theory

As the descriptions of incidents in which one or more hostages developed Stockholm Syndrome have shown, Stockholm Syndrome is a complex phenomenon.

Conditions Promoting the Syndrome

There is no agreement on exactly what conditions promote Stockholm Syndrome; however, based on hostages' cases histories, a number of variables have been proposed by experts in this area. These are listed in table 1.2. Investigators differ in the inductions they make based on the case histories available to them. Probably for ethical reasons, almost no empirical research has been carried out to test these inductions. Research is made more difficult because investigators frequently do not specify the nature or direction of the relationship expected between various elements they identify.

The syndrome is strengthened by aspects of the situation that decrease the psychological distance between the hostage and captor, and that increase the likelihood that the hostage will turn to the captor, and not to others, for help in dealing with the traumatic experience. Note that some of the variables thought to promote the syndrome are opposites, or contradictory. For example, abuse is seen by Strentz (1982) as decreasing the likelihood and strength of the syndrome. Because abuse is likely to increase the intensity of the experience, Ochberg (1977), on the other hand, probably sees abuse as likely to develop and increase the syndrome's strength.

Psychodynamics Underlying
Classic Stockholm Syndrome

No one universally accepted theory exists concerning psychological mechanisms responsible for the development and maintenance of Stockholm Syndrome, though an excellent synthesis of the disparate extant

TABLE 1.2
Variables Observed to Promote the Development of Stockholm
Syndrome in Hostages

Subject Characteristics

- Age (nature of relationship not stated; Crelinsten 1977; Milgram 1977)
- Sex (nature of relationship not stated; Crelinsten 1977)
- Captors' having strong personalities and/or strong beliefs that are communicated in a non-hostile manner (Turner 1985)
- The hostage having a weak personality (Turner 1985)

Variables That Encourage Interaction or Reduce the Psychological Distance between Hostage and Captor

- The absence of gagging of hostages and of hooding of hostages and captor (Turner 1985)
- Hostage's being permitted to make eye contact with captor (E. E. Flynn 1990)
- Infrequent rotation of "guards" of hostages (Turner 1985)[a]
- Guards' being permitted to speak with the hostages (Turner 1985)[a]
- Reducing hostage-captor language differences (Turner 1985)
- Reducing prejudice or preexisting stereotypes that might put psychological distance between hostage and captor (Turner 1985)
- The relationship of the hostage to the terrorist's cause (presumably, the less a "we-they" stance exists, the more the syndrome will appear; Crelinsten 1977)
- Increasing psychological distance of a hostage from his/her government (Ochberg 1977; Wesselius and DeSarno 1983)

Variables That Reduce the Likelihood That Hostages Will Turn to Persons Other Than the Captor for Nurturance and Protection

- The hostage's being held in total isolation (E. E. Flynn 1990)
- Whether the hostage is alone or with others (presumably, being alone strengthens syndrome; Crelinsten 1977; Milgram 1977)
- Whether the hostage knows other hostages also being held (presumably, not knowing them strengthens syndrome; Crelinsten 1977; Milgram 1977)
- Whether the hostage is with his/her family (although presence of family probably increases stress, it decreases isolation, thus the effects of family could go in either direction; Milgram 1977)
- The homogeneity and size of the group taken hostage (presumably, the greater the heterogeneity and size of the group, the less likely the possibility of the hostages' organizing against the captors and the more likely the development of the syndrome; Crelinsten 1977)

Variables Increasing Hostage-Captor Contact and/or the Likelihood that Hostages Will Turn to the Captor for Nurturance and Protection

- Dependence upon captor for survival (presumably, the greater the dependence, the greater the syndrome; Ochberg 1977)
- Increasing captor-captive interdependence, including increasing the threat of imminent common death (Hacker 1976; but see note 2)
- Increasing duration of captivity (Elshtain 1985; Milgram 1977; Ochberg 1977; Wesselius and DeSarno 1983)
- Increasing the time which the hostage and captor spend together (Hacker

TABLE 1.2 *(Continued)*

1976), so long as the interaction is not negative (Strentz 1982) and so long
as factors leading to negative identification are not present (Turner 1985)
- Increasing physical proximity between captive and captor (Hacker 1976)
- Increasing the amount of hostage-captor contact (Wesselius and DeSarno
  1983)
- Increasing the amount of face-to-face hostage-captor contact (Turner 1985)
- Reducing the hostage's ability to psychologically insulate herself or himself
  from the captor, as might be accomplished through busy work (Strentz
  1982)
- Having hostages and captors who are unsophisticated about Stockholm Syndrome and other psychological phenomena, though knowledge of the syndrome can also help hostages use the syndrome to their advantage (Turner
  1985)

Variables Increasing Hostages' Arousal Level
- Increasing the amount of violence during the takeover period (Turner 1985)
- The intensity of the experience (presumably, the more intense, the greater the
  strength of the syndrome; Ochberg 1977)

Variables Decreasing Hostages' Arousal Level
- Decreasing the amount of random violence, unprovoked violence, and taunt-
  ing of hostages once the takeover has been accomplished (Turner 1985)[b]
- The lack of negative experiences such as rape or beatings at the hands of
  captors (Strentz 1982)[b]
- How the hostages are treated by their captors (presumably, the better they are
  treated, the more likely is development of the syndrome; Crelinsten 1977)
- The relative benignness or harshness of the captors (presumably, the greater
  the benignness relative to harshness, the greater the syndrome; Elshtain
  1985)

[a] In this case, the syndrome would be with the guards, though elsewhere in this chapter
we have not differentiated between guards and captors.
[b] One problem with this position is that captives who have had negative contact with
abductors still have developed the syndrome and that, once the syndrome has developed,
hostages are not likely to perceive abuse as abuse. Rather, they rationalize the abuse, seeing
it as deserved or as something the captors had to do or were pushed to do by outside forces.

explanations is provided by E. E. Flynn (1990). Hypotheses regarding the
psychodynamics underlying the syndrome have been offered by numerous
experts. Strentz (1982) emphasizes hostages' *regression* to an infantile mode
of behaving, wherein hostages fear separation from their captors and cling
to them. He sees the bond developing in hostages when they take the
view that they, like the captor, want to go home but can't because police
are pointing guns at them.[1]

Hacker (1976) emphasizes hostages' *identification with the victim dimension of their captor*, which he does not see as differing from *identification with the aggressor*, and *victim solidarization*, wherein the victim projects his or her own victim status onto the captor. According to Hacker, identification with the captor occurs because both the hostage and the captor fear that they may be killed by police and other rescuers. The longer the ordeal and the greater the threat of "imminent common death," the stronger the identification that develops between captor and captive.

Symonds (1982) utilizes the concepts of *frozen fright, traumatic infantilism,* and *pathological transference* to make sense of the syndrome in hostages. Frozen fright develops as the hostage comes out of shock and begins to perceive the reality of the situation. In frozen fright, hostages are affectively paralyzed, enabling them to focus their cognitive and motor functions solely on survival, with concentration centered on the terrorist. In this state the hostage responds to the captor with cooperative, friendly behavior. As this state continues and the hostages are still not rescued, they will feel overwhelmed and develop traumatic psychological infantilism wherein they respond to the captor with appeasement, submission, ingratiation, cooperation, and empathy.[2] As captivity continues and the hostages are still alive, they will begin to perceive the captor as giving their lives back to them. At this point a hostage develops a pathological transference to the terrorist, wherein the terrorist is seen as the "good guy" and authorities, police, and family, because they have not gotten the hostage out of this situation, are seen as the "bad guys." This transference will persist long after hostages are released because they fear that any expression of negativity toward the captors may invite retaliation.

Noting that the syndrome always develops within a context of confinement and helplessness, Soskis and Ochberg (1982) emphasize that the purpose of the syndrome's development is the generation of hope within an otherwise hopeless situation. Because the captor is the source of that hope, the hostage feels gratitude toward the captor.

One idea shared by all four groups of experts is that the terror created in the hostage by the captor creates feelings of absolute dependence and helplessness in the victims. In fact, all except Soskis and Ochberg (1982) liken the helplessness of the hostage to that of an infant, and the dependence of the hostage on the captor to the dependence of the infant on a parent.[3] Beyond this initial similarity, considerable variability exists regarding the psychological mechanisms proposed to underlie the syndrome, yet there appears to be a moderate amount of consistency regarding the phenomena associated with Stockholm Syndrome that require explanation: (1) hostages' belief that the captor is an omnipotent, caring protector and that it is the police who are trying to kill them; (2) the hostages' clinging to their captor; (3) their blind obedience to the captor; (4) their gratitude to the captor for permitting them to live; and (5) their absence of anger at the captor despite nightmares and fear that the captor will come back again to get them.

Each of the four groups of experts described above has made important contributions to our understanding of Stockholm Syndrome. Each brings a different perspective and each attempts to explain somewhat different psychological phenomena associated with the syndrome. Their contributions provide different pieces of the puzzle that is Stockholm Syndrome. There is no one accepted understanding of the syndrome's psychodynamics and the various hypotheses suggest that our understanding of them has been fragmented. In chapter 2 we will provide an overarching theory, referred to as Graham's Stockholm Syndrome theory.

Summary and Conclusion

Most of what is known of captives bonding with captors comes out of anecdotal accounts of hostage incidents during the past twenty years. Examination of several of these incidents in detail brings a number of paradoxical aspects of Stockholm Syndrome to light. The paradoxical nature of the syndrome suggests that we, as a public, as mental health professionals, and even as former hostages, do not really understand it. The mental health sciences have described captives bonding with captors but have done little to further our understanding of the phenomenon.

Three widely accepted indicators that Stockholm Syndrome has developed are (1) positive feelings by the captives toward their captors; (2) negative feelings by the captives toward the police and authorities trying to win their release; and (3) positive feelings by the captors toward their captives (cf. Kuleshnyk 1984). Studies of the psychodynamics thought by experts (such as Symonds and Hacker) to underlie the syndrome reveal neither a widely accepted understanding of the psychodynamics at work nor an extant comprehensive theory that explains them. Some of the psychodynamics underlying a number of the paradoxes have been explained, others remain. For example, why do victims blame themselves for their captors' abuse of them, or otherwise rationalize it? Why do small kindnesses by captors impact so powerfully on hostages' attitudes toward captors, making the kindnesses appear to supplant the impact of terror? Do cognitive distortions occur because a hostage has the syndrome or does the syndrome develop because the hostage cognitively distorts?

In the next chapter we will examine a phenomenon similar or identical to bonding with a captor: bonding to an abuser.[4] In examining this phenomenon in a wide range of situations (child abuse, wife abuse, etc.), we attempt to identify the conditions conducive to its development, its aspects, and the psychodynamics underlying it. Thus, while the core definition of Stockholm Syndrome has been conceptualized as involving only three feelings (Kuleshnyk 1984), in the next chapter we will develop the construct further. We will find that many more psychodynamics or indicators may be associated with Stockholm Syndrome than have been identified in the hostage literature to date. This identification process will permit researchers to study these phenomena empirically, perhaps even subjecting them to experimental test. In addition, we will present Graham's Stockholm Syndrome theory, which addresses the psychodynamics of the syndrome that Strentz (1982), Symonds (1982), Hacker (1976), and Soskis and Ochberg (1982) sought to explain, plus more.

Also, we will introduce the concept of "Generalized Stockholm Syndrome," which explains how Graham's Stockholm Syndrome theory applies at both an individual and a societal level. In chapters 3 to 5 we will demonstrate how Graham's Generalized Stockholm Syndrome theory explains the responses of oppressed group members to their oppressors, and, more specifically, women's bonding to their oppressors, men. We will also show how women as a group develop femininity, love for men, and heterosexuality as part of a hostage psychology.

Graham's Stockholm Syndrome Theory: A Universal Theory of Chronic Interpersonal Abuse?

As our descriptions of several hostage-taking incidents have revealed, Stockholm Syndrome involves the bonding of hostages to their captors and is not only an apparently inexplicable but also a complex phenomenon. Earlier work of others regarding various "hostage" groups (e.g., battered women, abused children) allowed us to identify precursors to the development of Stockholm Syndrome and its psychodynamics and aspects (Graham and Rawlings 1991). These phenomena, and the extension of the theory from an individual to a societal level, comprise what we refer to as Graham's Stockholm Syndrome. The work of others has allowed us to identify themes observed for a wide range of "hostage" groups and thus to create what we believe to be a universal theory of chronic interpersonal abuse. This new understanding of Stockholm Syndrome allows us to show how a victim's Stockholm Syndrome can be generalized to those who are not a person's captors or abusers. This generalization will provide us with a way of understanding women's femininity, love of men, and heterosexuality.

Bonding to an Abuser/Captor as a Survival Strategy: Graham's Stockholm Syndrome Theory

Roots of Stockholm Syndrome Theory

In developing Stockholm Syndrome theory, Graham began with a conceptualization of Stockholm Syndrome that emerged from the literature on hostages whose captors were political activists, criminals, mentally disturbed, or prisoners (see chapter 1). Although a universally accepted definition of Stockholm Syndrome does not exist, Kuleshnyk (1984) proposed that the syndrome is present if one or more of the following feelings is observed: (1) positive feelings by the captive toward his or her captor; (2) negative feelings by the captive toward the police and authorities trying to win his or her release; and (3) positive feelings by the captor toward his or her captive.

Graham (1987) attempted to ascertain the precursors, parameters, and psychodynamics of this syndrome more fully, and thereby to develop the construct of Stockholm Syndrome further, beyond that described in the classic hostage literature. She was particularly concerned with the psychology of hostages, not the psychology of captors. Toward this end, she examined the psychological literature of nine different "hostage" groups to see if bonding to an abuser or captor (Stockholm Syndrome) occurred in other "hostage" groups as well, even though eight of the nine groups are not commonly thought of as hostage groups.

Bonding to an abuser was found in all nine "hostage" groups studied: concentration camp prisoners (Bettelheim 1943; Eisner 1980), cult members (Alexander 1979; Atkins 1977; Bugliosi, with Gentry, 1974; Mills 1979; Yee and Layton 1981), civilians in Chinese Communist prisons (Lifton 1961; Rickett and Rickett 1973; Schein, with Schneier, and Barker 1961), pimp-procured prostitutes (Barry 1979), incest victims (E. Hill 1985), physically and/or emotionally abused children (Alexander 1985; Coleman 1985; Finkelhor 1983; Kemp and Kemp 1978), battered women (Dutton and Painter 1981; Ehrlich 1989), and POWs, as well as hostages per se (see chapter 1). The list of nine is not necessarily an exhaustive list of all groups that display Stockholm Syndrome. For example, although not included in the groups studied, other groups, such as prisoners (Biderman 1964) and children and spouses of alcoholics, may also show bonding with their guards/abusers. Even infant, nonhuman social animals, such as birds, dogs, and monkeys, were found to bond to their abusers (Rajecki, Lamb, and Obmascher 1978; Sackett et al. 1967; Scott 1963; Seay, Alexander, and Harlow 1964). The apparently pervasive nature of this phenomenon suggests that bonding to an abuser (Stockholm Syndrome) both is instinctive and plays a survival function for hostages who are victims of chronic interpersonal abuse.

TABLE 2.1
Comparison of Classic Stockholm Syndrome Theory and
Graham's Stockholm Syndrome Theory

Components	Classic Stockholm Syndrome Theory	Graham's Stockholm Syndrome Theory
Based on:	Anecdotal evidence obtained through hostage interviews	Anecdotal evidence cited in: Hostage literature Concentration camp literature Literature on civilians in Chinese Communist prisons POW literature Cult literature Child abuse literature Battered women literature Incest literature Pimp-procured prostitute literature
Indicators:	3	66 potential aspects and 9 major indicators
Conditions promoting:	(See table 1.2)	Perceived threat to survival Perceived inability to escape Perceived kindness Isolation
Psychodynamics:	No comprehensive theory	Comprehensive and universal theory which may apply to all interpersonal chronic-abuse groups

From her examination of nine different literatures, Graham identified (1) a set of four conditions she hypothesized to be *precursors* of Stockholm Syndrome; (2) a list of sixty-six aspects (behaviors, attitudes, and beliefs) associated with victims in "hostage" situations in which bonding with an abuser occurred, which Graham referred to as potential *aspects* of Stockholm Syndrome (and which are listed in the appendix); and (3) the psychodynamics associated with situations in which bonding to an abuser occurred, which Graham synthesized and hypothesized to be the *psychodynamics* underlying Stockholm Syndrome (see also Graham and Rawlings 1991). See table 2.1 for a comparison of Classic Stockholm Syndrome theory and Graham's Stockholm Syndrome theory.

We refer to bonding to a captor/abuser as Stockholm Syndrome because Graham's theory was inspired by hostages' stories, including Lang's (1974) description of the 1973 bank holdup in Stockholm, Sweden, described in chapter 1. We use the word "hostage" for persons who others might argue are more appropriately called "prisoners" for two reasons: (1) we base our concept on the identification of parallels between the situations and responses of those commonly thought of as hostages and chronic interpersonal-abuse victims not commonly thought of as hostages, and (2) the term "prisoner" implies that the captive did something to deserve the captive status and therefore is being punished, a connotation we want to avoid.[1]

Hypothesized Precursors of Stockholm Syndrome

Because Graham (1987) found that bonding to an abuser or captor occurred under a certain set of conditions in each of the nine "hostage" groups, she proposed that Stockholm Syndrome describes a unitary phenomenon observed whenever four conditions co-exist. These four *precursors* are the following:

1. perceived threat to survival and the belief that one's captor is willing to carry out that threat
2. the captive's perception of some small kindness from the captor within a context of terror
3. isolation from perspectives other than those of the captor
4. perceived inability to escape.

Although these four conditions are thought necessary to the development of the syndrome, they are probably not sufficient. As discussed in chapter 1, other necessary conditions may be those encouraging humanization, those promoting interaction and reducing the psychological distance between captor and captive, and the captive's wanting foremost to survive.

Each of these precursors, with the possible exception of kindness, exists on a continuum, that is, a victim shows more or less of each precursor. The precursors are not either present or absent, but rather present or absent in degrees. Aspects of these conditions will be examined in more detail.

Perceived Threat to Survival

While most people view physical violence as a more serious offense than psychological violence, both battered women and prisoners of war report that threat of physical violence is more psychologically debilitating than actual physical violence. *Emotional* abuse, such as the threat to maim or kill, is often perceived as a threat to *physical* survival. For these reasons, psychological violence may promote the development of the syndrome as much or more than physical violence. This makes sense. A person who threatens to shoot you may be the one knocking on your door, calling you on the phone, turning into your driveway, or waiting around the next corner. Every moment is filled with fear until you are finally shot. Once shot, you can relax because you now know where and how the shooting occurred, how seriously you were hurt, what you need to do to take care of the wound, etc. (cf. Browne 1987, p. 115).

Threat to psychological survival occurs any time a person's psychological survival is threatened. Emotional abuse can pose a threat to a person's psychological survival, particularly if that person is a child and if the emotional abuse is chronic and severe. Threat of abandonment is experienced by some as a threat to physical and/or psychological survival. This is particularly so if the victim is dependent on the person threatening abandonment, as a child may be. Incest is a form of physical and emotional abuse that threatens a child's psychological survival and sometimes even her or his physical survival. Extreme sexual or emotional abuse may produce fragmentation of identity, as in multiple personality, or psychic annihilation, as in psychosis. Threat to psychological survival can also occur, for example, when someone threatens to kill your children, when someone continues to sexually abuse your children and there is nothing you can do to stop it, or when someone prevents you from seeing your children.

Perceived Kindness

A person whose survival is threatened perceives kindness differently from a person whose survival is not threatened. For example, a small kindness—one that likely would not be noticed under conditions of safety—appears huge under conditions of threat and/or debilitation. Angela Browne (1987) reports that some battered women experience the *cessation* of violence by their partners as a show of kindness. When prisoners of war are deprived of food, sleep, and human contact, and then are given these things but not enough to satisfy their basic human needs for them, they often perceive their torturers as kind (cf. Amnesty International 1975). Bettelheim (1943) found that Nazi concentration camp prisoners had a strong need to see at least some of the high-ranking members of the Gestapo as kind and sympathetic to them. Because Bettelheim—himself a prisoner—never actually saw evidence of the officers' kindness or sympathy, one deduces that his co-prisoners' claims were cognitive distortions. These examples are provided to expose the peculiar nature of the perception of kindness by victims within a context of terror.

Isolation

The victim's isolation from persons other than the captor/abuser is ideological and usually also physical in nature. For example, a wife batterer is not likely to permit his wife to maintain ties with her family unless her family is giving her messages that strengthen or at least do not contradict his messages to her (for example, "You made your bed, now lie in it," "You just need to be a better wife," and "A woman's place is with her husband").

Abusers use a variety of strategies to isolate incest victims by discouraging them from telling others who might help if told about the abuse. The strategies include threats to kill the child or the other parent, threats backed up by violence against animals, claims that the abuser will go to jail or that the family will break up, and claims that others will not believe the child or will blame the child should the child tell. In hostage cases where victims are in physical contact with one another, as in Chinese Communist prisons, the abuser uses techniques that isolate victims from one another. These include planting informants or spies, punishing captives for being friendly to each other, encouraging captives to hate one another, punishing captives who refuse to abuse another captive, and, among victims, creating social pressure to show pro-captor/abuser attitudes (see, for example, Rigney 1956).

The victim's internalization of the captor's/abuser's belief that the victim deserves the abuse, experienced by the victim as shame, serves to further isolate the victim from others and others' perspectives, which differ from the perspective of the abuser.

Perceived Inability to Escape

A captor will usually use violence or the threat of violence to prevent a victim's escape. Examples are threats made to battered women by abusive partners that "I'll kill you if you leave me." Similar threats are made to members of other "hostage" groups as well. The incest victim may be told by her father that he will be sent to jail, that the family will be split up, and/or that she will be blamed if she reports the sexual abuse to others. Cult members are typically told that they will go to hell if they leave, for the outside world is evil. They also may know they will be killed if they leave the cult.

Outsiders usually are not aware of the threat the captor (overtly or covertly) communicates to the captive. Watson et al. (1985) describe a male hostage in a skyjacking who, upon finding a pistol left in a lavatory of the airliner by a captor, called to his captor, "Hey, you forgot your gun." Claude Fly (1973) describes his captors handing rifles to him as police worked to win his release; Mr. Fly did not turn the rifles on his captors. The point being made here is that hostages and outsiders view the hostages' ability to escape differently. What looks to outsiders as an opportunity for escape may look like a test (a trick) or a death trap to hostages. It is *hostages'*, not outsiders', perceptions of hostages' ability to escape that determines whether or not hostages develop Stockholm Syndrome.

Despite fear narrowing hostages' perceptions of options available to them, their perceptions are probably more accurate than outsiders'. Being there, hostages both have more information than do outsiders and are forced to live with terrifying contingencies that outsiders probably cannot even imagine. Outsiders' perceptions are often distorted by a need to believe that, if they were taken hostage, they would be able to escape.

Graham, Ott, and Rawlings (1990) studied the degree of threat to survival, isolation, and inability to escape, as well as the amount of kindness shown by abusive partners to women in shelters and women in emotionally abusive relationships. They found that, in such relationships, the measures of threat to survival, inability to escape, and isolation were so closely associated that it would be very unlikely to see a high degree of one of these three precursors—for example, isolation—unless one also saw a high degree of threat to survival and inability to escape. Thus, if a woman was being isolated, one can be fairly sure that her survival was also being threatened and that her options for escaping her partner were diminished. Strong associations among these three precursors may exist for other "hostage" groups as well.

The nature of the conditions that Graham found existed whenever bonding to a captor occurred leads us to apply the word "victim" to members of the nine "hostage" groups. To deny the victimizing nature of the conditions under which Stockholm Syndrome develops, encourages us to overlook the conditions important to the development of Stockholm Syndrome, to fail to see the survival function of Stockholm Syndrome, to deny the reality of the captive, and to engage in victim-blaming.

Psychodynamics Underlying Stockholm Syndrome in "Hostage" Groups

The confluence of the four precursor conditions can be seen as giving rise to the psychodynamics that account for the apparently bizarre behaviors of people exhibiting Stockholm Syndrome. Graham (1987; see also Graham and Rawlings 1991) hypothesized that the following psychodynamics underlie Stockholm Syndrome in the various hostage groups.

An abuser (or captor) terrorizes a victim, who cannot escape, by threatening his/her (physical or psychological) survival. This terrorization could be the result, for example, of someone holding a gun to another's head and playing Russian roulette, or of ongoing childhood sexual abuse. Because of this traumatization, the victim needs nurturance and protection, and because the victim is isolated from others, he or she must turn to the abuser for nurturance and protection.[2] Because of the need for nurturance and the will to survive, and because there appear to be no means of escaping further terrorization, the victim actively searches for expressions of kindness, empathy, or affection by the abuser. If the victim perceives that kindness, she or he becomes hopeful that the abuser will end the terrorization and permit her/him to survive.[3]

With the perception of kindness and hope, the victim denies any feelings of danger, terror, and rage that the abuser creates in her or him. The denial occurs because the terror, and thus danger, is experienced as overwhelming (that is, as threatening psychic annihilation), and the rage, if expressed, invites retaliation by the abuser. Such denial allows the victim to commence bonding to the positive side of the abuser.

Having found some hope that the abuser will let her or him live, the victim tries to enlarge upon and intensify any perceived caring felt by the abuser toward the victim, and thereby to turn the abuser into someone who cares too much about the victim to continue the terrorization. The victim therefore works to keep the abuser happy, becoming hypersensitive to the abuser's moods and needs. To determine what will keep the abuser happy, the victim tries to get inside the head of the abuser, that is, to think and feel as the abuser thinks and feels, thereby taking on the abuser's worldview. Because the victim's very survival is at stake, she or he becomes hypervigilant to the abuser's needs, feelings, and perspectives. Thus, not only is the victim compliant, but actively working to anticipate the needs of the abuser. Her or his own needs (other than survival), feelings, and perspectives must take second place to those of the abuser. In addition, the victim's needs (other than survival), feelings, and perspectives only seem to get in the way of the victim's doing what is necessary for survival (they are, after all, feelings of terror). For example, it is unimportant to the victim if she or he has a headache, except to the extent that the headache gets in the way of keeping the abuser happy. But if the abuser has a headache, the victim will do everything possible to relieve the abuser's headache and ensure the abuser's well-being, therefore denying the victim's own needs, feelings, and perspectives.

The victims unconsciously try to view the world as the abuser does, for only by doing so can they anticipate what they need to do to keep the abuser happy and feeling kindly toward them. They thus see the abusers/captors as the "good guys" and those trying to win their release (e.g., parents, police, therapists, or friends) as the "bad guys," for this is the captor's view. Similarly, the victims perceive themselves to deserve abuse at the hands of the abuser, because that is the way the abuser perceives things. For similar reasons, the victims displace their repressed anger at the abuser onto the police. They also transfer the abuser's anger and destructiveness onto the police, whom they see as more likely to kill them (or get them killed) than the abuser/captor. If victims are subjected to the Stockholm Syndrome precursor conditions for a prolonged period of time (e.g., months or years), even their sense of self comes to be experienced through the eyes of the abuser, replacing any former sense of self that once existed.[4]

Why would a bond develop under these conditions? If victims deny their own terror, the danger they are in, and their rage, how can they understand their strict compliance with the captor's every order, their state of extreme arousal, and their hypervigilance to the abuser's needs, wants, and moods? Having denied the danger, terror, and rage, victims look to their environment and to their internal motivations for cues to explain their behavior and state of extreme arousal (cf. D. J. Bem 1972; Festinger 1957; Schachter and Singer 1962). Seeing themselves being compliant and even hypervigilant to the abuser's needs, they interpret their physiological arousal and behavior as indicating they have strong positive feelings for the abuser (cf. Walster 1971; Walster and Berscheid 1971).[5] The more extreme the state of arousal, the stronger the bond experienced by the victims. The more hypervigilant the victims are relative to the kindness shown by the abuser, the stronger the bond is interpreted to be. The harder the victims have to work to win over the abuser, the stronger the victims' bond to the abuser (cf. Walster and Berscheid 1971).

If victims are given the opportunity to leave their abuser after being subjected to the precursor conditions for a prolonged period, they will have an extremely difficult time doing so. Having denied the violent, terrifying side of the abuser as well as their own anger, the victims see no reason to leave the abuser. At the same time, intense, unconsciously driven "push-pull" dynamics characterize the victims' orientation toward the abuser. These dynamics involve powerful, survival-based feelings of being *pulled* toward the abuser (because it is the mutual bonding between victims and abuser that convinces the abuser to let victims live and that gives hope to victims) and of being *pushed* away from the abuser (because the abuser is threatening the victims' survival, even though this may be recognized only unconsciously). "Pull" forces are expressed as cognitive distortions, for example: victims believe they must help the abuser because the abuser needs them; victims see the abuser himself as a victim who would stop being abusive if he were given enough love; victims believe they are the only ones who really understand the abuser; and victims want to protect the abuser, because they perceive that the abuser has protected them. These cognitive distortions provide an interpretation of the victims' behavior *to the victims themselves*. The content of the distortions, and the fact that the distortions provide meaning to the victims about their own behavior, help the victims believe they are in control.[6] The cognitive distortions provide the only sense of control in a life-threatening relationship, and thus cannot be abandoned. "Push" forces are experienced as terror and anger, though victims almost never *express* these emotions to the abuser because they fear it will threaten their survival.

A number of mechanisms make it difficult for the victim to separate psychologically from the abuser following prolonged captivity. Two such mechanisms are fear of losing the only positive relationship available to the victim during this prolonged period of isolation—marked by terrorization and the resultant craving for nurturance, protection, and safety—and fear of losing the only identity that remains, namely, her or his self as seen through the eyes of the abuser. These fears are expressed variously: fear of abandonment, of being lonely, of not being able to live without the abuser, and of not knowing who one is without the abuser, feeling empty, and so on. The greater the victim's fears, the greater was her or his isolation from perspectives other than the abuser's, and the greater the damage to the sense of self. In the case of child victims, this view of self may be the only sense of self they have ever experienced; in the case of adult victims, this view of self may have replaced a previous sense of self. In any case, living without the abuser, and thus without a sense of self, is experienced by the victim as a threat to psychic survival. Loss of their only "friend" and of self as experienced through the abuser's eyes requires victims to take a leap into a terrifying unknown, which is difficult even for people in healthy environments. It is considerably more difficult for someone whose survival depends on the fragile feelings of predictability and control produced by cognitive distortions and the whims of a terrorist.

The victims' feeling that the abuser may return to "get" them another time, and that this time the abuser might not be so nice (i.e., might not let them live), serves to keep the victims loyal to the abuser long after the ordeal is over. Victims feel certain that the abuser will get them again—after all, he's done it before, and that's proof that he could do it again. They might live the rest of their lives fearful of showing any disloyalty, preparing for the time when the abuser might catch up with them again and thus being never fully separate from the abuser psychologically. If the abuser wants the victim close by, the victim will feel panic away from the abuser. This panic becomes understandable when we keep in mind the fact that the victim sees things from the *abuser's* point of view. Thus, if the abuser wants the victim close by, the victim will see being apart from the abuser as a form of disloyalty. As a result, the released victim lives in fear of her or his physical survival, afraid that the abuser will return to punish any such disloyalty. The fears persist even if the abuser dies or is sent to prison. The extent and depth of such fears are revealed by the fact that the victim fears having even disloyal *thoughts* about the abuser.

The need to master the terror created by the hostage-taking experience may keep the victim in the terrorizing situation for a longer time than would otherwise be necessary. To master the terror created by the trauma, the victim must (1) process her or his (positive and negative) feelings surrounding the life-threatening ordeal, and (2) develop feelings of control (e.g., recognizing previously used survival strategies that could be used again). Only if the victim masters the terror will the fear of being reterrorized subside.

Aspects, Major Indicators, Cognitive Distortions, and Long-Term Effects Associated with Graham's Stockholm Syndrome

Aspects

Graham compiled a list of people's responses to different hostage situations so that they could eventually be subjected to empirical testing. Aspects of victims' psychology—attitudes, feelings, beliefs, or behaviors—observed in the various "hostage" groups were viewed by Graham as potential components of the Stockholm Syndrome. To date, sixty-six different potential aspects of Stockholm Syndrome have been identified by Graham; they are listed in the appendix. Because this conceptualization was developed to test the usefulness of hostage-captor dynamics in understanding the responses of members of a wide range of hostage groups, as well as to test whether (or which) responses are aspects of Stockholm Syndrome, we use the words "captive" and "captor."

Major Indicators

Because efforts to identify all aspects of Stockholm Syndrome and to empirically verify their association with the phenomenon continue, the following list of nine aspects (major indicators) can serve as a guide for identifying the presence of the syndrome. In assessing its presence, one looks for a combination of indicators. Any one of them could be present and the person may still not have the syndrome. The syndrome is described by a continuum, that is, it is present in degrees rather than an all or nothing phenomenon. The major indicators are also described by a continuum.

1. Captive shows symptoms of ongoing trauma or of Post-traumatic Stress Disorder (PTSD).
2. Captive is bonded to her/his captor (actually the bond is bidirectional, but here our focus is on the psychology of the captive).
3. Captive is intensely grateful for small kindnesses shown to her/him by captor.
4. Captive denies captor's violence against her/him when violence and/or threats of violence *are* actually occurring, or captive rationalizes that violence. The captive denies her/his own anger at captor, to others, and to herself or himself.
5. Captive is hypervigilant to captor's needs and seeks to keep the captor happy (to increase the chances of the captor letting her/him live); this hypervigilance is undirectional, or not bilateral. To do this, captive tries to "get inside the captor's head."
6. Captive sees the world from the captor's perspective; he or she may not have his/her own perspective. Captive experiences own sense of self through the captor's eyes.

7. In accordance with no. 6, captive sees outside authorities (e.g., police) trying to win her/his release as "bad guys" and sees captor as "good guy." Captive sees captor as protecting him/her.

8. Captive finds it psychologically difficult to leave captor even after her/his physical release has been won.

9. Captive fears captor will come back to get her/him even after captor is dead or in prison. She or he fears thinking disloyal thoughts about captor for fear of retaliation.

Cognitive Distortions

Table 2.2 provides a list of cognitive distortions associated with Stockholm Syndrome in a study of college-age women in dating relationships and/or in a study of emotionally and physically battered women (Graham et al. 1993; Graham, Ott, and Rawlings 1990). I propose that these cognitive distortions are likely to occur in any human victims of chronic interpersonal abuse.

The vast majority of the cognitive distortions listed in table 2.2 have the effect of reducing the victim's terror. Because it requires a lot of psychic energy to maintain a cognitive distortion, the large number of distortions that are used to help reduce terror should not be taken lightly: it suggests that terror reduction is important to survival and to effective coping *during* ongoing abuse. Other distortions are also survival strategies. For example, the victims' belief that they must win their abuser's love in order to survive helps them work toward that end. (Recall the importance to the hostages' survival of the abuser's bonding to them during the Stockholm bank siege described in chapter 1.) Distortions involving the victims' taking the abuser's perspective help victims anticipate the needs of the abuser by helping them stay "tuned in" to the needs, wants, and perspectives of the abuser. A number of the distortions help victims believe they have some control over the abuse. These include self-blame for the abuse, belief that they control whether the abuser abuses them, perception of the abuser as a victim, and belief that if one gives enough love, the abuser will stop abusing.

Three of the distortions listed in table 2.2—seeing the abuser as omnipotent, seeing small kindnesses as huge, and seeing the relationship

TABLE 2.2
Cognitive Distortions of Stockholm Syndrome Victims

- Narrowed perceptions; perceptions are focused on the immediate, that is, on surviving in the here and now.
- Denial of abuse: don't see themselves as abused when they actually are.
- Minimization of abuse: minimize the extent of the abuse ("It's not so bad. Other people have it worse").
- Rationalize abusers' abuse, seeing the cause of the abusers' abuse as being outside the abuser, or externally motivated.
- Self-blame.
- See their abuser as good and themselves as bad, or switch back and forth between seeing abuser as either all good or all bad.
- See their abuser as more powerful than the abuser actually is.
- Take on their abuser's perspective as their own. This includes:
  - Seeing themselves as the abuser sees them.
  - Hating those parts of themselves that abuser criticizes or says is reason she or he is angry at them.
  - Believing they have to be perfect or they are worthless and thus deserve abuse.
  - Believing they do not deserve love and affection from others or even from themselves.
  - Seeing their abuser's needs, wants, and desires as their own.
  - Seeing those trying to help them escape the abuser and his/her abuse as "the bad guys" and the abuser as "the good guy."
- See small kindnesses by abuser as large kindnesses. Small kindnesses by abuser create hope that abuser will stop being abusive in future.
- See violence by abuser as a sign of his caring or love.
- Believe their relationship with their abuser would be perfect if the abuse were not occurring.
- See their abusers as victims rather than as perpetrators of abuse against them.
- Believe that if one is kind enough to, and gives the abuser enough love, the abuser will let them live and possibly even stop abusing them.
- Believe that they love their abuser.
- Believe that to survive they must have their abusers' love or caring.
- Are thankful and grateful to their abusers that the abusers have not killed them.
- Believe that if they even think a thought that is disloyal to their abuser, the abuser will know and retaliate.
- Believe that their abusers will come back to "get them" even when their abusers are dead or in prison.

with the abuser as perfect if it were not for the abuse—may be the result of contrast effects. For example, compared to the victim who is fighting feelings of total helplessness, the abuser appears totally powerful. The displays of kindness, while small, provide enormous hope in a context of otherwise overwhelming terror. Only the distortion of seeing the abuser as omnipotent is not clearly beneficial to victims of chronic, inescapable abuse; however, it may be beneficial in the short-term if it serves both to encourage victim compliance and to communicate to the abuser that he or she is taken seriously by the victim.

Two cognitive distortions deserve further explanation: the victims' belief that they love their abuser, and self-blame. The victims' misattribution—that love, not terror, is responsible for their arousal and behavior—is *a cognitive distortion that develops when victims see no way to escape.* Stockholm Syndrome would not develop without this misattribution (cognitive distortion), nor would the syndrome persist without its continuance. This is so because, as Walster and Berscheid note, "Once the subject has . . . identified the experience as love, it is love" (1971, p. 47). If victims were to reinterpret their arousal and hypervigilance as due to something other than love or caring, the bond would vanish, though the behavior and arousal might remain the same.[7]

Victims often rationalize abuse by blaming themselves for its occurrence, believing that they control whether and when they are abused (see "Rationalize abuser's abuse" in table 2.2). (But, as Wortman [1976] observes, one does not have to be victimized to believe one exercises control over uncontrollable, chance events.) Empirical research indicates that persons who perceive they have control, even when they don't, adapt better to stress and demonstrate more endurance (Glass, Reim, and Singer 1971; Glass, Singer, and Friedman 1969; Lefcourt 1973; Richter 1959). But why would victims blame themselves for their own abuse? There are at least two reasons: (1) To help ensure survival, victims take the perspective of their abuser, and the abuser believes he or she is justified in abusing the victim; (2) if victims see themselves as to blame for the abuse, then they believe they are able to stop the abuse. The misperception that they have control encourages them to try to influence outcomes; the alternative is to give up, which, as Richter (1959) shows and Turner (1990) warns, may result in death.

Self-blame as a cognitive distortion, then, represents an attempt to feel in control in a situation over which the victim has little or no control. I propose that the less control the victim actually has and the more severe the consequences of not having control (that is, the more severe the abuse), the more likely it probably is that a victim will self-blame. In essence then, self-blame enables a victim to not feel like a victim—a very useful distortion: it allows one to deny one's abuse in order not to be overwhelmed, and in order to create a bond with one's abuser. Consequently, the victim will spend considerable effort trying to figure out what she or he is doing wrong to cause the abuse. Another consequence is that the victim spends enormous energy attempting to change or improve herself or himself so that the abuse will end. Readers wishing to learn more about self-blame as a response to trauma are encouraged to consult Janoff-Bulman (1979), D. T. Miller and Porter (1983), Thornton et al. (1988), and Wortman (1976).

Associated with bonding to an abuser in humans, and possibly promoting or strengthening the bond, are cognitive distortions embodied in beliefs that the abuser is not responsible for his or her abuse, abuse is a sign of the abuser's love, the abuser is also a victim, and if given enough love the abuser will stop abusing.[8] It is not clear whether these cognitive distortions are responses to the victims' misattributions that love, not terror, is responsible for their high arousal and hypervigilance to the abuser, or if they are noncausally related to or cause the misattributions.

Cognitive distortions serve three primary functions. They help prevent victims from being overwhelmed by terror, which would render them unable to do what is needed to increase their chances of surviving. The misattribution that the victim's arousal and hypervigilance are due to love, not terror, creates both a bond between victims and their abusers and hope in the victim. When the victim defines the relationship as one of care, it is easy for the abuser to do likewise. Clearly, these cognitive distortions are in the service of survival: they reduce terror, provide hope of escape by winning over the abuser, and facilitate the bonding of the abuser with the victims and thereby increase the victims' chances of survival.

Long-Term Effects of Exposure to the Precursor Conditions

Graham and Rawlings (1991) theorized that prolonged exposure to the four Stockholm Syndrome precursors would cause victims to generalize abuser/victim (or captor/captive) psychodynamics to their relations with others. They identified four principal long-range outcomes of prolonged

Stockholm Syndrome: (1) splitting; (2) intense push-pull dynamics in relationships with others; (3) displaced anger; and (4) lack of sense of self except as experienced through the eyes of the abuser. Below, we will examine each of these long-term effects and describe the survival function of each.

Splitting is a process that occurs at an unconscious level wherein the victim sees her or his partner as all good and herself or himself as all bad, or alternately sees the partner as all good or all bad. If splitting did not occur, the victim would simultaneously see the abuser as both good and bad, and the bad would overwhelm the good. Recall that the victim sees the abuser as good because the abuser has shown the victim some small bit of kindness, but this small bit of kindness was shown within a context of terror. If the bad overwhelms the good, the victim may be overcome with terror and will likely lose hope of surviving. We propose that, after prolonged exposure to interpersonal abuse, victims will begin to engage in splitting in their relationships with others as well.

The *intense push-pull dynamics* seen in persons with Stockholm Syndrome have developed because, on the one hand, victims naturally *push* away from the person who is threatening their survival, but, on the other hand, to survive they must also *bond with (pull toward)* the very person who is threatening them *in the hope of winning him or her over*. These opposing forces are played out with an intensity expected of issues determining life and death. After long-term exposure to chronic interpersonal abuse, victims generalize these push-pull dynamics to their relations with others.

Victims of chronic interpersonal abuse, fearing retaliation if they express their anger at their abuser for the abuse done to them, will *displace* that *anger* onto themselves and others who have less power over them than does (or did) the abuser. Thus, another effect of long-term interpersonal abuse is displaced anger.

Yet another long-term effect of chronic interpersonal abuse is either a *loss of sense of self* or the lack of a sense of self (if one had not developed prior to the abuse). In an effort to survive, the victim takes on the perspective of the abuser, coming even to experience her or his own sense of self through the eyes of the abuser. Thus, the victim's sense of self comes to be experienced as the abuser's sense of the victim. Obviously, such a "self" is likely to be experienced as deserving of abuse, as that is apparently how the abuser sees the victim. In the absence of the abuser, the victim will no longer know who she or he is, exposing the lack of a real sense of self in the victim.

Because the symptoms—splitting, intense push-pull interpersonal dynamics, displaced anger, and lack of sense of self—parallel those seen in Borderline Personality Disorder (BPD), we have proposed that the four Stockholm Syndrome-conducive conditions not only give rise to the syndrome, but may eventuate in BPD if abuse is sufficiently severe and long-term. In less severe cases, the victim is likely to show only borderline personality *characteristics* (BPC). We conceptualize BPD and BPC as survival strategies, wherein the syndrome's psychodynamics are generalized to persons other than the abuser/captor. We also propose that BPD and BPC can develop at any age, even in adulthood, as a consequence of prior chronic, long-term interpersonal abuse (Graham and Rawlings 1991). Readers interested in empirical studies of the application of Graham's Stockholm Syndrome theory to various abuse populations are referred to Allen (1991), Graham et al. (1993), Graham, Ott, and Rawlings (1990), Lipari (1993), and Naber-Morris (1990).

Clarifications about the Ideas Presented Thus Far

Before describing Graham's Generalized Stockholm Syndrome, an extension of the theory presented thus far, we want to clarify two facets of Graham's theory. *People who develop the syndrome do not do so because they have a personality defect such as a weak personality, because they were previously abused, or because they were socialized in a certain way.* The syndrome appears to be a universal response to inescapable threat to survival. It is seen in humans and nonhumans, young and old, males and females, and peoples of different cultures. It occurs when animals, human and nonhuman, whose survival is threatened seek to survive. Under the right conditions—the four precursor conditions—anyone who seeks to survive will develop Stockholm Syndrome. This occurs whether, for example, the victim is an abused child, a battered women, a skyjacking victim, or a prisoner of war.

As described by Peter Hill (with Friend 1986), in the 1985 skyjacking of

TWA Flight 847 virtually all passengers developed the syndrome. Are we to presume then that the people who boarded that particular plane did so because of a personality defect? That skyjackers select planeloads of people on the basis of their knowledge of those people's personalities? That kidnappers wait until they see someone with a weak personality walking down the street before they pounce? More broadly, are we to assume that only people with weak personalities are held hostage and abused? This is absurd. Similarly, we would argue that battered women and abused children are not battered because of a personality defect or their socialization; *it is their abusers who have the personality defect and/or abusive backgrounds*.

People tend either to blame the victims of accidents and chance occurrences, seeing the victims as responsible for their ill fate, or to distance themselves from those victims by identifying ways in which they are not like the victim (Walster, 1966). The tendency to blame victims, called *defensive attribution* (Shaver 1970), is exacerbated when the consequences to the victim (and/or to others) are severe (Burger 1981; Walster 1966), when the victim is more socially respectable (successful and altruistic as opposed to despicable and dishonest; C. Jones and Aronson 1973), and when the observer making the attribution sees himself or herself as a potential victim and as similar to the victim (Shaver 1970; Burger 1981). This distortion or distancing helps us defend against the idea that bad things can happen to us as well.

Anyone, therefore, can be taken hostage and abused. Chance factors to a large extent determine who becomes a victim. The chance factors may be the socioeconomic class into which one is born, the parents to whom one is born, the time and airline one chooses to fly to a particular location, the time one happens to be walking along a particular street, the persons one happens to meet, and so on. Believing that a victim is different from oneself, that the victim was a victim because he or she behaved in a way that caused the victimization, or that the victim has a character weakness that led to the victimization *helps us feel safer,* but it does not help us understand why people develop the syndrome.

If you think that you would respond differently than other hostages, consider the following possible scenario. A person holds a gun to your head and tells you, "If you try to escape I'll kill you." Are you likely to try to escape while that person is aiming a gun at your head? You could go for the gun and most likely be killed, or you could try to convince your captor to let you live. Wouldn't you do exactly what other hostages do: try to survive by making the most of aspects of the situation in which you find yourself, namely, by assessing and making use of any good-will that your captor shows you. Like other victims, you are likely to search diligently for some sign that your captor has positive feelings, somewhere, for you. If you catch a glimpse of caring, you, like other victims, are likely to try to win your captor/abuser over. If you are lucky, you will. Do you do this because you have a weak personality? Because you were socialized to be compliant or submissive? No, you do it for survival.

Victims with the syndrome do not stay with their abusers because they have bonded with the abusers; rather, they bond with their abusers because they see no way to escape. A hostage who sees a safe way to escape does so. A hostage who physically leaves the abuser and then returns does so because of fears of retaliation for not returning (even though the victim may think otherwise).[9]

Graham's Generalized Stockholm Syndrome

In this section we will argue that there exists an additional phenomenon—Generalized Stockholm Syndrome—in which the victims generalize Stockholm Syndrome dynamics to persons they perceive as similar to the abuser/captor and who show them some kindness. Generalized Stockholm Syndrome can develop in any one of three situations where Stockholm Syndrome is present. In one of these situations, a special type of Generalized Stockholm Syndrome—*Societal Stockholm Syndrome*—develops. In chapters 3–5 we will show that Societal (culturally based) Stockholm Syndrome characterizes women as a group in their relations to men as a group.

Basis of Generalized Stockholm Syndrome

Generalized Stockholm Syndrome results from having one's physical and/or psychological survival threatened by one or more individuals and then being shown kindness by *other* individuals who are perceived as similar to the threatening individuals in some ways. Generalized Stockholm Syndrome is explained in its simplest form by two psychological concepts: Graham's Stockholm Syndrome theory and stimulus generalization. Graham's theory predicts that, because the victim is suffering despair and needs nurturance as a result of terror created by the threat to survival, he or she bonds to the first person who provides emotional relief. The bond is particularly likely to develop if the person who provides emotional relief is the abuser, because kindness by the abuser creates hope that the abuse will stop.

Stimulus generalization accounts for a great deal of learning and is so reliably demonstrated in animals (including humans) that it is referred to as a scientific law in the field of psychology. Here an animal that has learned to give a certain response to a certain stimulus will also give that response to stimuli other than the original stimulus, as long as the other stimuli are sufficiently similar to the original one. To understand the importance of stimulus generalization to bonding, consider the following Stockholm Syndrome-conducive situation: An abuser behaves kindly after being abusive and threatening the victim's survival. The abuser's kindness creates hope in the victim that the abuser will discontinue the abuse and let the victim live. This hope pushes the victim to try to get on the good side of the abuser, which requires the victim to see the world from the abuser's perspective and to remain hypervigilant to the abuser's wants and needs. In the efforts to keep the abuser happy (nonviolent), the victim bonds to the abuser.

So how is stimulus generalization relevant to this situation? The law of stimulus generalization would lead one to expect a traumatized victim to show the same responses (hope, hypervigilance, bonding) to someone other than the abuser if this other person showed the victim kindness *and* was perceived by the victim to resemble the abuser. The resemblance could be physical, behavioral, historical, or of any other type that induces the victim to perceive the two individuals as similar (though this perception may not be conscious). However, this set of events is all the more likely to unfold if the victim perceives that this other person, like the abuser he or she resembles, is able to both abuse and, thus, end abuse.

Furthermore, a stimulus generalization gradient exists which reflects the fact that the more similar a stimulus is to the original stimulus, the greater is the likelihood of generalization. This gradient would lead us to expect that the more a person who shows kindness to a traumatized victim resembles the abuser, the more likely the victim is to respond (and bond) to that person as though that person were the abuser (and as though that person could stop the abuse), and the stronger the bond would be. Thus Graham's theory and the law of stimulus generalization predict that the more any person or group is perceived as being like those who have threatened one with violence, the more any acts of kindness by that person or group will lead a traumatized victim to develop the syndrome.

To use an example that foreshadows the arguments to follow, if a man threatens a woman's life and both a man and a woman (who are similar in all respects except gender) immediately and simultaneously show her kindness, the victim would be expected to bond more tightly with the man who shows her kindness than with the woman, because of the man's greater physical (gender-based) similarity to the (male) traumatizer. (This hypothetical example assumes that the victim uses gender as a dimension for differentiating people, as most people do, and that the man and woman are otherwise equally similar to the abuser.)

Situations Leading to Graham's Generalized Stockholm Syndrome

On the basis of the law of stimulus generalization, we identify three situations in which Graham's Generalized Stockholm Syndrome is likely to develop: (1) Threat of violence is shown toward a victim by one person, then kindness is shown to the victim by another person who is similar to the violent person in some ways. The victim will now develop Generalized Stockholm Syndrome in relation to the kind person. (2) Threat of violence is shown by members of one group toward members of another group, then one or more individuals from the violent group show kindness toward a member of the victimized group. As a result, the member of the victimized group will develop Generalized Stockholm Syndrome in relation to the one or more kind individuals from the violent group. (3) Threat of violence is shown by members of one group toward members of another group, and most or all members of the violent group

TABLE 2.3
Elaborations of Graham's Stockholm Syndrome Theory

Prototypical Case	
Stockholm Syndrome	Individual victim bonds to abuser who shows kindness.

Elaborations	
Generalized Stockholm Syndrome	Individual victim/oppressed group bonds to kind person/oppressor group resembling abuser/oppressor group.
Situation 1	Individual victim bonds to a kind individual who resembles abusive individual.
Situation 2	Individual member of oppressed group bonds to one or more kind individuals of oppressor group.
Situation 3 (aka Societal Stockholm Syndrome)	Oppressed group bonds with oppressor group (most or all of whose members abuse members of oppressed group and most or all of whose members show some kindness to members of oppressed group).

also show some kindness toward most or all members of the victimized group. As a result, members of the victimized group would be expected to display Generalized Stockholm Syndrome in relation to all members of the violent group. The third situation leads to a specific type of Generalized Stockholm Syndrome—namely, Societal Stockholm Syndrome. Table 2.3 describes the relationship of these situations to one another. In the following pages we will illustrate each of these three situations.

Situation 1

Situation 1 Generalized Stockholm Syndrome characterizes the behavior of certain traumatized *individuals* toward specific *individuals* in their lives, one violent and one kind, irrespective of the broader social context within which these interactions occur. Thus, if one person threatens a second person with violence and then a third person is kind to the second, traumatized person, Generalized Stockholm Syndrome will be said to have occurred if the second person then bonds to the third, kind person. As an example, if one young man victimized a second young man, threatening the second youth's survival, and a third young man, a passer-by, stepped in to help the second man, the second youth would be expected to sustain, perhaps for many years or even for life, the feeling of a strong bond to the third youth. This bond would be expected to endure (thereby showing the strength of the bond), even if the second youth had never seen the third one before or did not see him again after the incident. If the third party is not abusive or exploitative, the bond has the potential to promote healing.

A story aired on national television provides a further illustration of Situation 1 Generalized Stockholm Syndrome. A soldier was seriously wounded in Vietnam and was seeking, twenty years later, a member of the armed forces medical staff who had cared for him while he was still in Vietnam. He credited this staff member, a woman, for saving his life by creating in him a will to live. He still felt a strong need to reconnect with this medical staff member. The show was aired to help him locate her.

Another example of Situation 1 Generalized Stockholm Syndrome is provided by a male hostage's response in the TWA Flight 847 skyjacking to two hijackers and to Nabih Berri's Amal militia men who subsequently guarded them. Watson et al. (1985) report: "[Hostage Jimmy Dell] Palmer said the Amal men 'went out of their way to be nice,' but he declared, 'I will never forgive and forget' the hijackers, who murdered fellow passenger Robert Dean Stethem" (p. 19). It was to the "nice" Amal captors that hostages bonded, after having just been exposed to the brutality of two earlier captors (but see Hill, with Friend, 1986).

Francine Hughes, Linda Lovelace, and Patricia Hearst also provide examples of Situation 1 Generalized Stockholm Syndrome. According to McNulty (1980), Francine Hughes was battered by her husband, who continued to abuse her after she divorced him. The more he battered her, the less caring and remorse he showed. When she met a policeman, George Walkup, who was kind to her, she became emotionally attached to him. Although she had spent little time getting to know Walkup, and although she did not see him for a year, her attachment to him persisted (McNulty 1980).[10]

Linda Lovelace (Lovelace, with McGrady, 1980), whose real name is Linda Marchiano, reported that she was forced at gunpoint to engage in all kinds of sexual acts for money by her captor, Chuck Traynor. The rehearsals she attended while starring in *Deep Throat* and the contacts she developed following the success of the film enabled her to successfully escape from Traynor. Once away, she purportedly bonded to the first man she met who showed her kindness, David Winters. As she stated, "I clung to him the way a drowning person would hang onto a life preserver, the way a poisoned man would reach for an antidote. For the first time in my life, I fell in love" (p. 243).

Patricia Hearst, held hostage for a year and a half by the Symbionese Liberation Army (S.L.A.), was kept blindfolded in a closet, raped by S.L.A. members, and carried to new locations in a garbage can. The leader of the S.L.A. gave her a choice: she could either be released, which she knew would mean execution, or she could join them. She "chose" to survive—and to do this meant participating in the illegal activities of the S.L.A. Although she worked to be liked by the members of the S.L.A., because she knew her survival depended on it, Patricia Hearst reports that she did not develop an attachment to her captors (Hearst, with Moscow, 1982). However, others suspect that her father insisted that she not report anything that might embarrass the Hearst family, even though this act jeopardized her legally (Alexander 1979). In any case, she developed attachments with her prison guard, Janey Jimenez, and with her bodyguard—the first two people other than family members who showed her kindness after her capture by the F.B.I. (Hearst, with Moscow, 1982; Jimenez, with Berkman, 1977). Hearst subsequently married her bodyguard.

All three of these women were held hostage by brutal captors who repeatedly threatened their lives, and all three bonded to the first kind persons with whom they came in contact. In the case of Francine Hughes, the bond was to a policeman. Policemen are generally perceived as strong, as are abusers by their victims. Although Linda Lovelace described David Winters as "seemingly the opposite of Chuck" (Lovelace, with McGrady, 1980, p. 242), her descriptions of the two men suggest otherwise. David, like Chuck, was involved in show business, and David, like Chuck, lived off of Linda (David by signing Linda's name to bills and Chuck by trading Linda's sexual favors for goods). However, unlike Chuck, David lived extravagantly (Lovelace, with McGrady, 1980). Patricia Hearst bonded to her prison guard (Jimenez, with Berkman, 1977) and to her bodyguard (Hearst, with Moscow, 1982). Both were her guards, as were the men and women of the S.L.A. who held her hostage.

In contrast to Graham's Situation 2 and Situation 3 Generalized Stockholm Syndrome (see below), in Graham's Situation 1 Generalized Stockholm Syndrome the identity of the person who is traumatized may have been selected without regard to race, sex, ethnicity, class, sexual orientation, or other characteristics. For example, a person might be victimized because a man decided he would assault any person who next walked past him.

Situation 2

Situation 2 Generalized Stockholm Syndrome characterizes the responses of *individuals of an oppressed group* to specific, kind *individuals of an oppressor group*. Oppressor-oppressed groups describe the situations of rich-poor, white-black, male-female, and heterosexual-homosexual groups, for example. The occurrence and nature of trauma and the occurrence of kindness *are predictable,* based on the group membership of the individuals involved. However, contact with kind members of the oppressor group *is random*—it is a matter of chance whether or not a specific member of the victimized group will encounter a particular member of the oppressor group.

As an example, if men as a group are violent to women as a group, and then an individual man shows an individual woman kindness, this lone woman would be expected to develop Generalized Stockholm Syndrome in relation to this specific kind man. An example of this would be the woman who purports not to trust men—that men are not trustworthy— but who feels that her husband or boyfriend is an exception.

The key elements of Situation 2 Generalized Stockholm Syndrome are that, although transactions (and thus bonding) occur among individuals, group membership typically determines who is a victim and who is a traumatizer. For example, in rape cases, the rapist is more likely to be male and the rape victim female. For reasons such as this, Brownmiller (1975) and Dworkin (1983) have argued that women marry kind men in an attempt to obtain protection from male violence (such as rape). If women do marry men for this reason, even though they may not consciously recognize it—and if women are emotionally bonded to the men they marry, then Situation 2 Generalized Stockholm Syndrome is occurring.

Another example of Situation 2 Generalized Stockholm Syndrome is provided by observations made by Bruno Bettelheim (1943) while he was a prisoner in various Nazi concentration camps during World War II. Few doubt that the Gestapo constituted an oppressor group and Jews constituted an oppressed group during this time in history. It was within this social context that Bettelheim observed other prisoners expressing positive feelings for some members of the Gestapo. These members were "a few officers who were rather high up in the hierarchy of camp administrators" (p. 451). The prisoners "insisted" that these officers were "genuinely interested in them and even trying, in a small way, to help them" (p. 451). The smallest acts of kindness by an officer (e.g., an officer wiping off his feet before entering their barracks) aroused these feelings in the prisoners. Bettelheim himself could find no evidence that these officers were in fact sympathetic, despite the prisoners' "eagerness . . . to find reasons for their claims" (p. 451). Undoubtedly, the extent of the prisoners' eagerness to believe was proportional to the extent of their need for the officers in fact to be "just and kind," and thus also proportional to the extent of their despair.

Situation 3

If one (inescapable) group threatens another group with violence but also—as a group—shows the victimized group some kindness, an attachment *between the groups* will develop. This is what we refer to as *Societal (or Cultural) Stockholm Syndrome*) and it is expected to develop under Situation 3 Generalized Stockholm Syndrome conditions. That is, it is expected to develop in a culture in which it is socially mandated and socially predictable that members of the oppressor group will both victimize and be kind to members of the oppressed group. However, the identity of the particular member of the oppressor group who metes out the violence or shows kindness to any particular member of the oppressed group is random and may be determined by variables such as physical proximity.

Because the transactions between oppressor and oppressed group members are pervasive and the traumatizers are omnipresent, members of the victim group perceive that they cannot escape the abuse and therefore look to their traumatizers for nurturance and protection. A Stockholm Syndrome psychology is expected to generalize to *any and all* interactions with members of the violent group, even members of that group who are not themselves violent, or who are less violent, toward members of the victimized group.

As with Situation 2, the trauma experienced by the members of the oppressed group in Situation 3 is not random—it can be predicted on the basis of group membership. However, unlike Situation 2, the kindness encountered from members of the oppressor group can also be predicted on the basis of group membership. And the members of these victimized groups who develop the most Generalized Stockholm Syndrome are seen by other members of their (oppressed) group as "Uncle Toms" in the case of blacks, "male identified" in the case of women, and "heterosexist" in the case of homosexuals.

Co-occurrence of Situations

Whereas Situation 1 can occur to anyone (anyone could be kidnapped off the street, for example), Situations 2 and 3 can occur only with members of an oppressed group. *Stockholm Syndrome should be strongest when Situations 1, 2, and 3 are simultaneously present,* for instance, when it occurs in a culture described by Situation 3 wherein a member of the oppressor group who strongly typifies members of that group expresses kindness toward members of the oppressed group who have recently been victimized by other members of the oppressor group from whom they feel they cannot escape. Note that it follows, then, that bonds arising out of threat and kindness between members of different oppressor-oppressed groups should be stronger than bonds arising out of threat and kindness between members of the same group.

Conclusion

A review of the literatures of nine different hostage groups revealed the following overlooked facts about the phenomenon of bonding to an abuser (Stockholm Syndrome): (1) It is seen in a wide range of hostage groups. (2) Despite its pervasiveness among diverse hostage groups, mental health professionals have failed to question whether it might be a unitary phenomenon observed under conditions of captivity and abuse. (3) When it *is* recognized for particular hostage groups, it is viewed quite differently; for example, battered women who bond to their abusers are seen as masochistic (Young and Gerson 1991), while "political" hostages who bond to their abusers (captors) are seen as smart but unpatriotic (Rabinowitz 1977). (4) Virtually no empirical research on the phenomenon of bonding to an abuser had been conducted for *any* hostage group. In response to this situation, Graham proposed four conditions (perceived threat to survival, kindness, and inability to escape, and isolation) to be precursors of Stockholm Syndrome, a set of Stockholm Syndrome psychodynamics for captives, and sixty-six potential aspects of Stockholm Syndrome, nine of which are seen as "major indicators." Stockholm Syndrome develops when individuals—traumatized, unable to see a way to escape, isolated from others, and offered some small show of kindness by the abuser/captor—realize (though perhaps only at an unconscious level) that their only hope of surviving lies in befriending the abuser/captor and they attempt to do so. Because this befriending or bond must develop with the very person who is threatening their survival, its development can only be accomplished through considerable cognitive distortion. The cognitive distortion of denial is used unconsciously in the service of denying the risk of danger and trauma and has the effect of facilitating the development of the bond. Based on literature reviews of nine different hostage groups, Graham proposes that Stockholm Syndrome will develop any time the four precursor conditions exist, regardless of the hostage group involved. Differences in people's Stockholm Syndrome responses are therefore attributed to differences in precursor conditions. All precursor conditions and Stockholm Syndrome responses are seen to fall along a continuum, such that individuals may show different degrees of each.

Graham also proposed that Stockholm Syndrome psychodynamics can generalize to nonabusive others who resemble former abusers and who have shown only kindness. This generalization of Stockholm Syndrome psychodynamics can occur at both individual and group levels.

Several variables need to be considered in predicting Generalized Stockholm Syndrome, including similarity of the kind person to the threatening person; whether the person is the first kind person to make contact with the victim; the extent of emotional relief (including the degree of protection offered) that a person provides to the victim relative to what is being provided by others, including the abuser; and the pervasiveness of the precursor conditions in oppressor/oppressed group relations within the culture.

The law of stimulus generalization leads us to predict that oppressor-oppressed group relations, when characterized by the presence of the four Stockholm Syndrome precursor conditions, cause the bonding of oppressed to oppressor group members as well as strengthen the bond of individuals from the oppressed group to particular individuals of the oppressor group. In fact, the law of stimulus generalization leads us to predict that Societal Stockholm Syndrome characterizes the "group psychology" of oppressed groups (when the four precursor conditions describe oppressed/oppressor group relations).

Generalized Stockholm Syndrome involves survival strategies that resemble what psychiatrists refer to as Borderline Personality Characteristics, reflecting psychiatry's tendency to pathologize victims' survival responses to unhealthy interpersonal environments. These characteristics are expressed along a continuum: at one end are no BPCs and no generalization of captor/captive psychodynamics to relations with persons other than the captor (this is the prototypical Stockholm Syndrome scenario). At the other end of the continuum are Borderline Personality Disorder and generalization of captor/captive psychodynamics to relations with all members of the oppressor group (Situation 3 Generalized Stockholm Syndrome) or even with all people. In between these two extremes are Situation 1 and Situation 2 Generalized Stockholm Syndrome.

The following are unique aspects of Graham's Stockholm Syndrome theory:

1. It is a synthesis of information from literatures regarding the psychologies of a wide range of hostage groups.
2. It uses the language of hostage situations ("captor," "captive," "Stockholm Syndrome") as a lens for viewing the situation of groups not typically seen as "hostages" in the hope that this perspective will help us to see the situations of these other hostages in a new and useful way.

3. It emphasizes the role of the *context* within which bonding to an abuser occurs.
4. It views bonding to an abuser/captor as a survival strategy.
5. It asks whether bonding to an abuser/captor is a *unitary phenomenon* which will be observed whenever certain contextual (precursor) conditions are present in any "hostage" group.
6. It asks whether bonding to an abuser/captor is so pervasive as to occur in any interpersonal relationship characterized by inequality and kindness and thus whether the concept describes oppressor-oppressed group relations.

In the following chapters, we will ask to what extent the four precursors of Stockholm Syndrome characterize the treatment of women as a group by men as a group, and to what extent the psychology of the group, women, reflects the presence of the nine major indicators of Stockholm Syndrome.

THREE

"Here's My Weapon, Here's My Gun; One's for Pleasure, One's for Fun": Conditions Conducive to Women's Development of Societal Stockholm Syndrome

> The only way we can come out of hiding, break through our paralyzing defenses, is to know the full extent of sexual violence and domination of women. . . . In *knowing*, in facing directly, we can learn how to chart our course out of this oppression. (Barry 1979, p. 5)

In this chapter, we ask whether the four conditions conducive to Stockholm Syndrome exist at a societal level in male-female relations. In addition, we consider the possibility that cultures may differ in the extent to which Stockholm Syndrome-conducive conditions exist in male-female relations. Accordingly, we describe criteria for assessing the severity of the four precursor conditions in any culture. In the next chapter, we will clarify the construct of Societal Stockholm Syndrome (Situation 3 Generalized Stockholm Syndrome, as discussed in chapter 2; see table 2.2) by assessing its presence in females as a group, and we invite its empirical examination. More generally, in chapter 4 we will examine male-female relations to demonstrate how one might go about assessing the presence of Stockholm Syndrome and its preconditions in the relations of any two power-imbalanced groups of people within a culture (e.g., children and adults, blacks and whites, homosexuals and heterosexuals, poor and rich).

Our application of the words "hostage" and "captor" to women and men initially may seem strange. We use these terms here to test their applicability to power-imbalanced group-group relations. That is, does looking at groups from the perspective provided by a hostage-captor or victim-abuser relationship reveal dynamics that were not apparent before? Does it make the actions of members of these groups appear more comprehensible than before? We hope that, in reading this, you will bear with us until we have presented the theory of Societal Stockholm Syndrome and our application of it to male-female relations. Then you can determine for yourself whether this conceptualization is useful and appropriate.

Some readers may object to our use of the word "victim" as compared to "survivor." Like Diana Russell (1986), we use "victim" in order to emphasize the victimizing situational factors impacting on the person, whether or not she or he survives, manifests good survival skills, and responds as a victor. We hope this wording will help *reduce* victim-blaming by increasing our appreciation of the powerful impact of situational variables on people's psychology. Use of the word "victim" can help remind us (assuming the theory is correct) that it is the situations creating victimization that must be changed, not the victims themselves (see Caplan and Nelson 1973).

We will now examine the extent to which the four conditions conducive to Stockholm Syndrome are evident in male-female relations at a societal level. In exploring this question, we should bear in mind that conditions that are pervasive and long-established are easily overlooked or appear "natural."

Male-Female Relations and Societal Stockholm Syndrome

Three of the four precursors of Stockholm Syndrome (perceived threat to survival, inability to escape, and kindness) concern the *perceptions* of victims and not the objective conditions surrounding the victims. If a victim does not perceive the objective conditions, they cannot influence her or his thinking and behavior. One of the difficulties in obtaining an answer to the question, "Do women perceive that men threaten women's survival?" is that victims who show the syndrome *deny* the danger of their situation and the fact that they are being abused. Yet at the same time they also report incidents that sound abusive to anyone else. The reader may recall that such denial is an indicator of the presence of the syndrome. Similarly, victims who perceive no way to escape terrorization deny their inability to escape in an effort to cope with their terror. For these reasons, in this chapter we will not ask about women's conscious perceptions in assessing the presence of Stockholm Syndrome precursors in male/female relations. Rather, we will ask the following four questions concerning objective conditions impacting on women's lives: (1) Do men threaten women's survival? (2) Can women escape from men? (3) Are women isolated from outsiders and perspectives other than those of men? and (4) Are men kind to women?

As shown in table 3.1, these four questions can be used to evaluate how conducive any culture is to the development of Societal Stockholm Syndrome in its female members. The same four questions could be asked about members of any subordinate group relative to another, dominant group (e.g., children and adults, blacks and whites, homosexuals and heterosexuals). Note that the issues being considered under each of the four major questions in table 3.1 assess the extent of the syndrome in females at both cultural (for example, the percentage of men, compared to women, who are "bosses" within a culture) and individual levels (e.g., the number of brothers versus sisters with whom a female is raised), though broad cultural issues are more often emphasized. The list in table 3.1 is not exhaustive, yet space limitations will allow discussion of only a few of these issues.

We hypothesize that the severity of the four Stockholm Syndrome-conducive conditions determines the severity of Societal Stockholm Syndrome in women of different cultures. If the conditions do not characterize a particular society, Societal Stockholm Syndrome will not characterize the dynamics between women and men in that society. If the four conditions do characterize the society, the *extent* of that characterization will determine the *severity* of the syndrome. In addition, within a society, the nature of individual women's relations with individual men will produce variability in the extent of their Situations 1 and 2 Generalized Stockholm Syndrome. It should be clear then that Societal Stockholm

TABLE 3.1

*Some Criteria for Evaluating the Likelihood That Female Members
of a Culture Will Develop Societal Stockholm Syndrome in Their
Relations with Men*

To What Extent Is Females' Survival Threatened by Males?

- To what extent is femaleness derogated by males (for instance, through religion, street behavior, pornography, laws, medical practices, education, employment practices)?
- To what extent does a culture run by males ask females to sacrifice their lives and happiness for others' sake, especially men's sake?
- To what extent does the culture communicate the message to females that their minds and bodies belong to men (for instance, through laws, rape, rituals, tradition, popular entertainment, religion)?
- When infanticide occurs, to what extent are female infants more likely to be killed than male infants?
- To what extent is female behavior, particularly "femininity" or female submissiveness to males, controlled by men through force, threat of force, social ostracism, threat of social ostracism, or custodial access to children?
- To what extent are beauty standards for women (created by men for the purpose of attracting and keeping men) psychologically debilitating for women (e.g., in terms of self-concept)? To what extent are these standards life-threatening for women (as in the case of anorexia)?
- What proportion of females are murdered by males?
- What percentage of those living in poverty are female? What percentage of females are living in poverty? To what extent are men (e.g., through laws, social policy) responsible for these figures as a result of the laws and social policies they create/support?
- What are the prevalence rates for rape, wife abuse, incest, and other forms of female sexual abuse?
- To what extent do cultural practices reveal that women are not valued (for instance, through suttee, lack of quality care and life experiences for elderly women) once their male partners have died?
- To what extent do females of a culture fear any of the above, regardless of incidence and prevalence rates of the above?

To What Extent Are Females Able to Escape Males?

- To what extent are females required to turn to male experts for legal remedies, education, employment, and medical care?
- To what extent are the fields of psychiatry and psychology controlled by men? Are more women than men forcibly placed in mental institutions and/ or forced to have shock therapy or drug therapy (because they don't behave in "appropriate" ways)?
- How prevalent are depictions in the media of women as subservient? How prevalent is pornography in which women are shown as having less power than men and/or as being aggressed against by men through sex?
- To what extent is heterosexuality forced upon women, so that lesbianism is neither publicly visible nor sanctioned and thus not a real option for women?
- To what extent is female sexuality controlled by men (for instance, through compulsory heterosexuality, forced abstinence, or genital mutilation)?

TABLE 3.1 *(Continued)*

- To what extent does the culture sex-type people? How inaccessible is transsexualism?
- How restrictive are the roles and jobs open to women, as compared to men? How much segregation is there between men's roles and jobs versus women's roles and jobs?
- How many male, as opposed to female, bosses is a woman likely to have?
- How many male, as opposed to female, children is a woman likely to raise?
- To what extent is a woman expected or required to raise sons who are masculine?
- How much knowledge of weaponry and self-defense arts do men have relative to women?
- To what extent do men exercise more control than women in creating and running social institutions such as law, medicine, religion, education, psychiatry, etc.?
- How often and to what extent do rapists, wife batterers, incest perpetrators, and others who commit violent crimes against women get off without being punished?
- Do what extent are females blamed for their own victimization, particularly when the perpetrators are male?
- How high are men's employment rate and income relative to women's?
- Can only men vote? What percentage of legislators are men? What percentage of the leaders of the country are male? What percentage of jurors are male? That is, to what extent do men, relative to women, participate in creating laws and administering justice?
- How inaccessible to women are women's organizations, particularly feminist organizations, that are created and maintained by and for women?
- What percentage of men, relative to women, own property in their own names, operate businesses, inherit money (and how much relative to women), and make and sign legal contracts on their own?
- What percentage of women have their marital partners chosen by their fathers or other male relatives rather than selecting them themselves?
- To what extent are daughters, as opposed to sons, expected to care for ailing parents, especially fathers?
- To what extent are females taught to look after others and particularly males? To what extent are females taught to put being a wife and mother before their own career?

To What Extent Do Males Show Kindness toward Females?

- Does the culture create roles for women and men which require men and women to work cooperatively with one another? For example, do men earn money, power, and/or prestige which they can share with women in exchange for women's domestic, sexual, reproductive, and/or emotional work?
- To what extent does the culture mandate that men should treat women in ways that are portrayed as kind (as with chivalry and alimony, child support)?
- To what extent are women in positions or situations in which it benefits men to show women kindness?

- To what extent do men share their income, power, prestige, expertise, or wisdom with women? To what extent do men share their products (e.g., technology) with women?
- To what extent do men protect and defend women? To what extent do men share emotional closeness or intimacy with women? To what extent do men support and promote women's personal (psychological, physical, professional) growth?
- To what extent are men in the culture required to offer women some protection and safety, however small, particularly when women have been victimized by men?
- To what extent do males demonstrate to females that they value females' opinions, contributions, etc.?

To What Extent Are Females Isolated from Persons Having Perspectives Different from Those of Men?

- What percentage of time do women spend alone or with males, as compared to with females? When females do spend time with other females, how often are one or more males present?
- To what extent do issues of class and race divide women, keeping them from coming together and from hearing and valuing one another's perspectives?
- What percentage of a woman's life is lived with a male figure in the home?
- How many male versus female siblings does a female have?
- How many years lived with versus without a father figure in the home? How many with only a father figure in the home?
- Are females encouraged to be psychologically dependent on males? Are they told that there is something wrong with women who don't marry a man?
- Does the culture discourage females from having close female friends? Does it discourage females from living together or having frequent contact with one another?
- Are females taught to feel shame for having close friendships with other females? For living with other women without men? For associating primarily or exclusively with other females?
- Are females taught that a mature woman gives most of her energy to her husband or to men as opposed to other women?
- Are females taught to feel shame for having needs? For wanting others to help them satisfy their needs? For asking others to help them satisfy their own needs?
- Are females taught to take care of men's needs before taking care of their own?
- Does the culture provide more benefits or privileges to females who align themselves with males than to females who align themselves with females?
- Are females taught that what men say is more important than what women say? That is, how likely is it that a female's (versus a male's) voice will be heard? How likely is it that a female will hear another female's voice when that other female has spoken? Are women taught to trust women and what women say?
- To what extent are women silenced or not listened to regarding the conditions of their lives?
- Are women who report sexual abuse and/or wife abuse believed? Do others stay connected to them, or are they ostracized?

TABLE 3.1 *(Continued)*

- Does the culture feel and act as though it is more important for a male child to develop his own voice than for a female child to develop her own voice? Are people more accepting of the independent views of male children than of female children?
- Does the culture support or encourage competition between females, particularly as regards males?
- To what extent do the jobs and/or responsibilities assigned to females involve ongoing contact with men?
- Are men more likely than women to be mentored? Are men more likely to have a male mentor than women are to have a female mentor?
- Are immediate bosses (or employers), teachers, co-workers, or other persons with whom one has daily contact more likely to be male than female?
- Does the culture discourage or show indifference to, as opposed to encourage, women possessing a feminist ideology? Is a feminist ideology inaccessible to women? For example, does the educational system act as though feminist theory does not exist? Does the educational system, by omission or commission, deny that feminist theory is a legitimate alternative theory? Does the culture denigrate feminism, feminist values, or persons espousing such values?
- What percentage of females have never belonged to a feminist organization? Are these organizations inaccessible to women?
- What percentage of women do not possess feminist values or a feminist ideology? How likely is a female child to have parents who disparage a feminist ideology and values? How inaccessible are feminists in the community so that a woman with a feminist ideology would have difficulty finding others who shared her values?

Syndrome and the conditions producing it are not either just present or absent; rather, they are present (or absent) in degrees according to the individual and the conditions.

Do Men Threaten Women's Survival?

All unequal power relationships must, in the end, rely on the threat or reality of violence to maintain themselves.
(Clark and Lewis 1977, p. 177)

A study of violence against women seems necessary to an understanding of the psychology of women since it would seem that virtually all women are affected by the threat of male violence if not its actual occurrence.
(Leidig 1981, p. 191)

Here we will consider if male violence exists in such a way and to such an extent as to threaten women's survival. Men are currently pushing their power to the limit: they now have the ability to determine whether our planet will survive. There is no doubt that men threaten everyone's— and virtually everything's—survival.

History reveals that groups of human beings are capable of systematically killing members of other human groups. Humans have killed other humans: six million Jews, hundreds of thousands of Native Americans, and over 110,000 Japanese, the latter within a matter of seconds at Hiroshima and Nagasaki. John Hodge (1975) estimates that 150 million lives were lost in the slave trade of blacks from Africa. More than 5,000 blacks were lynched in the United States between 1882 and 1939. Just as a child who witnesses her mother being battered by her father feels physically threatened, women who witness male-male violence also feel physically threatened. The observation of violence among others creates fear of physical violence and thus constitutes emotional violence.[1]

Women's fear of male violence against us (women) is justified. Approximately half of those killed in each of these groups were women, and the killers of each of these groups were almost entirely men. In addition, men are known to have made women their primary targets.

For example, Woods (1974) notes that "the most reliable estimates suggest that in the course of three hundred years they executed about nine million people" branded as witches. Kors and Peters (1972) argue that witchcraft in Europe dated from 1100 to 1700, a period of six hundred years, with the last witch "legally burned in Europe as late as the 1780's" (p. 15). Thus, nine million executions may be a conservative estimate if the period was actually twice as long, though this figure is usually given as an upper limit. Who are "they" that executed the witches and who were the witches? Williams and Williams (1978) note that the "accusers were mostly men, [and the] accused mostly women" (p. 4). For example, "Fourteen of twenty put to death as witches at Salem [Massachusetts] in 1692 were women. Twenty-five of thirty-one convicted of witchcraft were women. One hundred four of one hundred forty-one accused witches were women" (p. 202). And who was considered a witch? Starhawk (1982) notes that "accusations of Witchcraft were mostly directed at women in the lower strata of society. Especially at risk were widows, spinsters, and those who were unprotected by a man" (p. 188). Accusations against wealthy or prominent citizens were suspect. Monter (1969) cites sixteenth-century Jesuit Martin Delrio as defining witchcraft as "an art by which, through the power of a contract with the Devil, wonders are wrought which pass human understanding" (p. viii). In other words, a witch was someone associated with some event or happening that another, an accuser, did not understand. The gap in understanding was filled by the presumption that the person (woman) was in cahoots with the devil. For example, a woman might be branded as a witch if she handed an apple to a child and the child subsequently died of chicken pox, even if the child never actually ate the apple. Clearly, no one was immune to the accusation of witchcraft, thus everyone, but especially women, lived in terror.

What was the purpose of the killings of so many people, primarily women? Starhawk (1982) notes that these killings occurred during a time, the Renaissance and Reformation, when "constricting chains of dogma were [being] thrown off, a time of questioning and exploration, of the birth of new religions and the reevaluation of corruption in old institutions, a time of discovery and enlightenment" (p. 185). The witch hunts served to "undermine the possibility of a revolution that would benefit women, the poor, and those without property" (p. 189). Certainly, the killings ensured women lived in fear that if they stepped out of line— which included doing anything that anyone else did not understand or getting on the wrong side of anyone else, especially men—they would be killed. This history and others like it in other parts of the world should leave no doubt in today's women's minds that men are capable of killing women, of using violence for the social control of women, and that men will settle for the flimsiest of reasons as rationalizations for the killings. In other words, history tells us that it doesn't take much of an excuse for it to be considered legitimate to kill a woman.

National victimization surveys indicate that males are more likely to be victims of violence than females. However, those surveys do not assess the prevalence of violence by intimates such as husbands and boyfriends. These surveys therefore grossly underestimate the amount of violence to which women are exposed, as most of the violence against women is perpetrated by male intimates. Furthermore, while violence targeted at women is "predatory," that directed at men tends to involve "exchanged blows." Also, women are much more likely to be the victims of sexual violence, the most frightening form of violence, than are men (M. D. Smith 1988). And, the perpetrators of violence, whether of males or females, are primarily males.

Femicide (The Killing of a Woman by an Intimate)

Although men are more likely than women to be murdered, women are more likely than men to be murdered by a member of the other sex and by a spouse. MacKinnon (1987) reports that "four out of five murdered women are killed by men; between one third and one half [of murdered women] are married to their murderers. When you add boyfriends and former spouses, the figures rise" (p. 24). Dobash and Dobash (1977/78) reported finding that more than 40 percent of women who are murdered are murdered by their husbands. By comparison, only 10 percent of male murder victims are killed by their wives. In a review of this literature, Okun (1986) noted: "Wives make up 52% of spouses murdered, husbands, 48%. Husbands are six to seven times more likely than wives to have initiated the violence in the incident leading to their eventual death; Wolfgang found that nearly 60% of husbands murdered were killed after they had initiated violence, compared to 9% of wives killed in 'victim-precipitated' murders" (p. 36). Men are also more likely than women to kill their spouses and their children and then to kill themselves.

Walter Gove (1973) found that "for women the shift from being single to being married increases the likelihood of being murdered, while for men the shift decreases their chances" (p. 51). Gove obtained similar findings for single as compared to married women as regards "accidental deaths." It is, of course, likely that many accidental deaths were in fact murders. Such statistics served as the impetus for Blinder's (1985) remark, "In America, the bedroom is second only to the highway as the scene of slaughter" (p. ix).

Looking beyond the murder of women by intimates, we find virtually all mass murderers are men, and most of their victims have been women (Levin and Fox 1985). These findings indicate that women's survival *is* threatened by male violence. In the following pages we will discuss some of the more common types of violence men commit against women.

Wife Abuse

Even women who are not murdered by their battering partners find their survival continually threatened. Hilberman and Munson (1977/78) describe the battered women they studied: "The women were a study in paralyzing terror. . . . [T]he stress was unending and the threat of the next assault was everpresent. . . . There was chronic apprehension of imminent doom, of something terrible always about to happen" (p. 464). Walker (1979) reports that battered women believe that their abusers would or could kill them. The women she has studied report being "trapped in a deadly situation" (Walker 1984, p. 40). Walker (1979) estimates that 50 percent of all women are battered by their husbands at some time in their marriages. MacKinnon (1987) reports that "between one quarter and one third of married women experience serious violence in their homes— some studies find as many as 70 percent" (p. 24).

Ann Jones (1980) describes the case of Mary McGuire, whose battering husband "made her watch him dig her grave, kill the family cat, and decapitate a pet horse" (p. 298). Browne (1987) found that 83 percent of the women in her homicide group (that is, women who had killed their abusive partners) and 59 percent of women in her "control" group (that is, women who had not killed their battering partners) had had partners who threatened to kill them. If men did not threaten women's physical survival, why would we need battered women's shelters or "refuges" for women (Martin 1977)? Interestingly, despite the threat to these women's physical survival, Ewing (1987) argues that "many battered women who kill [their abusers] do so primarily as a matter of *psychological* self-defense—that is, to prevent their batterers from destroying them mentally and emotionally" (p. 6; Ewing's emphasis).

Abuse threatens women's lives in other, less obvious ways as well. Suicidal ideation, suicide attempts, and actual suicide are directions taken by many battered women (Browne 1987; Gayford 1975; Pagelow 1981; Rounsaville and Weissman 1977; Walker 1984). Such action is the only way many women see of ending the abuse, short of murdering their abusers. Despite the clear threat of wife abuse to the welfare of women, the legal system has been relatively unresponsive to the reality of battered women's lives. See Dutton (1989) for insight into ways the legal system, run predominantly by men, fails women who are repeatedly battered by their spouses.

Rape of wives by husbands is a form of wife abuse. As regards sexual abuse in marriage, I am aware of no findings of husband sexual abuse by the wife (though men report experiencing sexual withholding as abusive). Sexual abuse by husbands, however, is well documented (see, for example, Finkelhor and Yllo 1985). In other words, sexual abuse in marriage is directed primarily at women by men. Finkelhor and Yllo studied a representative sample of women in the Boston area who had a child between 6 and 14 years of age living with them. They found that 10 percent of the married or previously married women had husbands who had used "physical force or threaten[ed] to try to have sex with them" (pp. 6–7). (Only 3 percent of these same women reported having been sexually assaulted by a stranger.) This figure is almost certainly an underestimation, as abuse victims often do not recognize abuse as abuse, and thus are not likely to report it as such. Finkelhor and Yllo note that "the sanitized image of marital rape routinely omits the component of terror" which these women experience (p. 18).

In a study of a representative sample of women at least 18 years of age in the San Francisco area, Diana Russell (1982) found similar results: 14 percent of the married women reported having been sexually assaulted by their husbands, whereas only half that many reported having been sexually assaulted by a stranger. These women perceived rape by their husbands as having more damaging, long-term effects than rape by strangers.

As of January 1985, in approximately twenty-seven states marriage to a man meant he could legally force the woman to have sex with him anytime he desired (Finkelhor and Yllo 1985). These statistics were worsening in 1985, however. Twelve states had just exempted cohabiting boyfriends from conviction for marital rape. Also, five states exempted from conviction men whom women had consented to have sex with in the past, thus legally sanctioning date rape (Finkelhor and Yllo 1985).

Lenore Walker (1979) found that almost all the women in her battered-women sample reported being sexually abused by their batterers. Most of them characterized the sexual abuse as rape. All of them reported being forced to engage in "unusual," "bizarre," "kinky" sex (p. 118). Irene Frieze (1983) observed that "marital rape is typically associated with battering and may be one of the most serious forms of battering" (p. 552). Finkelhor and Yllo (1985) reported that "we asked many of the women who had also been battered to compare the effects of the marital rape with the effects of other abuse. All but three of the women reported that the sexual assaults were more devastating" (p. 134). In her study of the relationships of women who killed their battering husbands, Browne (1987) found that "for many women in the homicide group, physical intimacy changed from joy to the most threatening part of the relationship" (p. 43). Fifty-nine percent of women in the nonhomicide, battered-woman "control" group and 76 percent of women in the homicide group had been raped by their battering partners. Forty percent of the women in the homicide group reported that they had been raped "often."

Rape by a partner with whom one has shared intimacy, trust, and love—a person with whom one lives and sleeps every day and must continue to live and sleep—threatens one's psychological survival. Browne quotes one of her subjects as saying of her batterer, "It was as though he wanted to annihilate me. More than the slapping, or the kicks . . . as though he wanted to tear me apart from the inside out and simply leave nothing there" (p. 103). Sophia, a participant in a study on rape in marriage by Finkelhor and Yllo (1985), was quoted as saying, "When he forced me to have sex with him, that was more than just physical. It went all the way down to my soul. He abused every part of me—my soul, my feelings, my mind. . . . It was just as much a mental rape as a physical rape, and I don't think that there is anything worse than that" (p. 135).

Although data that describe the frequency with which women feel their psychological survival is threatened by marital rape are currently unavailable, there are enough anecdotal reports to suggest that this is not an uncommon response.

Rape

Most rapists are male and most rape victims are female (Brownmiller 1975; Leidig 1977, cited by Leidig 1981). Prevalence statistics, based on interviews with 930 randomly selected females (18 years of age and older), were compiled by Russell (1984). These statistics revealed that 44 percent of the women in her sample had been victims of completed or attempted rape. (Only 8 percent of these assaults were reported to the police.) Fifty percent of the women who were raped were raped more than once. The probability of being raped increased by over 12 percent for each successive age-cohort of women. Life-table analyses revealed that in her lifetime a woman has a 26 percent chance of being raped and a 46 percent chance of being assaulted with intention to rape. Furthermore, these statistics reflect underdisclosure, for some respondents expressed an unwillingness to reveal some of their experiences.

Many if not the majority of rape victims view their ordeals as life-threatening. This view affects how they respond to sexual assault. Based on a study of ninety-four women who had experienced rape or attempted rape, Bart and O'Brien (1985, pp. 52–53) determined the following:

Two principal patterns of the woman's dominant fear or concern at the moment of attack are fear of being murdered and/or mutilated or fear of being raped.

When women were most afraid of being murdered or mutilated they were more likely to be raped. Often a woman who had this fear said that she hoped that by going along with the rapist she would deter him from further and more horrible violence. . . .

Women who were most afraid of being raped were more likely to avoid rape. They spoke of their *determination* not to be raped as well as their refusal to think about the possibility of death. . . .

Not all women mentioned either of these fears. It is significant that of those who did, over half the women who stopped their rapes said that fear of rape and determination not to be raped was their main concern. Almost all the raped women said their primary concern was fear of death or mutilation.

Although their sample was not representative, 51 percent of Bart and O'Brien's subjects reported a fear of death, mutilation, or beating; 31 percent reported a fear of rape and a determination not to be raped. Information regarding the presence or absence of these fears was either missing or unclear for 17 percent of their sample.

It is possible that aspects of the rape situation determine a woman's resistance and whether she fears rape or death and mutilation more. These aspects may be measurable, such as (perceived) presence versus absence of a weapon. Or the aspects may be difficult to specify and study, such as nuances of the rapist's behavior that suggest a willingness to kill. Burnett,

Templer, and Barker (1985) examined the efficacy of a variety of predictors (presence of a weapon; woman's height and weight, dominance, death anxiety, locus of control; and whether she knew her assailant) on women's resistance to sexual assault. Resistance was defined as screaming, fighting back, running, and/or trying to escape. Sixty-three percent of the variance in resistance was accounted for by the presence of a weapon and by the woman's death anxiety. Examining ten studies of rape, Katz and Mazur (1979) found that 21 to 59 percent of rapes involved the use of a weapon. Burnett et al. also found that the presence of a weapon was associated with decreased resistance to assault ($r = -.72$), as was fear of being killed. The significance of these variables is all the more telling because the woman's demographic, physical, and personality variables (with the exception of death anxiety) were not associated with whether she resisted.

Although studies using representative samples have not assessed the percentage of women who fear for their lives during rape or sexual assault, two things are clear. Many women fear being killed by rapists, and this fear translates into submission to rape.

Incest

Incest is a form of sexual violence that is primarily directed against female children by adult male perpetrators (Finkelhor 1980; Herman, with Hirschman, 1977). Herman and Hirschman found that 92 percent of incest victims are females and 97 percent of the offenders are male. On the average, incest begins when the victim is between 6 and 11 years of age (Browning and Boatman 1977; Giarretto 1976; Maisch 1972), and most cases last for one to five years (Tormes 1968). Herman (with Hirschman 1981) found that the daughters, not the fathers, ended the incest, whether by running away, marrying early, or getting pregnant at a young age. However, once incest has occurred, even if it does not recur, the victim harbors the fear that it will recur at any time and thus is never again able to feel safe from abuse. Therefore, in a sense, for the victim, once begun, incest never ends.

Incest can take both overt and covert forms. Covert incest refers to sexually motivated behavior that stops short of physical touching and does not require secrecy but which reveals an intrusive sexual interest in the daughter by the father (or other adult authority figure). Examples of covert incest are fathers constantly talking about sex with their daughters, interrogating their daughters about the daughter's sexual behavior, leaving pornographic materials lying around, spying on daughters while they are undressing, and courting their daughters. While overt incest is frequently backed by physical child abuse, covert incest is reinforced by threat of abandonment (a threat to children's physical and psychic survival; Herman, with Hirschman, 1981). All children are hostages of parents in the sense that they are totally dependent on their parents for survival. Children's survival is threatened by their underlying fear of parental abandonment as well as by actual and threatened physical violence. In approximately 50 percent of overt incestuous families, the father is physically abusive. Thus, children's submission to the father's overt sexual abuse is virtually guaranteed. Beyond the threat to survival that ensures submission, the incest itself is experienced as a threat to psychic survival. It is not uncommon for victims to dissociate during overt incestuous acts. (Dissociation is a psychic process, involving the breaking off of a group of mental activities that then function as if they belonged to a separate personality, which comes into play whenever events threaten to overwhelm the psyche of the victim.) Examination of long-term outcomes associated with incest (for instance, drug abuse, suicide, self-mutilation, borderline personality disorder, multiple personality disorder) reveal the severity of this threat to survival.

The findings of Diana Russell (1986) suggest that "a minimum of one in every six women in this country has been incestuously abused" (p. 16), where incestuous abuse was defined to include "any kind of exploitative sexual contact or attempted sexual contact" occurring between relatives before age 18 (p. 59). Sixteen percent of her randomly selected female sample had been sexually abused by a relative before 18 years of age. Four and a half percent had been sexually abused by their fathers. According to Russell, this means that "160,000 women per million in this country may have been incestuously abused before the age of eighteen, and 45,000 per million may have been victimized by their fathers" (p. 10). A study of 796 college students by Finkelhor (1980) revealed that 19 percent of the women and 9 percent of the men had been sexually victimized, primarily by men in their intimate social networks. Still, these rates are almost certainly lower than the actual prevalence of sexual abuse. Many victims of incest do not remember the incestuous events, blocking out large portions of their childhood from memory. Repression of this type is so frequent among incest victims as to be diagnostic.

Sexual Harassment

The term "sexual harassment" is used to refer to male behaviors that occur in seemingly disparate locations but seem to have similar functions. Sexual harassment in the workplace is defined by Farley (1978) as "unsolicited nonreciprocal male behavior that asserts a woman's sex role over her function as worker" (pp. 14–15). The harassing behaviors include "staring at, commenting upon, or touching a woman's body; requests for acquiescence in sexual behavior; repeated nonreciprocated propositions for dates; demands for sexual intercourse; and rape" (p. 15) (note that the sexual harasser acts on the presumption that a woman's body belongs to him, not her). What makes this form of harassment particularly vicious is that it is backed up by either an abuse of power or a threat of such, should the woman refuse. Farley identifies a variety of "penalties" used by men to help secure female compliance: "verbal denigration of a woman sexually; noncooperation from male co-workers; negative job evaluations or poor personnel recommendations; refusal of overtime; demotions; injurious transfers and reassignments of shifts, hours, or locations of work, loss of job training; impossible performance standards and outright termination of employment" (p. 15). Thus, the message to women is, because I am a man or because I am higher in the hierarchy, your body belongs to me.

Pulling from a variety of sources, Russell (1984) identified the functions of sexual harassment, which include

1. Maintaining the traditional male prerogative of male sexual initiative (Goodman 1978);
2. Expressing male hostility against women (Grayson, n.d.);
3. "Compensat[ing] men for powerlessness in their own lives" by granting individual men control over individual women (Bularzik 1978, p. 26);
4. Asserting "a woman's sex role over her [other] function[s]" (Farley 1978, pp. 14–15), thereby

5. Keeping women in a subordinate position (Farley 1978);
6. Limiting women's access, for example, to particular jobs (Bularzik 1978), especially jobs that are "nontraditional" for women.

An additional function is that the harassment sexualizes the interaction, communicating to women that we are, first and foremost, objects that exist for men's sexual pleasure.

The above functions also apply to harassment on the street. The street harasser communicates to women that the street belongs to him, not her; that she is not free to go where she likes, when she likes; that if she behaves as though she is free, he will prove to her that the street is his by sexually violating her. Sexual harassment by the "man on the street" is so frequent in women's lives that we have learned to see this behavior as normal for men and inescapable for women. In fact, sexual harassment is publicly viewed as harmless (Bernard and Schlaffer 1983). This view belies the moments of terror that women feel, not knowing what the perpetrator might do next, or what might aggravate him into an even more overt display of the physical control he can exercise over the situation. The common view of sexual harassment as harmless also belies the long-term (gender-typical) psychological damage that almost certainly accrues from the physical intimidation, the leering, the grabbing and pushing at women's bodies as though they belong to men rather than to the women themselves, the sexually humiliating comments (e.g., being called "pussy"), and the laughter at our expense. Even when not accompanied by physical assault, "street hassling" has been likened to "small-scale assaults" (Bernard and Schlaffer 1983) and "little rapes" (Medea and Thompson 1974).

Poverty

"Low income" means fighting for survival. It means worrying about basic needs such as food and shelter. It usually also means living in a high violence area. By definition, then, low income is equated with threat to survival. Female-headed families comprise more than half the poor families in the United States (Ehrenreich and Piven 1984). Below low income economically are the homeless. The homeless are barely surviving: sleeping on the streets in the dead of winter, being totally vulnerable to violence, not knowing from where their next meal is coming or, indeed, if it is coming at all.

The new homeless of the 1980s (and 1990s) are more often women and children than were the old homeless of the 1950s and 1960s. Unlike the old homeless, who were comprised mainly of older men who made enough money to sleep in cheap hotels, the new homeless more often sleep in the streets or in public places, even in winter, and have substantially less income, correcting for inflation, than the old homeless (Rossi 1990). Although poverty is not of many years' duration for most Americans, for single mothers and blacks it is long term (Belle 1990). Why might this be the case?

Oskamp (1989) notes that "women workers with a bachelor's degree earn $616 *less* per year than male workers who have not completed high school" (pp. iii–iv). Using statistics reported by the Current Population Reports, Rotella (1990) revealed that, between 1955 and 1987, the female-to-male earnings ratio for people working year around and full time ranged from .58 in 1975 to .65 in 1987. Thus, during this period, for each dollar that full-time male workers, who worked the year around, earned, female workers earned between 59 and 65 cents. Although some of the reasons women earned less than men were their lower levels of education and work experience, half or more than half of the pay difference was due to sex discrimination. It is an often-repeated finding that, as the proportion of women in a field increases, the wage level decreases (Ferber and Lowry 1976; Hodge and Hodge 1965; Snyder and Hudis 1976).

A large number of experiments have been carried out wherein, typically, potential employers are given identical resumés but with the sex of the applicant varying. The findings of such experiments consistently reveal discrimination against women in personnel decisions. For example, Rosen and Jerdee (1974b) provided male bank supervisors attending a management institute a single hypothetical situation and asked them to make a decision about what they would do. Situations varied by sex, but all other information received by the bank supervisors (the subjects) was identical. The following issues were assessed: (1) whether the subjects were more likely to promote to branch manager a male versus female employee; (2) whether the subjects would more likely send to a conference an "older, unpromotable female" or "a younger, highly qualified male," or whether the subjects would more likely send to a conference an "older, unpromotable male" or a younger, highly qualified female; (3) whether the subjects were more likely to follow the request of a male versus a female supervisor to terminate or transfer an employee; and (4) whether the subjects were more likely to grant a child-care leave of absence to a male versus a female employee. In instances (1) through (3), the bank managers discriminated against females: they were more willing to promote a male than a female candidate; they would send to a conference a highly promotable male employee more often than a comparable female employee; and they would follow the request of the male supervisor more frequently than that of a female supervisor in decisions regarding subordinate employees. Similar findings have been obtained by numerous other investigators (see, for example, Cecil, Paul, and Olins 1973; Cohen and Bunker 1975; Dipboye, Fromkin, and Wiback 1975; Fidell 1970; Levinson 1975; Rosen and Jerdee 1974a; Rosen, Jerdee, and Prestwich 1975).

When confronted with a male versus a female employee who sought a child-care leave of absence, the bank managers in Rosen and Jerdee's study were more likely to grant the females a leave. While this finding may look like discrimination against men, as was argued by Rosen and Jerdee (1974b), consider that employers often argue that males should receive preferential treatment in employment *because* they are more committed to their jobs. Child-care leaves, or other absences from employment, by women are cited as proof that males are more committed. Such absences in employment are used to keep women out of jobs, at lower pay, and in lower-level employment. One way of interpreting this last finding, then, is: bank managers are more willing to jeopardize the employment history of a female than a male employee.

These findings help us understand why women are poorer than men— women are consistently discriminated against in personnel decisions. But they don't help us understand why women (and children) are the *fastest-growing* segment of the American poor. One of the reasons is the recent change to no-fault divorce laws (see Weitzman 1985) and another the increase in divorce rates. These two factors conspire to reveal that many, if not most, women are just one man away from poverty. Rotella (1990), citing statistics from the U.S. Department of Commerce and the U.S.

Department of Labor, reported that 34 percent of families maintained by women lived below the poverty line in 1987, while only 6 percent of husband-wife families did so. The situation was even worse for families with children. Forty-six percent of families with children that were maintained by women lived below the poverty line in 1987, while only 8 percent of husband-wife families with children did so. These statistics were considerably more grim for black and Hispanic mother-led families than for white mother-led families: in 1987 approximately 60 percent lived below poverty level.

Weitzman (1985) examined the economic situation of ex-wives and ex-husbands as a function of the length of their marriages and as a function of the predivorce family income. She found that, for couples married less than ten years, one year after the divorce, ex-husbands' incomes were three-quarters of what they were prior to the divorce, while ex-wives' incomes were between a quarter to a half of their predivorce income. Comparison of ex-husbands' and ex-wives' postdivorce per capita income (calculated by dividing income by the number of people in the household) with their predivorce per capita incomes revealed an even greater discrepancy, due to the fact that 90 percent of minor children stayed with their mothers, and thus wives shared their already smaller incomes with children. A similar pattern of findings was obtained for couples married eleven to seventeen years. But the women who suffered most from divorce were those who had been married 18 or more years. Weitzman (1985, p. 332) found that men married this long

> have a much higher *per capita* income—that is, they have much more money to spend on themselves—than their former wives at every level of (predivorce family) income. Even where the discrepancy is smallest, in lower-income families, the husband and every member of this postdivorce family have *twice* as much money as his former wife and his children. In higher-income families, the discrepancy is enormous. The husband and each person in his postdivorce household—his new wife, cohabitor, or child— have three times as much disposable income as his former wife and the members of her postdivorce household.

Perhaps surprising to many, it was the women married the longest (that is, eighteen or more years) and with the highest predivorce family incomes ($40,000 or more) who experienced "the *greatest downward mobility* after divorce" (p. 334). Accordingly, these were also the women who expressed "the most distress with their financial loss and . . . the strongest feelings of outrage and injustice" (p. 334). Another finding that may be a surprise to many is that, regardless of the length of marriage, "as family income [went] up, divorced wives experience[d] greater 'relative deprivation.' That is, they [were] relatively worse off than their former husbands, and they [were] relatively worse off than they were during marriage" (p. 325). Furthermore, Weitzman's findings are based on the presumption that ex-husbands complied fully in making all court-ordered alimony and child support payments. Thus, her findings *overestimate* the postdivorce income of ex-wives (and children) and *underestimate* the postdivorce income of ex-husbands. The survival of women (and children) trying to make it without a husband's income is threatened as long as discrimination against women in employment continues to occur, women are not economically compensated for domestic work, including child care, performed while men are out building their careers, and courts give priority to the needs of men over women and children (cf. Weitzman 1985).

Beyond the violence that the *threat* of living in poverty or homeless poses for many, if not most, women, and in addition to the violence incurred by *actual* poverty, is the less recognized violence done to women by employment discrimination. What is the psychological effect on women who are denied employment because they are female? Who are paid less for their work than men, despite comparable credentials and performance? Who are unable adequately to support themselves and their children without a man's income? Who are reminded on a daily basis that society considers them not as good and/or not as valuable as men? These systematic, pervasive practices are also forms of violence against women.

A Continuum of Violence

Liz Kelly's (1987) research on violence in women's lives uncovered a continuum of violence to which women are exposed (see also Leidig 1981). At one end of the continuum are such frequent events as sexual harassment (e.g., catcalls or lewd remarks made by strangers on the street) and pressure to have sex. Virtually all the women in Kelly's sample had been exposed to these forms of violence, usually on many occasions. Many reported having to deal with sexual harassment daily. Their *ways of coping* with such events included "ignoring them, not defining them as abusive at the time and, very commonly, forgetting them" (p. 53). Thus, the incidence of these forms of violence was almost certainly underreported. At the other end of the continuum are less frequent forms of violence such as domestic violence, rape, and incest, which were still encountered by a shockingly large percentage of women (note, however, that Kelly's sample was not representative). Here again, incidence was likely to be underestimated for a variety of reasons: for instance, many women did not report having experienced domestic violence unless the violence recurred over time.

In addition, because Kelly's sample was relatively young and perhaps highly selective in other ways, elder abuse is not shown on the continuum, though it is committed primarily by sons against elderly, poverty-stricken mothers (Schlesinger 1988). Other forms of violence, such as hunger and cold, which accompany homelessness—a way of life for increasing numbers of women (and children)—are also not represented on the continuum. Nonetheless, the notion that male violence against women can be described by a continuum ranging from frequent to infrequent forms and from more to less severe and threatening is an important one. Another dimension along which forms of violence against women differ is sexual/nonsexual. It is important that all the forms of violence listed in Kelly's continuum, except domestic violence, involve sexual violence against women, and, as we have seen, domestic violence also often encompasses sexual abuse.

Kelly warned that the location of violence at different points along the continuum did not relate in any simple fashion to its effects on the women. She noted, for example, a finding by McNeill (1983) that "what women fear most when they are flashed at is death" (p. 49). Medea and Thompson (1974) reported that women experience common, subtle forms of violence ("little rapes") as threats of actual physical assault.

The concept of a continuum of violence reveals that violence is a very real part of every woman's life. The forms of violence that occur most frequently are not conceptualized as violent or abusive or even unusual by most women, however. In fact, they are viewed as normal male behavior. Kelly's continuum puts these everyday forms of violence in context.

Graham, Ott, and Rawlings (1990) also found evidence of a continuum of violence against women. In recruiting subjects for their study, they sought out three different groups of women in intimate relationships: emotionally and physically abused, emotionally abused only, and non-abused. However, cluster analysis of their data revealed that, among women with live-in heterosexual partners, there were no distinct abused and nonabused groups. Rather, male-female relationships were described by a continuum of abuse. *All* male-female relationships were more or less abusive. Even among dating couples Graham, Foliano, et al. (1990) found that 42 percent of the women in the sample, mainly college freshman, had experienced at least some physical abuse in their current relationship. Seventy-eight percent had experienced at least some emotional abuse in the same relationship. One third of this sample had been dating six months or less!

Bart (1983; Bart and O'Brien 1985) has identified a heterosexual sex-rape continuum. At one end is consensual sex (both parties equally desire sex). At the other is rape. In between are altruistic sex (one party submits out of guilt, duty, or pity) and compliant sex (one party submits because the consequences of not submitting are worse than those of submitting). Using Bart's conceptualization, Kelly found that most women "felt pressured to have sex in many, if not all, of their sexual relationships with men" (p. 56). Yet she found that women perceived sex as coercive only when physical force or the threat of physical force was used. An event usually was not called rape by women unless the perpetrator was a stranger, it happened at night and outdoors, physical force was used, and they resisted. Moreover, Scheppele and Bart (1983) found that women tended not to define nonphallic rape (for example, digital penetration) as rape. These findings reveal that most women strongly resist perceiving an event which happened to them as coercive or rape, but that most of the sexual experiences of most women involve altruistic or compliant sex.

Like Bart, Efron (1985) found that three fourths of the women in her sample (solicited through a variety of women's groups affiliated with churches, feminist organizations, etc.) reported being sexual on occasions when they did not want to be. Thirty percent reported some sort of sexual trauma and, in 44 percent of these cases, the trauma was rape. In three fourths of these rapes, the sexual aggressor was someone close to the woman (a relative, acquaintance or date, a lover, a husband, or a friend).

The most representative study of sexual violence and victimization among college students, and clearly the most extensive, was carried out by Koss, Gidycz, and Wisniewski (1987). Their sample was comprised of 6,159 students (3,187 of which were women). Using questions that assess male sexual aggression and female victimization along a continuum of sexual violence, Koss et al. found that 54 percent of the women students reported having experienced some form of sexual victimization. Koss et al. interpreted these findings as lending support to A. Johnson's (1980) observation, "That sexual violence is so pervasive supports the view that the locus of violence against women rests squarely in the middle of what our culture defines as 'normal' interaction between men and women" (p. 146).

Findings regarding a continuum of violence support MacKinnon's (1983) analysis of the reason rapists are rarely convicted in court. Mac-Kinnon pointed out that, because rape is legally defined as the use of more force than is found in normal male sexual behavior, and because that amount of force is considerable and does not take into account the point at which women begin to feel violated, rape is practically defined out of existence. In other words, according to the (predominantly male) legal system, it is acceptable (legal) for men to be violent to women when they are being sexual with us; it is acceptable (legal) for "normal" heterosexual intercourse to contain elements of rape.

As Kelly (1987, p. 59) points out, an implication of the construct of a continuum of male violence is that

> a clear distinction cannot be made between "victims" and other women. The fact that some women only experience violence at the more common, everyday end of the continuum is a difference in degree and not in kind. The use of the term "victim" in order to separate one group of women from other women's lives and experiences must be questioned. The same logic applies to the definition of "offenders."

At MacKinnon's (1987) request, and based on a random selection of 930 San Francisco households, Russell calculated the likelihood of a woman *not* being sexually assaulted or harassed in her lifetime. It was only 7.8 percent.

Men's Violence against Women Affects All Women

Incest, battering, rape, and sexual harassment are simply the most recognized forms of male violence that threaten women's physical and psychological survival. Other forms include poverty and a form of abuse frequently associated with poverty, elder abuse (Schlesinger 1988). Information on these forms of violence alone should confirm that men do threaten women's survival, even though some women would claim that "Men don't threaten me. I've never experienced any of that violence." As Andrea Dworkin has said (Reingold 1987, p. 72), "Although one in three girls in this country will be incestuously abused before she's 18, but [you are] not one of them—and if a woman is raped every three minutes, but [you have] never been one of them; and one woman is beaten every 18 seconds, but [you are] not one of them," no one can deny that we live in a hostile world that terrorizes women and girls, threatening our psychic and physical survival.

Letters received by Ellen Goodman (1993), in response to President Clinton's efforts to end discrimination against gays in the military, suggest men are frightened by the kinds of violence to which they themselves subject women on a daily basis. Approximately nine out of the ten letters received by Goodman were written by men. The male writers sounded panic-stricken that they would have to take showers and sleep in barracks with homosexual men (as though military men haven't always done this). Very clearly, the men didn't want other men looking at them the way they—men—look at women! Nor did they want other men treating them the way they treat women. Goodman notes, "The fascinating thing to this—female—reader was that nearly all the letter writers shared the same perspective: that of straight men worrying about being victims of sexual assault, harassment, lusting, or just plain ogling. *This garden variety homophobia*—fear of homosexuals—*was fear of becoming the object of unwanted sexual attention.* Being the oglee instead of, say, the ogler" (emphasis added). Goodman points out that the threat posed to straight men by gay men who might treat them as straight men treat women is the closest that most men may come, even in fantasy, to imagining the everyday real-life experiences of women. The closest they may come to imagining a trip past a construction site, unease in a fraternity house, fear that a date could become date rape. In short, the closest men come to worrying about male sexual aggression.

A writer from Idaho put it in this rather charming vernacular, "Some of the gays are not little pansy guys but big hulking guys and if a small man said no, what is to stop him?"

Apparently, most of the men who wrote Goodman found it frightening to even *imagine* being treated as men routinely treat women.

However, the story of male violence against women does not end with the more recognized forms of damage such as incest, battering, and rape, or even its more subtle forms. Remembering that the *emotional* assault involved in these physical acts often is reported as the worst aspect by victims, let's consider if emotional violence by men against women does not also occur in other, more subtle and more frequent ways.

It is a consistent, worldwide finding that potential parents prefer to have male over female children (see, for example, Campbell 1991; Krishnan 1987). How might parents communicate this preference to children? What effects do such communications have on daughters? What effects do they have on daughters' sense of self and self-esteem?

At the beginning of a course we teach, "The Psychology of Women," we ask students to write a short paper describing one or more times they feel they have been discriminated against because of their sex. Each year I receive stories from female students describing the pain of having to work while their brothers play. A common example is day after day, including holidays, the girls were required to help prepare meals, set the table, and clean up after meals, as the males play or sit around talking or watching TV. The stories divulge the confusion experienced by young women— girls, really—about why they have to do so much more work than their brothers. The wounds created by these common, everyday experiences of girls apparently fester for a number of years, as the writers of these stories are college women. Other stories describe how adults say girls should not climb trees, or a myriad of other activities, simply because they are girls. A sizable number of the stories describe the pain girls feel because boys do not want them on the neighborhood football, basketball, or baseball team, that they can't play because they are girls, or that they were chosen last and reluctantly to play on a team. (Who teaches boys that such behavior is acceptable?) In some of the stories, the girls respond by proving to the boys that they can play the sport better than any of the neighborhood boys. The skilled female player frequently continues to meet with rejection by the boys because she is a female. Other girls respond by giving up sports to do "feminine" things, which some of them learn to enjoy more than the more active, masculine activities. The reader can undoubtedly think of other examples of emotional violence commonly exacted upon the psyches of girls, in the name of teaching them their "appropriate" sex roles.

A woman may not have been personally touched by rape, battering, or incest, but where is the woman who has not suffered repeated psychological damage from at least one of these more "subtle" forms of violence? Are these other forms of violence trivial? Yes—as the air we breathe is trivial, as the food we eat is trivial. And if women daily take in poison in these "trivial" ways, we cannot escape widespread damage to the systems that sustain psychological life (cf. Horney 1967). Whether or not a woman directly experiences the more recognized forms of male violence, does not the existence of the more subtle forms, along with the knowledge that men's violence is directed at women *because we are women* and that any woman can be their target, threaten every woman's psychic survival?

It may be that women have lived with male violence for so long that it is no longer visible to us. We may find it impossible to imagine a life without male violence, a life in a safe world.

A notable aspect of much of men's violence against women is that it is directed at our sexual organs (see Barry 1979; Barry, Bunch, and Castley 1984; Rich 1980). In this regard, violence against women differs from violence against male members of other groups such as Native Americans, Jews, and blacks in that it is more likely to be directed at women's than at men's sexual organs. I use the term "female sexual terrorism" to refer to the fact that all females, *because we are female,* are potential targets of violence directed at our sexual organs by males. Examples of the way sexual violence is more likely to be directed at women can be seen in situations in which both men and women are held prisoners, and in which there is no obvious reason that the sexes should be treated differently. We will provide two such examples from different parts of the world that will show the pervasiveness of female sexual terrorism. Both examples concern violence inflicted upon male and female prisoners by *governments,* showing that this differential treatment operates at broad institutional levels and is not just the work of a few deranged individuals.

Ka-Tzetnik 135633's (1981) account of her and her brother's experience in the Nazi concentration camp of Kozentration Zenter provides one example. (The name given her at the camp, Ka-Tzetnik 135633, signifies both the particular camp and her inmate number. Her name prior to being sent to the camp was Daniella.) It is important to note that Daniella provides no indication that abuse was directed at the sexual organs of her brother while prisoner. However, Daniella and all other female prisoners at the camp were continually threatened with sexual abuse of all types. One type was flogging, which was carried out when prisoners failed to satisfactorily meet the demands of prison officials, but which had an unusual character because the prisoners were female. A flogging for female prisoners involved the prisoner's being led nude

> into the square. . . . Strung on the barbed wire along both sides of the Execution Square—eyes [of prisoners forced to watch the executions]. Eyes beyond count. . . .
> Each [woman to receive a flogging] is strapped over a separate stool—the feet to the forelegs of the stool, arms to the hindlegs, face down. . . .
> The Master-Kalefactress cracks her knout down on the back of one of the kalefactresses. . . .
> Bludgeons . . . swing down in unison on the naked bodies. Without pause, without letup. The shrieks split the heavens. . . .
> The black van stands by. Kalefactresses hurl in the mangled bodies of the "purgated" [to be sent to the crematorium]. (Ka-Tzetnik 1981, p. 138)

An additional type of sexual abuse was meted out to attractive, unmarried, female prisoners who had no venereal diseases, such as Daniella: they were sent to "the Joy Division" to serve as "whores" for Nazi soldiers heading to the front. The German word for whore and a number were branded across their chests, and the women were forcibly sterilized. If Nazi soldiers, serviced daily by the women, "were not satisfied with the 'enjoyment,' they had only to report it, . . . [giving] the girl's breast number" (p. 161). After three such reports, a woman was flogged and sent to the crematorium. A third type of sexual abuse involved forced experimental surgery on women's sexual organs.

The sexual violence used by governments to torture women political prisoners in Latin America provides another example. Bunster (1984) makes clear that, while females are exposed to all the torture methods used on males, they are also treated to sexual torture, used only on females. When initially brought to a detention center for interrogation, female prisoners, while blindfolded, are fingered and pawed particularly on their breasts, buttocks, and genitals. As the interrogation heightens, a group of men tears the clothes from the woman's body while beating and slapping her. Their actions are accompanied by "crude verbal abuse and vile ridicule of her naked body" (p. 99). Along with other forms of sexual torture, cigarettes are extinguished on her breasts and nipples. She is subjected to massive gang rape by males. Rape by trained dogs may also be used. Mice, which scratch and bite in their disorientation, are put in her vagina. Bunster notes that such sexual violence is seen by the governments as "the key" in controlling women, that is, in teaching them to "retreat into the home and fulfill the traditional role of wife and mother" (p. 98), and not be political activists.

Why is much of men's aggression against women sexual in nature?[2] Why wouldn't men use the same kind of violence against women as they use against men? The answers may lie in patriarchy's use of anatomical sex differences for determining individuals' membership in oppressor and oppressed groups. That is, because we use individuals' sexual organs as the basis for discriminating membership in the oppressor group (male) and the oppressed group (female), males may direct violence and threats of violence against females' sexual organs. (Jane Elliot, in *The Eye of the Storm,* demonstrates with third graders that virtually any dimension along which people can make discriminations, such as eye color, is easily turned into grounds for creating oppressor and oppressed groups.) *The purpose of such directed violence is to help ensure that female sexual organs are seen as subordinate and male sexual organs are seen as dominant.* (Consider in this regard the fact that Sigmund Freud so strongly believed that the penis was superior that he based his whole psychology of women on this belief, arguing that women's envy of the penis produced their heterosexuality.

In addition, the label "castrating," assigned to women whom men perceive as assuming too much power in their relationships with men, reveals a publicly recognized relationship between the penis and dominance.)

If the superiority of the penis over the vagina is being established through male sexual violence against females, then males benefit from this violence in their everyday interactions with females if they remind females that they, males, have a penis, and the women have a vagina. The more frequently females (and males) are reminded of the dominance of the penis over the vagina, the more rewards *all* men reap from some men's sexual violence against women. Consider the following example, provided by Kaschak (1992), quoting Chernin (1985, p. 85), demonstrating one way in which men attempt to remind women (and themselves) of women's inferiority: "When Emma Goldman spoke against conscription, the crowds would yell 'strip her naked,'" (p. 85). Kaschak asks, "Would a man be threatened this way by a crowd of women? . . . It reminds her of her place—in a woman's body. And that is equivalent to vulnerability and shame, that in itself puts her in danger and diminishes her" (p. 85).

Interestingly, much of our graffiti is concerned with genitalia, even among elementary school children. Lucca and Pacheco (1986) found bathroom graffiti of boys contains sexual content twice as often as that of girls. Eleven percent of the girls' graffiti concerned genitalia, while 19 percent of the boys' did. Although genitalia were absent in girls' *drawings* in restrooms, half the boys' drawings portrayed genitalia.

The sexualization of men and women takes yet another form: the sexualization of male/female interactions. Society's use of sexual organs—to make group membership determinations—may account, then, for why males, much more than females, sexualize interactions. (For empirical evidence that males are more likely than females to sexualize interactions, see Abbey 1982, 1987, and Abbey and Melby 1986.) For example, females who are trying only to be friendly are viewed by males, much more than females, as being promiscuous and seductive (Abbey 1982). At work, it is common for co-workers and employers to remind female employees that we are first and foremost female, through actions so blatant as to be viewed as sexual harassment and through remarks so familiar and routine that they are not recognized as harassment. Street harassers remind women after work hours that we are simply "cunt" or "pussy," and thus subordinate. By compulsively sexualizing their interactions with females, males remind both themselves and females that males are dominant.

People are required to announce their sex to others frequently and in many ways, thereby helping to ensure that the sex of interacting parties remains central to male-female interactions. For instance, we wear distinctive clothing, emphasizing our sex differences (e.g., bras and low-cut blouses to emphasize women's breasts). With our language we force speakers to identify the sex of persons (and even animals) being discussed. We are given first names that are likely to communicate our sex. (For an entertaining examination of the myriad ways we announce our sex, see Gould 1972.) Furthermore, strong social norms govern such events so that when individuals try to desexualize themselves or others, they are likely to meet with ridicule, reeducation, or rejection. It is perhaps for these reasons that people are uncomfortable interacting with a baby (or even an adult) unless they know its sex.

The dominance of the penis over the vagina is maintained in everyday, "normal" sexual interactions between males and females through cultural rules concerning "appropriate" sexuality: sex should only occur between cross-sex individuals. Males should initiate sex, or "take" (or "make") a woman. Females should be unwilling participants in sex or should not like sex as much as men. (If females sought sex with men as much or more than men seek sex with women, sex between men and women would not communicate the dominance of the penis unless men rejected sex with women under these conditions.) Sex should occur in the missionary position, with the man on top. And on and on. Dworkin (1987) notes that "the laws regulating intercourse in general forbid those sex acts that break down gender barriers and license those sex acts and conditions that heighten gender polarity and antagonism. The laws that say who to fuck, when, how, and anatomically where keep the man differentiated in a way that seems absolute" (p. 150). All these cultural rules operate to ensure that both men and women see the penis as dominant over the vagina, and thus men as dominant over women. They also operate to ensure that both women and men see sexual violence in heterosexual intercourse as "normal."

Interestingly, it is the presence or absence of a penis, not a vagina, that determines whether someone is considered a male or a female. A person with a penis and a vagina is considered male. A person with no vagina and no penis is labeled female. People's biological sex is not the only thing defined in terms of the penis, without regard for the vagina. Scheppele and Bart (1983) found that all but 4 percent of the women in their sample who had been forced to have nonphallic sex (including digital penetration of the vagina) considered themselves rape avoiders, whereas 93 percent of those forced to have phallic sex defined the experience as rape. As Scheppele and Bart note, "Rape, therefore, is what is done with a penis, not what is done to a vagina" (p. 75). The importance people attach to the penis as compared to the vagina—in, for example, defining biological sex and rape versus rape avoidance—suggests men have been effective in convincing men and women alike that the penis *is* superior.

In conclusion, women's sexual organs may be the essential battlefield on which the war for male domination is fought. The more violent a sexual crime against women, the greater the social distance between men and women, and the more clearly that distance is emphasized. Sexual violence reveals the extent to which women are not men. This theory would help explain why sexual violence is experienced as more hideous, more psychically violent, and thus more frightening to women than other crimes.

Our society's use of sexual organs to make dominant versus subordinate group membership determinations accounts for the exaggerated way in which we obsessively advertise our gender (our sex) to others, for the compulsive sexualization of male-female interactions by males, for the social mores that males, not females, should be the initiators (and thus dominant) in sex, and for the tremendous violence meted against women's bodies by men. Male sexual violence against women and "normal" heterosexual intercourse are essential to patriarchy because they establish the dominance of the penis over the vagina, and thus the power relations between the sexes. The sexualization of people and male/female interactions is central to the practice of patriarchy because it keeps group membership (and thus power relations) salient. Thus, when a male sexualizes an interaction with a female, he is doing work for patriarchy. When a male sexually violates a female, he is doing work for patriarchy. Men's sexual violence against women is the primary vehicle through which the dominance of the penis over the vagina is established.

Can Women Escape from Men?

If women as a group were able to escape male violence, we would not be men's victims. Women as a group obviously have not yet found a way to stop or escape rape, wife abuse, incest, sexual harassment, or other forms of male tyranny. Individual acts against women are publicly credited to women's masochism, failure as wives, inappropriate dress, or seductiveness. However, viewed collectively, these acts make it clear that the purpose of male violence against women is male domination. Naturally, a system designed to enforce male domination is not going to provide women with real protection or escape from male violence.

Only one percent of rapists are arrested, and only one percent of those arrested are convicted (Russell 1984). Those who are convicted serve little time before being put back on the streets. Some are freed because the prisons are overcrowded. Women are encouraged to walk in groups, to not go out at night, or to go out only in the company of a male. Rather than effectively stopping rape by locking up rapists, our system "locks up" women. Probably because women do stay off the streets, "more rapes take place in or near the home than any other single place" (Gordon and Riger 1989, p. 14). Despite women's best precautions, we are not safe from rape in this culture.

Many battered women who try to leave their batterers are pursued by them. And this is when a battered woman is most likely to receive her severest beating or to be killed (Browne 1987; Ewing 1987; Serum 1979a, 1979b, cited by Okun 1986). Those who call the police and turn to the criminal justice system for help find that neither is willing to provide protection. Outsiders who don't want to "get involved" because *they* fear the batterer nonetheless expect the battered woman to stand up to him. (The recent trial of Joel Steinberg in New York City provided examples of this [Ehrlich 1989]. Police who fear for their own safety in making domestic violence calls but who nevertheless minimize the danger to which battered women are exposed provide another.) Women who kill their batterers because they have tried every other means of escape (to no avail) frequently are given stiff prison sentences. The system that does not protect victims' rights to freedom from abuse zealously protects their abusers from the victims' acts of self-defense (see Browne 1987; Ewing 1987).

It certainly seems no accident that, in a patriarchy, men as a group are required to use weapons and train for combat in the name of "serving their country," while women are not. Throughout their lifetimes most women remain ignorant of how to use guns. Still fewer train for combat. Thus women are even denied training in self-defense against male violence. Fear that women will develop weapon and combat skills may be at the heart of the heated controversy of whether women should be allowed to serve in combat.

It is impossible for women to remain in this culture and completely escape men. Men create the norms of our culture (for example, they define appropriate behavior for males and females, they define women's purpose in life as seeking to love and marry men, and so forth). Men control society's institutions (such as marriage, law, religion, psychiatry [and thus mental institutions], medicine). Men are the societal experts, whether as gynecologists, child-care experts, or generals in the military. Men are socialized to use their size and strength to their advantage, including to dominate women. As a result of all this, men are able to reward those women who behave as men desire and to punish those who do not (Polk 1976). Women who don't conform to men's rules can, for example, be *legally* jailed (as are battered women who kill their husbands in self-defense; Browne 1987; Ewing 1987); raped (by husbands, cohabiting partners, or dates with whom they have had consensual sex in the past; Finkelhor and Yllo 1985); and/or deemed crazy, forcibly put in mental institutions, and given shock treatments (Hudson 1987) or drugs to compel their submission. Because sources of power (normative, institutional, reward, expertise, psychological, and brute force, as noted by Polk 1976 and described above) are controlled by men, and because these sources of power guarantee that women cannot escape men, men create the conditions that ensure women's inability to escape them.

Because it is men who have power in patriarchy, they assign tasks to subordinates. They use their power to help ensure that tasks are carried out by those whom *they* choose. Whether the subordinates have contact with men or not, if they are carrying out the tasks men have assigned to them (as a group or as individuals), they have not escaped men. Men have assigned domestic, sexual, reproductive, and child-care services to women. They also feel entitled to women's emotional services, including ego-stroking, expressing feelings for them, and smoothing out social interactions.

Examples are provided by recent changes in laws which occurred because legislators (who are predominantly men) used their power to ensure that women will provide men the services they desire and that women will be unable to do otherwise. As noted by Finkelhor and Yllo (1985), legislators have been eagerly extending marital rape protections to cohabiting men (i.e., granting men freedom from prosecution for marital rape), but not to cohabiting women (i.e., not granting women the right to prosecute for marital rape), even though women, not men, have been making organized efforts to obtain such protections. According to Finkelhor and Yllo, "cohabiting men have been granted these privileges as a gift. No large group of cohabiting men has converged on the state houses demanding the right to rape their partners. Whereas, when women's-rights groups have lobbied hard for laws protecting unmarried cohabiting women, in many instances they have come away empty-handed" (p. 149). In a similar way, the U.S. Supreme Court (in *Webster v. Reproductive Health Services*) took women's reproductive freedoms out of women's hands and put them in the hands of (male) state legislators. Men have used and are using their power to ensure their access to women's sexual and reproductive services. Women have no comparable access to men's services unless men *choose* to provide those services. Legal changes such as those in our examples have prompted S. Johnson (1987, 1989) to argue that it is a waste of energy for women to push for legal reform, because men simply change the laws back or make them worse for women if the changes turn out not to be in men's interests. In sum, men use all their sources of power to ensure continued access to women and women's services.

Women who feel they are in egalitarian marriages may believe they have escaped male domination. However, even men who "let" their women have more freedom (e.g., to work outside the home) or who "help" their women with domestic chores retain control. They decide how much freedom a woman can have and how much they give.

Using their power to set norms and create social institutions (Polk 1976), men make women's escape still more difficult. The following are examples of ways in which this occurs:

- God is portrayed as male, omnipotent, and superior, giving divine sanction to hierarchical relationships (Lipman-Blumen 1984). People are taught that women's subservience to men is pleasing to God and anything less than that is displeasing. People are also taught to forgive and to love their enemies, which certainly helps maintain oppression. Probably because of our position in society, it is primarily women who are involved in organized religion (Lipman-Blumen 1984), though men are its leaders and the "legitimate" interpreters of the "word of God."

- Our history is male, for women's lives have been erased from official accounts or rewritten from men's perspective (Spender 1982). Each generation of women that fights male domination is led to believe that it is the first, that there is something wrong with it for not being willing to accept its "proper" role in society. Imagine the sense of purpose, entitlement, pride, and direction women resisters of male domination would feel if they knew that women had resisted all through history and if they knew how they fit into that quest.

- The lower incomes of women relative to men pressure women to marry, and to stay married, for purposes of economic survival. This is because, in general, any time women try to make it apart from men, their incomes drop substantially. This is true for divorced women, never married women, separated women, widows, and thus elderly women. Russo (1990), citing Eichler and Parron (1987), states, "Elderly women are among the poorest of the U.S. population: Among people age 65 and older living alone, 26% of White women, 48% of Hispanic women, and 60% of Black women live below the poverty level" (p. 372). (See also the section on poverty earlier in this chapter.)

- Women are encouraged to love and care for husbands, fathers, and grandfathers and to want and care for male children and grandchildren. Such prescriptions ensure that women will continue to be surrounded by men throughout our lifetimes. Women's efforts to look after ourselves are viewed as selfish and as disloyal to husbands and male relatives. Comparable prescriptions do not exist for men. Rather than being viewed as selfish, men who look after themselves are seen as smart, deserving, and "good catches."

- Attractiveness in women is defined as being small and thin (Garner, Garfinkel, et al. 1980; Silverstein et al. 1986), that is, weak (cf. L. Brown 1985), and as dressing in non-self-protective ways (for example, wearing high heels).

- Men much more than women are encouraged to strengthen their bodies through sports. This encouragement takes a variety of forms. Men's sports programs are heavily funded and are the object of mass viewing. Women's sports are neither well funded nor viewed as exciting entertainment. Differences in public attitudes regarding body building for males versus females reflect this differential encouragement of men versus women strengthening their bodies. Even with strong, *but feminine* and thin, role models like Jane Fonda and Madonna, female college students continue to express revulsion upon viewing slides of women, but not men, body builders.

- Lesbianism is viewed as perverse. Lesbians are denied civil rights.

- A child without a father is marked as illegitimate, a bastard. Public opinion is that an unmarried woman should not have children, that children need a father.

- Men's ideas and feelings are listened to and shown respect. Women's ideas are trivialized or ignored. This differential response is apparent when men and women propose the same idea during meetings. Women are told we are too sensitive or overly emotional or that we don't feel the "right way" (the way men want us to) when we express our feelings.

- Men invade women's physical space, touching our bodies, when they have not received invitation or permission (Henley, cited by

Parlee 1983). They feel free to intrude upon a lone woman or two women together in public. They interrupt and control topics of conversation when talking with women (Fishman, cited by Parlee 1983). Many of men's messages to and about women are in the form of sexist jokes and putdowns (Hite 1987). These invasive behaviors are considered acceptable when performed by men against women.

These examples show the extent of *every woman's* inability to escape men. Of course, women as individuals can reject male norms, but because men back up their norms with rewards and punishments (for example, a woman who is attractive to men is more likely to be hired than one who is not), going against men's norms is costly for individual women.

Are Men Kind to Women?

> The predicament of women a propos the dominant reality is complex and paradoxical, as is revealed in women's mundane experience of the seesaw of demand and neglect, of being romanced and assaulted, of being courted and being ignored.　　　　(Frye 1983, pp. 162–163)

Even if women's survival is threatened by male violence, which is inescapable, and even if women are isolated by men, a fourth element—women's perception of kindness from men—would be necessary for women as a group to develop Societal Stockholm Syndrome. In this section we ask if women perceive men as showing kindness.

Men are kind to women in a number of ways, creating hopes that they really do care about women and will stop their violence against us. Chivalry, male protection of women from other men's violence, courting behavior, love (including affection during sex), and heterosexual privileges (access to men's income, power, and prestige) that accrue to women for coupling with men provide examples of such kindness. These facts—that men show women these kindnesses, and that women perceive these acts as kind—are themselves sufficient for affirming the presence of the fourth precursor (some show of kindness, however small) in men's relations with women. However, further analysis reveals that none of these kindnesses comes free. We will examine each of these acts of kindness.

Chivalry

Chivalry is one of the first things that comes to mind when one thinks of male kindness toward women: men opening doors for women, lighting women's cigarettes, and so forth. But, as Richardson (1983) has pointed out, "Manners . . . provide the *modus vivendi* by which our cultural values are maintained and our self-images as 'males' or 'females' are confirmed" (p. 5). In other words, these chivalrous acts, performed almost unconsciously a thousand times a day, reinforce sex-role stereotypes. And, as Richardson (p. 6) notes, sex roles are an instrument of oppression:

> It is not a cultural accident that the personality traits associated with a *male's* performance in rituals between the sexes are precisely those traits which this culture values the most and considers socially desirable and mentally healthy activity: efficacy, authority, prowess, independence. Nor is it a cultural accident that the personality traits associated with the *female's* performance are exactly those that our culture writes off as immature and childlike: passivity, dependence, weakness, frailty, ineptitude.

The effect of chivalry, then, is to reinforce sex roles, a system geared to the creation of dominant males and submissive females.

Students in our "Psychology of Women" classes have routinely argued that the act of a man opening a door for a woman has nothing to do with sexism. It is simply one person being polite to another. If they are right, then men should feel complimented when women (and men) open doors for them. To test their presumption, we ask the women in the class to open doors for men and the men to wait at doors until a woman opens the door for them. We also ask them to record the responses they receive. (We invite readers to do the same.) The women learn that there is a sizable minority of men that refuses to go through a door held open for them by a woman, becoming irate if the women insist on "just being polite." The men report that women *will* open the door for them, but that the women frequently give them disapproving looks or say unkind things "under their breath" to them. These class observations are somewhat similar to the findings of Ventimiglia (1982): the most gratitude was shown by female recipients of door-opening by males, the most confusion by male recipients of door-opening by females, and the most disapproval and avoidance by male recipients of door-opening by other males.

In another "test" of the "just being polite" presumption, we ask half the students in our class to indicate whether they agree or disagree with each of the statements shown in part A of table 3.2. The other half of the students are asked to indicate whether they agree or disagree with the statements shown in part B of table 3.2. The students assume that everyone is responding to the same set of questions. (Readers may now want to answer the questions too, but will need to respond to both parts A and B.)

Typically, one hears snickering from the students responding to part B statements, suggesting that our social norms regarding polite behavior are not only sex-typed, but "inappropriate" for members of the other sex. As the reader probably suspects, students endorse part A statements more often than part B, providing additional evidence that social norms regarding what is considered polite depend on the sex of the individual, which suggests there is more going on here than people "just being polite." What could it be? We then ask students to look for underlying themes regarding what is considered polite for each gender. Do the behaviors considered polite for men have anything in common? Do the behaviors considered polite for women? We suggest to them that, because social norms are often invisible to us until we violate them, it will probably be easier for them to identify common attributes (or underlying themes) by examining part B statements. The reader who wishes to do so is now invited to look for common attributes defining those behaviors considered appropriate for each gender.

The sex-role reversed statements in part B create an image of a woman running in circles about a man, doing all kinds of things, while he— for the sake of politeness—just stands there. When one considers men performing the polite behaviors of women (see part B, "A Courteous Man . . ."), one realizes the extent to which social norms of politeness for *women* require women to *wait* for men, the actors. This social norm of female passivity appears to relate to another less prominent norm, namely, that women should look after the feelings of men. When one considers women performing the polite behaviors of men (see part B, "A Courteous

TABLE 3.2
Sex-Role-Typical and Sex-Role-Atypical Behaviors of a Courteous Man and a Courteous Woman

Part A. Sex-Role-Typical Behaviors

A Courteous Man . . .

1. Makes the first move in sex.

2. Calls the woman on the phone instead of waiting for her to call him.
3. Picks up for a woman something that she has dropped.

4. Holds a door open for a woman and waits until after she goes through the door before going through himself.
5. Carries a woman's luggage, or at least her heaviest piece of luggage.

6. Asks a woman out on a date instead of waiting until the woman asks him.
7. Decides what he and his date will eat and orders their meals when dining together at an expensive restaurant.

8. Seats a woman (that is, he pushes a woman's chair in as she sits down).
9. Offers to change a woman's flat tire and does so.

10. Buys a woman's drink.

11. Stands and lets a woman have his seat if there are no other seats available.

A Courteous Woman . . .

1. Waits for a man to make the first move in sex.
2. Waits for a man to call her when wanting to talk to him.
3. Lets a man pick up something for her that she has dropped, and she thanks him, even if she had already started to get it herself.
4. Says "thank you" and goes through a door that a man has held open for her.

5. Lets a man carry her heaviest piece of luggage, when he offers to do so, and then says something like, "Thank you so much. I couldn't have done this without your help."
6. Waits until a man asks her out when she wants a date with him.
7. Asks the man to decide what the two of them will eat and lets the man order her meal when dining together in an expensive restaurant.
8. Stands and waits for a man to seat her (that is, she lets him push her chair in as she sits down).
9. Lets a man change her flat tire, if he offers to do so, and afterward thanks him profusely, even if she would have preferred to change the tire herself.
10. Lets a man buy her a drink, if he offers, and because he has bought her the drink, she sits and makes polite conversation with him while she drinks it.
11. Accepts the seat a man offers her, thanks him, and expresses concern for his having to stand, when there are no other seats available.

TABLE 3.2 *(Continued)*

12. Gets a woman's coat and helps her put it on.	12. Lets a man get her coat and gives him a smile and a "thank you" upon his return, as he helps her put the coat on.
13. Drives when he and a woman are together, even if it is the woman's car.	13. Lets the man drive even if she owns the car.

Part B. Sex-Role-Atypical Behaviors

A Courteous Man . . .

1. Waits for a woman to make the first move in sex.
2. Waits for a woman to call him when wanting to talk to her.

3. Lets a woman pick up something for him that he has dropped, and he thanks her, even if he had already started to get it himself.
4. Says "thank you" and goes through a door that a woman has held open for him.

5. Lets a woman carry his heaviest piece of luggage, when she offers to do so, and then says something like, "Thank you so much. I couldn't have done this without your help."
6. Waits until a woman asks him out when he wants a date with her.
7. Asks the woman to decide what the two of them will eat and lets the woman order his meal when dining together in an expensive restaurant.
8. Stands and waits for a woman to seat him (that is, he lets her push his chair in as he sits down).
9. Lets a woman change his flat tire, if she offers to do so, and afterward thanks her profusely, even if he would have preferred to change the tire himself.

A Courteous Woman . . .

1. Makes the first move in sex.

2. Calls the man on the phone instead of waiting for him to call her.

3. Picks up for a man something that he has dropped.

4. Holds a door open for a man and waits until after he goes through the door before going through herself.
5. Carries a man's luggage, or at least his heaviest piece of luggage.

6. Asks a man out on a date instead of waiting until the man asks her.

7. Decides what she and her date will eat and orders their meals when dining together at an expensive restaurant.

8. Seats a man (that is, she pushes a man's chair in as he sits down).

9. Offers to change a man's flat tire and does so.

10. Lets a woman buy him a drink, if she offers, and because she has bought him the drink, he sits and makes polite conversation with her while he drinks it.	10. Buys a man's drink.
11. Accepts the seat a woman offers him, thanks her, and expresses concern for her having to stand, when there are no other seats available.	11. Stands and lets a man have her seat if there are no other seats available.
12. Lets a woman get his coat and gives her a smile and a "thank you" upon her return, as she helps him put the coat on.	12. Gets a woman's coat and helps her put it on.
13. Lets the woman drive even if he owns the car.	13. Drives when she and a man are together, even if it is the man's car.

Woman . . ."), the extent to which *men* are required to be active in the name of politeness becomes visible. Men are supposed to be the initiators in all types of interactions with females. We are forced to conclude, then, that social norms regarding politeness in males and females are not just about being polite: they operate to maintain sex roles that champion action in males and passivity in females. One has to question the psychological healthiness of social norms that oblige women to be passive if they are to be perceived as polite. Pitting action against politeness affords women no *real*, or healthy, choices about how to behave.

Psychologists Eugene Nadler and William Morrow (1959) reasoned that if chivalry was a form of antiwomanism then a scale measuring attitudes toward chivalry and attitudes toward openly subordinating women would correlate positively; if chivalry was a form of prowomanism, then scales measuring chivalrous attitudes and the open subordination of women would correlate negatively. Their Open Subordination of Women Scale measured attitudinal "support of traditional policies which openly restrict women to a subordinate position" and "stereotyped conceptions of women as inferior, hence deserving of subordination" (p. 122). The Chivalrous Attitudes toward Women Scale assessed attitudes regarding providing "superficial 'protection and assistance' in conduct toward women, . . . [showing] special 'deference' in conduct toward women, . . . [and showing] special pseudo-respectful 'deference' toward women as a value; and stereotyped conceptions of women as 'pure,' 'delicate,' unassertive, and relatively 'helpless' " (pp. 117–118). When these two scales were administered to a group of eighty-three men, a significant positive correlation was obtained. (A positive correlation was also obtained in an earlier pilot study.) The positive correlation indicates that the men who supported openly subordinating women were also the men who supported chivalry.

Though it is apparently ironic, the man who insists on opening doors for a woman often is the same man who argues that a woman should not be considered for a high-level job and that women should make less money than men. Similarly, it is entirely likely that the man who marries his wife to protect her from harm is the same man who beats her (for a case example, see McNulty 1980). Ted Bundy, a mass murderer of women, walked women to their cars at night to protect them from violent males. This behavior made it difficult for his friend, Ann Rule (1980), to believe he could have committed atrocities against women. Acts of protectiveness *appear* inconsistent with acts of violence. However, there is another way to look at this behavior: male protectiveness embodies an admission by men of men's malevolence toward women. Perhaps Ted Bundy protectively walked women to their cars because he knew how badly women need protection from men. Acts of protection by men may stem from familiarity with more base male attitudes and acts toward women. Chivalrous behavior may follow accordingly and may be the root of the small kindnesses men offer women.

Protection from Male Violence

It is to men that women turn for protection from male violence. A man who protects women is seen as kind, no matter what else he may do. Because the possibility of violence is ever present, women seek out the company of kind men for virtually continual companionship. This need for protection (and for other kindnesses which only men can provide under patriarchy) stimulates many, if not most, women to marry. In a sense, women, like Patricia Hearst (1982), marry our bodyguards and avoid or break off relations with men we feel do not protect us. In our gratitude for men's protection, women forget that it is men's violence against us that creates the need for such protection. We overlook the fact that our coupling with "kind" men strengthens our dependence on men, sets the stage for men's one-on-one oppression of us, and furthers our isolation from other women.

Donna Stringer (1986) argues that women gain physical protection from violent men by giving a man, usually a male partner, power over women's lives. In table 3.3, Stringer describes "rights," or "rewards," women receive when we give up our power to men. The table also shows the responsibilities of men to whom women have given up power. Notice that in exchange for physical safety, a woman is required to submit sexually to her (male) protector and to birth and parent his children. The point being made here is that women pay, and pay dearly, for the "kindnesses" we receive from men, including the kindness of protection from the violence of other men. However, Stringer notes that because men have the right to label women's behavior, even a woman who perceives herself as having given a man power over her life can be labeled as out of line and thus be subjected to male violence (as occurred in the witch trials occurring between 1300 and 1600 or as occurs daily to battered women). Thus men do act as protectors of women—but only for a price, and even then male protection is not guaranteed. So women can never "let down our guard." We must continually give up our power to men. Atkinson (1974) argues that men's protectiveness toward women is actually a protection of what they perceive as their own property (women).

Courting Behavior

Most women are aware that the time they will get the most attention, gentleness, and warmth from a man is during what is called the courting stage. With marriage, their work for him begins in earnest: washing his clothes, cooking his meals, cleaning his house (see Hartmann 1987). Once he is married, a man's amorous attention toward a woman quickly drops by the wayside, for he assumes she now belongs to him. For a few months or a couple of years of real kindness during courting, a woman offers a man a lifetime of domestic labor.

TABLE 3.3
Stringer's (1986) List of Male and Female Rights and Responsibilities Regarding One Another

Male		Female	
Rights[a]	Responsibilities[b]	Rights[a,b]	Responsibilities
To control women's sexuality	To physically protect her; to teach her about sexuality	Physical safety; to learn about sex	Sexual submission (only to the protector); exclusivity of sexuality
To label women and define women's experience	To protect her socially; to label her appropriately	To be legitimized through his labels	Loyalty; nurturance; live up to his labels (wife/mother, etc.)
To assert individual sexual needs and to reproduce for future generations	To procreate frequently—and impregnate; not to demand "weird" sex from "good" women	Physical safety; protection from "weird" sex; right to refuse sex with all but her protector	Sexual receptivity—but only to him or his designee; to birth and parent children
To own women	Financial support; physical support; physical protection	To be financially and physically supported	Provision of his physical and emotional needs; care for his physical possessions; to care for, and relinquish on demand, his children
To control women through money and to exploit women for economic gain	To support her financially during his lifetime; to leave her a financial legacy after his death	To be financially supported	Not to interfere with his means of supporting her (even if this means selling her body); not to make excessive demands; loyalty
To use physical strength if necessary	To use physical strength only when she makes it necessary by her behavior	Physical and financial support	Not to provoke physical violence; to act "right"; forgiveness/understanding when he does use physical violence

[a] Note that male rights are all *proactive* while female "rights" are *reactive* and depend on the male's executing his rights and responsibilities. Female "rights" could perhaps most appropriately be labeled "rewards" for staying within the female role.

[b] Because core values are most strongly embodied in Male Rights and Female Responsibilities, these are most resistant to change. The easiest reforms occur in the areas of male responsibilities and female rights. For example, removing male legal responsibilities for providing alimony payments occurred quickly and easily as did requiring women to enter the labor market to contribute to financial support for families. On the other hand, reducing male control of women through outlawing marital rape or spouse abuse have been difficult changes to achieve.

Reprinted with permission from D. M. Stringer (1986, March 9). A model for understanding male response to female efforts to change violence against women. Annual Conference of the Association for Women in Psychology, Oakland, Calif.

Heterosexual Privilege

The material and social advantages (kindnesses) women obtain through coupling with men are referred to as "heterosexual privilege." According to Bunch (1983), heterosexual privilege gives women "a stake in male supremacy" and thus "a stake in their own oppression" (p. 367). She warns that "heterosexual women must realize—no matter what [our] personal connection to men—that the benefits [we] receive from men will always be in diluted form and will ultimately result in [our] own self-destruction" (p. 367).

Because of the difference between women and men in average income, women know we will have a higher standard of living if we align ourselves with a man. Certainly, a high or just decent standard of living may be experienced as a kindness which particular men provide specific women, particularly since most women are "just one man away from poverty." However, it is men who keep women's pay lower than men's, creating women's need for this male kindness.

Power and prestige also belong to men more than women. But by coupling and otherwise aligning ourselves with men, women too can have these privileges, if only indirectly. Power and prestige are kindnesses which women reap from men, though again it is men who insure that most women do not have access to them in our own right.

Men's Love

Perhaps the kindness most valued by women is a man's love (affection). Frye (1983, pp. 134–135) offers an interesting perspective on men's love:

To say that straight men are heterosexual is only to say that they engage in *sex* (fucking) exclusively with (or upon or to) the other sex, i.e., women. All or almost all of that which pertains to *love,* most straight men reserve exclusively for other men. The people whom they admire, respect, adore, revere, honor, whom they imitate, idolize, and form profound attachments to, whom they are willing to teach and from whom they are willing to learn, and whose respect, admiration, recognition, honor, reverence and love they desire . . . those are, overwhelmingly, other men. In their relations with women, what passes for respect is kindness, generosity or paternalism;

what passes for honor is removal to the pedestal. From women they want devotion, service and sex.

Heterosexual male culture is homoerotic; it is man-loving. (Emphasis added)

Hacker (1981) also has noted the limitations of men's love of women, the compartmentalization which men show in marrying women but not wanting to have much to do with women. Men who marry nonetheless limit their associations with women in other situations. One example is the male physician who doesn't want female physicians as members of the hospital staff. Another is the poker player who doesn't want women to participate in his game. Similarly, hunters don't want women to join in their sport with them. Another example is the man who would not want to consult with a woman lawyer. Hacker notes, "Men will accept women at the supposed level of greatest intimacy while rejecting them at lower levels" (p. 171). But this is understandable if intimacy ("love-making") is the time that the bodily characteristics determining membership in dominant versus subordinate groups (male versus female) are most apparent and the time that the dominance of the penis over the vagina is reenacted.

Many women report that men are most kind to them during sex. Frye (1983) sees men's "love-making" as a tool for men's oppression of women, serving to ensure our submission to them. She calls into question the notion that sex is an act of kindness for men (p. 140):

> Fucking is a large part of how females are kept subordinated to males. It is a ritual enactment of that subordination which constantly reaffirms the fact of subordination and habituates both men and women to it, both in body and in imagination. . . . A great deal of fucking is also presumed to preserve and maintain women's belief in [our] own essential heterosexuality, which in turn (for women as not for men) connects with and reinforces female hetero-eroticism, that is, man-loving in women. It is very important to the maintenance of male-supremacy that men fuck women, a lot. So it is required; it is compulsory. Doing it is both doing one's duty and an expression of solidarity.

Although some women report experiencing Frye's language as assaultive, Frye uses this language because it is the language of men and thus reflects men's feelings about "making love" with women. This point is important: the word "fucking" is assaultive because the behavior that the word connotes is assaultive.

Heterosexual practice (in patriarchy) establishes male domination in women's most basic, private, and personal spheres (our bodies and our erotica). Given that male domination governs women's public lives (law, medicine, and so on), male domination in sexual relations ensures that male domination encompasses all aspects of women's lives. As domination becomes more complete, it becomes less visible. There are numerous examples of ways that heterosexual practice establishes male domination in women's most private and personal spheres: "normal" sex is carried out in the missionary position, in which the man is on top. The erotic stimulation from which women derive the greatest pleasure and are likely to achieve orgasm is trivialized as "foreplay." Only 30 percent of women achieve orgasm through sex involving penile penetration alone, but this is what is defined as "having sex." As a result, most women are defined as sexually deficient. Sex is defined from men's perspective and is what gives men pleasure. It is considered acceptable for a man to pressure a woman to have sex. Men rationalize this use of pressure by arguing that women say "no" when we really mean "yes" and by arguing that women need sex for our own good ("all she needs is a good fuck"). Men blame women for male sexual arousal, saying men cannot control their sexual urges. Men see women as objects for their sexual gratification. Men tell women they should perform sexual acts women don't want to perform because it makes men feel good. In most states, men have a legal right to have sex with their wives at any time they desire, and, as stated earlier, in some states this right is extended to cohabiting male partners and men with whom women have previously had consensual sex (Finkelhor and Yllo 1985).

The phenomenon Frye describes is neither new nor specific to American culture. Writing about ancient Greek culture, Michel Foucault (1976–1978, p. 215) made a similar observation:

> Sexual relations . . . were seen as being of the same type as the relationship between a superior and a subordinate, an individual who dominates and one who is dominated, one who commands and one who complies, one who vanquishes and one who is vanquished. . . . And this suggests that in sexual behavior there is one role that is intrinsically honorable and valorized without question: the one that consisted in being active, in dominating, in penetrating, in asserting one's superiority.

Furthermore, young males were criticized for playing the "passive" role in sex with older men because doing so *feminized* them. Women who (naturally) played the same inferior role were not so criticized because "it was in conformity with what nature intended and with what the law prescribed" (p. 216).

Clinical psychologist Dr. John Carta-Falsa (pers. comm., October 31, 1992) pointed out that, when men discuss with one another their sexual relations with women, they are being (covertly) sexual with one another. I would add to his observation that, when men get together to talk about "fucking" women, "scoring," or their sexual conquests, they are communicating to one another that, although they have sex with women, *their emotional bonds are with one another*. They are saying to their male companions, "You are more important to me than the woman with whom I had sex." (Perhaps this is why the individual females with whom men have sex are not all that important to many of them.) They are also communicating that their sexual relations with women are for the purpose of exploitation. Such talk by men puts the male listeners in the sex act with the male speaker and the woman. The companions are invisible, but they are there with the man doing the "fucking," sharing in his victory of the exploitation of a woman, the men's bonds strengthened by the sharing, united in their subjugation of femaleness.

In today's culture it takes degrading, humiliating, controlling, and/or inflicting pain on women for many men to "come," that is, to reach orgasm, or even just to have a sexual, erotic experience. The fact that pornography is a multibillion dollar industry financed overwhelmingly by men, says that it is not just a small minority of men who seek female degradation for their sexual pleasure. If men's love for women is healthy or real, it should not take degradation or humiliation of women, or inflicting pain on us, for so many—and perhaps most or even all—men to have the profound emotional and physiological experiences associated with sex.

Although Frye recognizes that sex ("fucking") can have other purposes, she argues that the sex promoted by our sexist culture is an act of hostility, not love. Certainly, the fact that men often refer to sex with women as "fucking," with all the negative connotations that this word involves, supports her claim. So does the profitableness of the pornography industry and the energy with which access to pornographic portrayals of women is defended by men. A theme running through pornography is unequal power relationships between men and women as played out, in every sort of imaginable way, with sex (cf. Donnerstein 1984; Efron 1985). Consider as well the "popular" group of high school boys of the Spur Posse who proudly claimed that they competed with one another to amass points for "sexual conquests" with female peers, as they denied allegations ranging from sexual molestation to rape. At least two of these youths boasted of having reached orgasm with more than sixty different "girls." The boys' parents blamed the girls while defending their sons as "red-blooded American boys." While the girls were taunted with the label "slut," the boys were cheered by their classmates (Smolowe 1993). Consider also that the courts have difficulty distinguishing between "normal" sex and rape due to the similarity in power dynamics and violence against women involved in both (see MacKinnon 1983, 1987). These examples suggest that sado-masochism is the model for normal heterosexual sex in our culture.

Frye (1983) argues that it is because sex in our culture is an act of hostility, not love, that gay men are so hated by straight men. Gay men are hated because they fuck men—not women. If sex were a communication of respect, as the culture claims it to be, men would not fear and hate men who fuck other men. (The reader may recall the fear expressed in letters to Ellen Goodman, discussed earlier in this chapter, by straight men who were threatened with being treated as men treat women.) In fact, if being fucked said something positive to and about the fuckee, men would want it only for themselves and would outlaw it for women. Yet, as Frye notes, "The one general and nearly inviolable limitation on male phallic access is that males are not supposed to fuck other males, especially adult human males of their own class, tribe, race, etc." (p. 142). When they do, the fucked male is seen as a woman.

In considering men's kindnesses to women—chivalry, male protection of women from other men's violence, love, and heterosexual privilege—it is necessary to keep in mind the context in which these kindnesses occur. Perhaps most influential to the development of Societal Stockholm Syndrome is kindness offered following traumatization caused by male violence or threats of male violence. Women are more likely to turn to men rather than other women for nurturance and support following traumatization—because we are isolated from other women who might provide us comfort and because we perceive that men are better able to protect us from male violence. (Only after men and their institutions fail to provide this support do most women turn to other women for it.) The more women need comfort and support, the more likely we are to bond to men when men provide them, even if the comfort and support provided are minimal. In fact, the less support we are given, the more dependent we become and the more grateful we are for any crumbs of kindness.

We present all these observations so that readers may determine for themselves whether men as a group show kindness to women, or more to the point, whether women perceive that men show them kindness. Some men are indeed genuinely caring toward women, at least on occasion. Some men swim against the general stream, working as individuals against societal oppression of women by men. However, it is beside the point whether a few men or groups of men feel actual (mutually empowering) love for women or are genuinely kind to women. Kind slaveholders may have made slavery more bearable for their slaves but that did not make the institution of slavery any less heinous. Also, kind, loving men can always do an about face and stop being kind and loving. The threat of withdrawal therefore serves as a means of social control of women, keeping women focused on men and working to keep men kind (cf. Stringer 1986). The only real kindness men can show to women is to join with women and support women in our struggle against male domination.

The "kindnesses" presented in this section are ones which our society mandates that all men provide women—even if only to some women and only if we are deemed to deserve them. They are worthy of examination *as a group* for that reason alone. Why would a culture characterized by male violence against women—a patriarchy—mandate male kindnesses toward women? Examination of the social conditions that give rise to women's need for such kindnesses and of the functions that these kindnesses play within patriarchy leads to the conclusion that patriarchy is *strengthened* by the kindnesses men as a group are mandated to show toward women. Through men's acts of kindness, women are given a stake in patriarchy (cf. Bunch 1983). These kindnesses wrap in a chivalric cloak the misogynistic core of our culture, disguising the actual situation of women.

If men's kindnesses toward women were really only kindnesses, a man would be pleased if another man or woman offered these kindnesses to him. He would be pleased if another man or woman lit his cigarette or pulled out his chair for him. He would be pleased to derive his income, prestige, power and even his identity from his partner. He would take pride in another man's or woman's offer to walk him to his car at night. But in fact, "one of the very nasty things that can happen to a man is his being treated or seen as a woman, or womanlike" (Frye 1983, p. 136).

Are Women Isolated from Other Women and from Perspectives Other than Those of Men?

Even if women's survival is threatened by male violence, women are unable to escape men, and men show women kindness, Societal Stockholm Syndrome would not be expected to develop for women as a group unless women were isolated from nonmale perspectives. Is there reason to think that women are thus isolated?

A woman whose time, emotional energy, and cognitive energy are devoted to men (and children) to the exclusion of other women, particularly other women of her own age group and life situation, is a woman who is isolated. Isolation takes one of two forms: physical and/or ideological, though physical isolation fosters ideological isolation.

Ideological Isolation

A woman who is exposed to the ideas, opinions, attitudes, feelings, and needs of men (and children), to the exclusion of exposure to the same in other women of like situation, is a woman who is *ideologically* isolated. Ideological isolation occurs whenever women do not have access to others who espouse women's perspectives as opposed to men's. Ideological isolation is likely to occur when women get together but one or more men are present. This is because most women try to take care of men and to ward off men's anger. Men therefore tend to become leaders of such groups

(Crocker and McGraw 1984) and to be more influential then women members of the group (Martin and Shanahan 1983). Most men get upset if women focus their attention on one another, and most women are afraid to upset men (see Mayes 1979).

A group consisting only of women can get together (at teas, coffees, and the like), but its members still remain ideologically isolated if they speak to one another giving men's perspectives, not their own. When ideologically isolated, we experience our problems, thoughts, and feelings as unique to us as individuals. As a result, we are prevented from recognizing the social/political basis of our situations and problems (cf. Allen 1970).

During the seventies, feminist consciousness-raising groups enabled women to realize that our common problems have a political basis, but few women were exposed to these groups. Support groups for special groups of women (lesbians, battered women, incest victims) emerged. Probably because of the enormous importance of community support to members of these groups, they are still active in many areas today. However, *all* women need community support for dealing with our special concerns. In such groups, members talk about their problems and begin to realize that problems they thought were uniquely theirs are shared by other women. This realization leads women to ask why they are all having particular problems, and they begin to see how male-female arrangements in our culture create common problems for all women (cf. Allen 1970). In this way, women talking together politicizes us, breaking down our ideological isolation as we develop a women's perspective (a perspective that grows out of an analysis of women's situation and is rooted in women's experiences). These analyses form the substance of what is called "feminism."

Most of the women students we teach at the University of Cincinnati do not know what feminism is and are afraid to be labeled as feminists. Feminism is referred to as the "f" word, as though it were naughty or something that should not be talked about in public. Dworkin (1983) offers a poignant observation: "Feminism is hated because women are hated. Antifeminism is a direct expression of misogyny; it is the political defense of woman hating. This is because feminism is the liberation movement of women" (p. 195). Women's not knowing what feminism is—a theory and social movement about *our* rights—strongly reveals the systematic isolation of women from perspectives other than those of our captors, men. Women's fear of being labeled as feminists reveals that men are successfully keeping women from fighting for our rights. Unless women fight for our rights as women, we are unlikely to ever escape male domination.

Physical Isolation

A woman who has little or no contact with other women is *physically* isolated. Most women are isolated from one another because most homes have one adult male and one adult female in them. Having most members of any oppressed group live one-on-one with their oppressors is probably the strongest possible arrangement for ensuring continued psychological enslavement (cf. Hacker 1981; Lipman-Bluman 1984). Whether the adult male is father or husband, the effect is the same: the woman is isolated from other women.

The role of homemaker physically isolates a woman, helping to ensure that the only people with whom she has any regular, sustained contact are her husband (a member of the oppressor group) and her children. The most isolated women may be those who are full-time homemakers, do not have gainful employment that gets them outside the home and in contact with others, and have many children, especially children under school age. Sex-segregated jobs (clerical worker, teacher, etc.) also are usually physically isolating, where women are paired with men or children whom they serve. Thus even in female-dominated fields of work, women are often isolated from one another. Even when we work with other women, we still usually work *for* men.

Male power has the effect of isolating women from one another. More precisely, the fact that women lack power over our own lives isolates us from one another. Male power and female powerlessness force most women, and pressure all women, to align ourselves with men for purposes of survival. The resulting isolation is both ideological and physical.

For example, the conditions promoting the development of Societal Stockholm Syndrome, already discussed in this chapter (men's threat to women's survival, women's inability to escape from men, and men's kindness to women), function together to isolate women from one another. Barbara Polk (1976) has identified four mechanisms used by males to maintain power over females: "through the use of brute force [threat to survival], by restricting options [inability to escape] and selectively reinforcing women within these options [selective use of kindness to females whom males think 'deserve' that kindness], through control of resources and major institutions [inability to escape], and through expertise and access to the media [inability to escape and ideological isolation]" (p. 403). These mechanisms for maintaining male domination are examples of the four conditions for development of Stockholm Syndrome. All of these manifestations of male power identified by Polk also serve to isolate women from one another by pressuring us to align ourselves with men.

Women as a group are in a position comparable to a hostage whose captor has a gun to her or his head and says, "Try to escape and I'll kill you." The only power that the hostage has is power gained *through* the captor, that is, power experienced vicariously and power that the captor chooses to share with the hostage ("If you're good, I won't kill you." "If you're good, tonight I'll let you sleep lying on the floor rather than sitting up in the chair"). The best thing for women (the hostages) to do in this circumstance, *in the short run,* is to align ourselves with men (our captors). Through alignment, women (the hostages) may decrease the likelihood of being the target of men's (the captors) brute force and may be rewarded for our "good behavior," as men (the captors) define that behavior.

As long as women have to attach ourselves to men to avoid violence and to indirectly share men's power, prestige, and wealth, there will be a sizable portion of women who will do so.[3] The one-on-one pairing of women with men—in an effort, for example, to escape violence from *all* men or to avoid poverty—helps to physically isolate women from other women. According to Walker (1979), even battered women "choose to be married to one man and endure sexual assaults from him rather than run the risk of being raped and assaulted by any number of men in their lives" (p. 126). The one-on-one pairing of men and women also keeps women competing with one another for men's attention and thus unable to form alliances, for we tend to see one another as enemies. Because men have direct access to power at a societal level, females' efforts to align ourselves with men go even to the most intimate, erotic relations that women share with others. We will say more about this in chapters 4 and 5, but for now we want to say that by aligning ourselves with men, women distance ourselves from other women.

One of the major vehicles men use to isolate women when men become threatened is to call women's sexual orientation into question. For a number of years, incoming graduate women at our university would form a women's group. Invariably, before the academic year was over, male students would begin questioning the sexual orientation of the women in the group and, almost as predictably, the women's group would break up. This example shows how the label "lesbian" can be used by men to keep women isolated from one another. Beck, with Glick and Annin (1993), reports that both lesbians and heterosexual women in the military "say they have sometimes agreed to have sex with men rather than be hit with an accusation of lesbianism" (p. 60). Obviously, the label can be used in an attempt to threaten *any* woman. Even when men do not use the label as a weapon, women know that it is there to be used whenever the men desire. Thus, even though no man has uttered a word, young women, of whatever sexual orientation, who are having a good time together know not to be "too friendly." Why does the label possess such power? Lesbians aren't perceived as putting men first. Women who don't put men first aren't given the privileges (rewards) received by women who align themselves with men, including some safety from male violence by *all* men. Women know, consciously or unconsciously, that men will use their power to teach women, with brute force if necessary, to put men first. Women hear men express hostility toward lesbians. Women may hear stories about men raping a woman they perceive to be a lesbian, as they tell her, "We'll make a woman out of you yet": they'll teach her to put men first. Women get the message. It is men who have the power and it is only by attaching ourselves to men that women gain access to that power. Women therefore think about how men would feel if we showed other females too much affection, *before* we show affection, if we do. We hold in restraint our relations with other women in an attempt to avoid male ire.

How often is this scenario played out? To what extent does it affect women's behavior? It's okay for women to go out together at night, but we shouldn't go out *only* with women and we shouldn't go out with other women too often. And if we see an interested male, we should be willing to desert our woman companion. In other words, males should come first. And if both a woman and a man ask a woman out, the receiver of the invitations should prefer to go with the male over the female. In other words, males should come first. When a woman has to choose between spending a Saturday with her husband, the person with whom she has lived for years, and spending the day with her best female friend whom she rarely sees, she should elect to spend the time with her husband. In other words, males should come first. The list goes on and on. And any woman who doesn't put men first is likely to be labeled a lesbian, no matter with which gender she prefers to have sex. For example, women in the military who reported men for sexually harassing them often were investigated for possible lesbian sexual practices (Beck, with Glick and Annin, 1993). And each time a woman puts a man first, she distances herself from either herself (as a woman) or from other women, or both.

To what extent are women separated from one another? Is our isolation evident in only minor areas of our lives, or does the isolation go deeper? One might think of interpersonal relations as spanning from the most intimate and personal to the most public and superficial. Does our isolation from one another span the entire continuum, or is it restricted to the more public and superficial relations with other women? In this regard, it is useful to examine to what extent men have isolated women from other women in our most private and intimate relations.

Adrienne Rich (1980) provides a convincing argument that men make heterosexuality compulsory for women. Rich draws upon Kathleen Gough's (1975, pp. 69–70) list of characteristics of male power to make her case:

> Men's ability to deny women sexuality or to force it upon [us]; to command or exploit [our] labor to control [our] produce; to control or rob [us] of [our] children; to confine [us] physically and prevent [our] movement; to use [us] as objects in male transactions; to cramp [our] creativeness; or to withhold from [us] large areas of the society's knowledge and cultural attainments.

Giving examples of each of the eight ways male power is "manifested and maintained," Rich (1980) shows how each characteristic "adds to the cluster of forces within which women have been convinced that marriage, and sexual orientation toward men, are inevitable, even if unsatisfying or oppressive components of [our] lives" (p. 640). Each manifestation of male power cloaks a wedge, separating women in the most personal and intimate aspects of our interpersonal lives, including the sexual.

Summary

In this chapter we have asked if the four conditions conducive to the development of Stockholm Syndrome describe conditions existing between dominant and subordinate groups of people. Male-female relations have been the arena for illustrating how one might test the applicability of these four conditions to group-group relations. We have presented facts and ideas that allow one to assess whether threat to survival, inability to escape, isolation, and small kindnesses characterize the relations between men as a group and women as a group. If the four Stockholm Syndrome-conducive conditions are present, and the evidence presented here suggests that they are, one would expect the nine major indicators of Stockholm Syndrome (described in chapter 2) to characterize women's psychology. The more severe the Stockholm Syndrome-conducive conditions, the more severe and thus the more apparent the major indicators of Stockholm Syndrome should be in our psychology. So that the reader can judge if women as a group do display Societal Stockholm Syndrome, in the next chapter we will describe evidence bearing on whether the major indicators of Stockholm Syndrome are manifested in women's psychology.

FOUR

En-Gendered Terror: The Psychodynamics of Stockholm Syndrome Applied to Women as a Group in Our Relations with Men as a Group

Because some or many men have committed crimes against women, all men benefit from the consequences. These consequences . . . include women giving up control to men; putting men's needs ahead of [our] own through fear of annoying, bothering, or "provoking" a man, thereby remaining incongruous with one's own beliefs and perceptions; and remaining "shuffling," second-class citizens. (Leidig 1981, pp. 204–205)

Victimizing behaviors . . . all serve to keep women in [our] prescribed place. . . . If all of these male behaviors place women in some sort of physical and/or psychological fear . . . , women remain helpless, dependent upon male protection, geographically limited, subservient, and frightened.

The behaviors mentioned above . . . fit with behaviors already described by psychologists as culturally-specific to psychologically healthy women. (Leidig 1981, pp. 198–199)

In the last chapter we examined the possibility that *all* women are exposed to conditions conducive to the development of Societal Stockholm Syndrome: threat to survival, inability to escape, isolation, and kindness.

Men's violence against women encourages women to bond with "kind" men for protection against other men, setting the stage for men's one-on-one oppression of women (Brownmiller 1975; Dworkin 1983) and the institutionalization of heterosexuality. This violence is mystified as normal under the guise of the masculine sex role.

In this chapter we ask if the conditions giving rise to Stockholm Syndrome, operating at a societal level, structure women's psychological development, creating a women's psychology based on Stockholm Syndrome. That is, is women's psychology accurately described by Societal Stockholm Syndrome psychodynamics? We consider women as a group and show how Societal Stockholm Syndrome psychodynamics appear in women's psychology. According to our theory, to the extent that Stockholm Syndrome-conducive conditions are intrinsic to the life situations of women in patriarchal culture, so that no part of women's lives is untouched by these conditions, Stockholm Syndrome psychodynamics should be present to some extent in *all* women's relationships with men, in women's relationships with *every* man, and in *every encounter* between a woman and a man. However, *because women differ in the extent and nature of our exposure to the four conditions* (for example, by virtue of social differences associated with class, race, and individual experiences), *women differ in the extent and* possibly *in the configuration* (that is, organization, pattern, or structure) *of Stockholm Syndrome manifested in our individual psychologies and in our individual relations with men.*

Application of Societal Stockholm Syndrome to Women as a Group in Regard to Our Relations with Men as a Group

This section presents the theory of Societal Stockholm Syndrome as it applies to women as a group. (Research bearing on the validity of the theory as regards different subgroups of women is described by Allen 1991; Graham et al. 1993; Graham, Ott, et al. 1990; and Naber-Morris 1990.) We will refer back to the nine major indicators of Stockholm Syndrome, identified in chapter 2, and will examine the applicability of those indicators to women as a group. We are interested in the extent to which, and the manner in which, the nine indicators might be present in women as a group. A list of the nine indicators and a brief summary of the evidence for Societal Stockholm Syndrome as manifested in women as a group are provided in table 4.1.

We do *not* propose that these indicators apply to women simply because we are women, but rather because of the nature of male-female relations in patriarchal culture. We propose that these indicators are produced by differential power relations, characterized by the four Stockholm Syndrome-conducive conditions, between the sexes; we do not see the indicators of Stockholm Syndrome as resulting from biologically-based sex differences.

Our discussion of each of the nine indicators of the Syndrome in relation to women as a group contains much material—material that calls for reflection. We encourage readers to take the time they need to mull over each of the following nine sections.

1. Captive Shows Symptoms of Ongoing Trauma or of Post-Traumatic Stress Disorder (PTSD)

The American Psychiatric Association defines Post-traumatic Stress Disorder (PTSD) as "the development of characteristic symptoms following a psychologically distressing event that is outside the range of usual human experience. . . . The stressor producing this syndrome would be markedly distressing to almost anyone" (p. 247). But McCann, Sakheim, and Abrahamson (1988) note that "it is increasingly recognized that some traumatic events are generally *within* the range of usual human experience" (p. 585). McCann et al. categorize PTSD symptoms as follows: *emotional,* which includes fear, anxiety, depression, lowered self-esteem, anger (though this may be absent where the victim fears retribution for expressed anger), guilt, and shame; *cognitive,* which refers to perceptual disturbances such as de-realization and dissociation; *biological,* which includes somatic disturbances such as increased ulcers, headaches, gastro-intestinal disturbances, asthma, and menstrual problems; *behavioral,* which includes suicidal behavior and personality disorders; and *interpersonal,* which includes sexuality problems, and relationship problems such as decreased trust and fear of getting too close. Some of these symptoms

TABLE 4.1
Evidence for Societal Stockholm Syndrome in Women as a Group

Indicators	Evidence
Captive shows-symptoms of ongoing trauma or of Post-Traumatic Stress Disorder (PTSD)	Full-blown PTSD symptoms not expected to surface until after male violence against women has ended and women feel safe. Still, early PTSD symptoms are present: depression, low self-esteem, fear of males, psychosomatic disturbances, eating disorders, anxiety, agoraphobia, simple phobia, panic disorder, obsessive-compulsive disorder
Captive is bonded to her/his captor.	Women's love of men (practical and dependent love). Women perceive violence as improving relationship and a sign of love. Women love men no matter what they do to us.
Captive is intensely grateful for small kindnesses shown to her/him by captor.	Women are thankful for being permitted to share men's money, power, and prestige even though it is men who prevent women from having direct access to these things (through lack of equal rights). Women are thankful for chivalry even though chivalry strengthens sex-role stereotypes. Women are grateful to rapists and batterers for not killing us.
Captive denies captor's violence or rationalizes that violence; denies own anger at captor.	Women see men as protectors even though it is men from whom we are being protected. Despite criminal justice system's protection of male rights and lack of protection for women victims of rape, incest, and wife abuse, women believe men will protect our rights. Anger at men is turned against self, other women, and children. Defensive attributions are made in response to other women's victimization.
Captive is hypervigilant of captor's needs; tries to keep captor happy.	Women provide men with domestic, sexual, reproductive, and emotional services. Women put men's needs before our own; are more aware of men's needs and feelings than own. Women respond submissively to men. Women alter our bodies so as to be attractive to men.
Captive sees world from captor's perspective.	Women see ourselves as men see us: less valuable, less competent, to blame for men's problems and our own victimization. We express ambivalence about being female and feminine. Prefer male first-born child. Attribute success to luck.
Captive sees those trying to win her/his release as "bad	Male identification; antifeminism, homophobia; heterosexism.

TABLE 4.1 *(Continued)*
Evidence for Societal Stockholm Syndrome in Women as a Group

Indicators	Evidence
guys" and captor as "good guy." Sees captor as protecting him/her.	
Captive finds it difficult to leave captor even after physical release is won.	(Women's release from male domination has not yet been won.) Women find it difficult to even imagine disengaging from men. Women fear that, without men, we will be alone and further isolated. Women feel that, without men, life isn't worth living.
Captive fears captor will come back to get her/him even after captor is dead or in prison.	(Women's release from male domination has not yet been won.) Science fiction writers attempting to imagine women's lives after separation from men have shown how rare and fragile the absence of fear is.

arise immediately upon victimization and may persist for some time afterward (e.g., fear, anxiety). Other symptoms arise immediately but are unlikely to continue (e.g., depression, anger). Still others may arise later and are associated more with long-term effects (e.g., self-esteem problems).

Our theory leads us to expect that symptoms of PTSD will become fully apparent in women only when men no longer threaten us with their violence and we have begun to feel safe. As long as men's violence against women continues, women as a group are not likely to show full-blown PTSD symptoms. Rather, women will show symptoms of ongoing traumatization, or symptoms likely to immediately arise upon victimization: fear, anxiety, and depression. Because retaliation is likely if anger is expressed, one would not expect to see women expressing a lot of anger at men. It is interesting therefore that symptoms of what may be construed as a traumatic stress reaction have repeatedly been noted in women as a group: otherwise unexplained physical and psychosomatic problems, clinging behavior, feelings of helplessness and powerlessness, depression, occasional seemingly illogical outbursts of anger and rage, ambivalence in relations with men, and low self-esteem. We will now examine the extent of such symptoms in women, using the two categories of fear of males and "mental disorders" to structure our discussion. We will note, when information is available, the extent to which women, as compared to men, show such symptoms. And we will attempt to establish whether such symptoms in women are tied to male violence against us.

Fear of Males

Girls from the first, second, fifth, and sixth grades, when contrasted with their male age-mates, were found by Brody, Hay, and Venditor (1990) to tend to report more intense feelings of fear. (*Both* girls and boys, in fact, reported more intense fear of boys than of girls.) Femininity in both girls and boys was associated with greater fear of boys. Further, associations between fear and sex role were stronger than associations between fear and biological sex. These findings suggest that intensity of fear of males is related to the roles people play, not just to their biological sex. Similar findings were obtained with regard to the feeling of hurt. Girls also expressed more intense feelings of being hurt by boys than by girls. And the intensity of the hurt expressed by girls was greater than that experienced by boys at the hands of either boys or girls. Femininity in males and females was associated with being hurt by boys. Brody et al. noted that social psychologists typically predict that feelings of fear and hurt will be associated with persons of lesser power.

Two indirect indicators of women's fear of men are suggested by the findings of studies summarized by Henley and LaFrance (1984): studies of women's personal space indicate that women, when given the opportunity to choose their seating arrangements, sit farther from males than from other females, and women, when being approached, prefer that men stay farther away from them than women (Henley and LaFrance 1984).

In a study of male and female partners who lived together, Graham, Ott, and Rawlings (1990) found it was not men's *actual* physical violence that was most associated with women's fearing for their lives, but rather the *threat* of men's violence. Statistical regression of questionnaire items concerned with physical and emotional violence onto the item "made me fear for my life" revealed that the two best predictors of women fearing for their lives were (1) not knowing when they were going to be slapped, hit, or beaten and (2) being threatened with a weapon. For women as a group, uncertainty about men's future actions, combined with the knowledge that men as a group *are* willing to carry out their threats against women, keep women in fear of our lives.

Robin Morgan (1989, p. 68) describes an experience familiar to every woman, whether she is walking on a city street, down a dirt road, to her locked car, or out in the fields:

> Suddenly there are footsteps behind her. Heavy, rapid. A man's footsteps. . . . She quickens her pace in time to the quickening of her pulse. She is afraid. He could be a rapist. He could be a soldier, a harasser, a robber, a killer. He could be none of these. He could be a man in a hurry. He could be a man merely walking at his normal pace. But she fears him. She fears him because he is a man. . . .
>
> She does not feel the same way—on city street or dirt road, in parking lot or field—if she hears a woman's footsteps behind her. It is the footsteps of a man she fears. This moment she shares with every human being who is female.

When we describe this experience in our Women's Studies classes and explain that every woman has gone through it, the men in the class are incredulous. Invariably, one man will ask the women students, in a disbelieving tone, how many of them have really experienced this fear. The women, equally shocked that a man wouldn't know they do experience it, respond with statements such as, "You've got to be kidding!" This dialogue strikingly exposes the extent to which fear is ever present in women's—but not men's—lives. It dramatically exposes what it means to be male—as opposed to female—in patriarchal culture. It dramatically reveals the extent to which fear and lack of fear can be taken for granted.

Jackson Katz, founder of an antiviolence group called Real Men in Boston, has found an effective technique of demonstrating that violence against women is a serious problem. He draws a line down the blackboard. On one side of the blackboard, he invites men to list things men do to avoid being sexually assaulted. Their typical response is "Nothing." On the other side of the blackboard, he invites women to list the things women do to avoid sexual assault. This side is quickly filled (Rogers 1993).

The wives of transvestites and transsexuals expressed concern to Dr. Carolyn Kowatch (pers. comm., March 20, 1993), a psychotherapist, that their husbands did not know to be afraid, and thus did not take appropriate precautions when they went out at night dressed as females. That is, the women were concerned that the men, having grown up male, had never learned the dangers of being female and thus did not know to be afraid and to take suitable precautions, like not walking down the street alone at night.

Gordon and Riger (1989) found that rape is what women fear most. When they think about it, "they feel terrified and somewhat paralyzed" (p. 21). Gordon and Riger found that 61 percent of women who live in any one of the twenty-six largest U.S. cities report feeling "very unsafe" or "somewhat unsafe" when out alone in their own neighborhoods at night. The group *least* likely to report feeling unsafe was young women aged 20 to 24 (Gordon and Rigor 1989)—the age group *most* at risk for sexual assault (Russell 1984)! Only 26 percent of this group reported feeling unsafe (Gordon and Riger 1989).

Table 4.2, from Gordon and Riger (1989), reveals the extent to which women take precautions in order to protect ourselves from male violence, particularly rape. It is important to note here that fear of rape is often denied. Women who report that they do not fear rape (that is, they "never" worry about it)—about a third of the women studied—also reported that they took measures to protect themselves from rape. Gordon and Riger report that these precautions are sometimes quite elaborate. Thus, actions taken by women to prevent rape may be a better measure of fear of male violence than acknowledged fear of rape. We invite the readers to answer the questions in table 4.2.

National victimization surveys indicate that males are more likely to be victims of violence than females. If this is the case, why do women report more fear of violence than men? As noted earlier, a major shortcoming of the national victimization surveys is that they do not assess the prevalence of violence by intimates such as husbands and boyfriends—and most of the violence against women is perpetrated by male intimates. These surveys therefore grossly underestimate the amount of violence to which women are exposed (Smith 1988). Furthermore, while violence targeted at women is "predatory," that directed at men tends to involve "exchanged blows." Also, women are much more likely than are men to be the victims of sexual violence, the most frightening form of brutality (Smith 1988).

TABLE 4.2
Correlation Between Fear and Use of Strategies by Gender

	% Who "Never" Do Activity[a]		% Who "Always" Do Activity[b]		Correlation of Fear with How Often Done	
	Male	Female	Male	Female	Male	Female
Strategies which women use more frequently than men:						
How often do you restrict your going out to only during the day time?	72	25	9	26	.3106	.5250
How often do you avoid doing things you have to do because of fear of being harmed?	78	32	6	15	−.0279	.3050
When you go out, how often do you drive rather than walk because of fear of being harmed?	56	18	13	40	.1335	.2925
How often do you not do things you want to do but do not have to do because of fear?	75	30	6	15	.1682	.2813
When you are looking for a parking place at night, how often do you think about safety?	15	5	33	71	.1512	.2350
How often do you ask for identification from salesmen or repairmen?	18	11	33	50	.0282	.2342
How often do you go out with a friend or two as protection?	50	10	4	51	−.0371	.2031
How often do you check the backseat of your car for intruders before getting in?	38	12	31	59	.0048	.1826
How often do you check to see who is at your door before opening it?	10	2	60	87	.2184	.1789
How often do you try to wear shoes that are easy to run in, in case of danger?	61	19	13	36	.1500	.1779

	% Who "Never" Do Activity[a]		% Who "Always" Do Activity[b]		Correlation of Fear with How Often Done	
	Male	Female	Male	Female	Male	Female
How often do you lock the outside door when home alone during the day?	12	3	63	79	−.0769	.1567
On the street, how often do you avoid looking people in the eye whom you don't know?	31	18	22	29	.1334	.1567
How often do you try to avoid going downtown when making plans to go out at night?	37	21	19	24	.1334	.1489
When you are out alone, how often do you try not to dress in a provocative manner?	63	18	10	58	−.0017	.1288
How often do you lock the doors when home alone at night?	87	.3	85	95	.0215	.1340
When in a car, how often do you lock the doors?	10	1	64	79	−.0665	.1288
How often do you cross the street when you see someone who seems strange or dangerous?	11	6	25	52	−.0247	.1261
How often do you stay out of parts of town you think are dangerous?	9	9	38	55	.2774	.1109
When walking on the street, how often do you make a point of being alert and watchful?	3	2	66	81	.1972	.1101
How often do you deliberately leave on lights or a radio when no one will be home?	14	5	57	65	.1504	.1037
When out alone, how often do you take something for protection like a dog or whistle?	73	50	6	23	.1961	.0656

TABLE 4.2 *(Continued)*
Correlation Between Fear and Use of Strategies by Gender

	% Who "Never" Do Activity[a]		% Who "Always" Do Activity[b]		Correlation of Fear with How Often Done	
	Male	Female	Male	Female	Male	Female
How often do you carry keys in your hand when going to your car?	20	4	44	82	.2260	.0596
Did you install or make sure there were special locks or bars on the doors?	43	28	57	72	.1081	.0452
Did you get an unlisted phone number?	60	43	40	57	.1985	.0399
When at a movie or on a bus, how often do you change seats if someone strange is nearby?	26	18	13	28	.0125	.0375
How often do you ask neighbors to watch your house when no one will be home for several days?	16	5	60	75	−.1094	.0323
How often do you get your house keys out before reaching your door?	15	4	50	81	.2216	.0265

[a] Percent of people who responded "Never" or "No" to questions about precautionary behavior.
[b] Percent of people who responded "Always" or "Yes" to questions about precautionary behavior.
Reprinted with permission from M. T. Gordon and S. Riger (1989). *The female fear*. New York: The Free Press. Pp. 16–18.

"Mental Disorders"

L. Robins et al. (1984) found several sex differences in the lifetime prevalence rates for fifteen psychiatric diagnoses. (A lifetime prevalence rate refers to the percentage of people who have *ever* experienced a disorder up to the time the people are interviewed.) Females were found definitely to have higher rates of "major depressive episode," "agoraphobia," and "simple phobia." Females were found probably to have higher rates of "dysthymia," "somatization disorder," "panic disorder," "obsessive-compulsive disorder," and "schizophrenia." Males, on the other hand, definitely had higher prevalence rates of "antisocial personality" and "alcohol abuse/dependence," and probably had higher "drug abuse/dependence." Diagnoses for which sex differences were not apparent were "manic episode" and "cognitive impairment." The diagnoses associated with men seem to describe someone who is selfishly looking out for himself and unconcerned about others (antisocial) and someone who feels sufficiently safe that he doesn't have to be constantly vigilant and/or doesn't want to be held responsible for his actions (alcohol and drug abuse/dependence). These male-typical diagnoses are more characteristic of a dominant than a subordinate. The diagnoses associated with women describe someone who is depressed, frightened but unable to acknowledge the source of fright (agoraphobia, simple phobia, panic disorder), unable to express unhappiness even to herself (somatization disorder), and someone who must be ever vigilant (obsessive-compulsive). The diagnoses associated with women describe characteristics of a subordinate.

Although we have used the psychiatric term "mental disorder," we view these symptoms of subordination as *normal responses* to an unhealthy social environment. Furthermore, we view them as survival strategies. We will now examine five "disorders" that are highly prevalent in women as a group: borderline personality disorder, depression, anxiety, agoraphobia, and eating disorders.

Sixty-seven to 86 percent of those with Borderline Personality Disorder (BPD) are female. BPD is characterized by dysfunctional behavior in five areas: (1) lack of sense of self; (2) intense, unstable affect; (3) "push-pull" dynamics and "splitting" (dualistic thinking) in interpersonal relationships, (4) impulsive, self-destructive acting out, and (5) temporary impairment of reality testing under stress (Herman and van der Kolk 1987). (The reader will note parallels between these five characteristics and the four long-term effects of Stockholm Syndrome we described in chapter 2.) There is growing evidence that a large proportion of female psychiatric patients receiving this diagnosis have experienced severe abuse, particularly sexual abuse (Herman 1992; Herman and van der Kolk 1987; Westen et al. 1990). While traumatized women are more likely to be diagnosed with BPD, traumatized men are more likely to be diagnosed with antisocial personality disorder.

A community survey by Cochrane and Stopes-Roe (1981) revealed that women reported more feelings of anxiety, depression, and inadequacy than men. Erdwins, Small, and Gross (1980) found that college students who described themselves as masculine (that is, high in masculinity and low in femininity), regardless of their sex, reported less anxiety than those who were androgynous (that is, high feminine *and* high masculine), feminine (high feminine and low masculine), or undifferentiated (low feminine and low masculine).

Phobias are a major clinical form of anxiety. One of the most common forms of phobia is agoraphobia, a condition that restricts the lives of over a million women (e.g., they may refuse to drive or leave their homes alone, and, in extreme cases, become housebound; Chambless and Goldstein 1980). The two most common ages of onset are late adolescence, when women are normally moving away from their families of origin, and the late twenties to early thirties. Women in the latter age group typically have "never experienced a period of autonomous functioning but transferred dependency on parents to dependency on an authoritarian, dominant husband" (Chambless and Goldstein 1980, p. 128). Agoraphobics fear that autonomous action will disrupt their interpersonal relationships with families of origin or husbands.

Also, research has repeatedly shown that women suffer from unipolar depression at approximately twice the rate that men do. This sex difference appears not only in the United States but also in Denmark, Scotland, England, Wales, Australia, Canada, Iceland, and Israel (Nolen-Hoeksema 1987), and it appears even in third- through sixth-grade schoolchildren (Alloy 1981, cited by Abramson and Andrews 1982). Weissman and Klerman (1977) point out that the greater preponderance of depression in females may be due to, among other things, (1) social discrimination against women, leading to "legal and economic helplessness, dependency on others, chronically low self-esteem, low aspirations, and, ultimately, clinical depression" (p. 106), and (2) femininity, which they conceptualize as creating "a cognitive set against assertion" and a type of "'learned helplessness,' characteristic of depression" (p. 106).

If, as we propose, dominants and subordinates are defined on the basis of bodily sexual characteristics, and trauma against women's bodies is used to maintain male dominance over women, one would expect women as a group to have ambivalence about our bodies, to have difficulty nurturing our bodies, and to feel out of control as regards our bodies. Over two thirds of college females, as compared to one half of college males, engage in "uncontrolled" excessive eating (Hawkins and Clement 1980). Twelve percent of college females, as compared to 6 percent of males, report self-induced vomiting (Halmi, Falk, and Schwartz 1981). Thirteen percent of college students show all the symptoms of bulimia, at a ratio of 87 women to 13 men (Halmi, Falk, and Schwartz 1981). Bulimics and anorexics, as compared to a normative sample of female and male college students, report a stronger drive for thinness, greater body dissatisfaction, more maturity fears, stronger feelings of ineffectiveness, stronger perfectionism, greater interpersonal distrust, and difficulty in labeling interoceptive emotions and sensations such as hunger (Garner, Olmstead, and Polivy 1983). Bulimics show cognitive distortions associated with having to look "perfect" (as defined by the culture) (Schulman et al. 1986). The greater incidence of bulimia and anorexia in women as compared to men suggests that women do feel less control over our bodies, less nurturing toward our bodies, and greater ambivalence about our bodies. But, in addition, eating-disordered women seem to have bought the culture's definition of who they should be (perfectly beautiful) and measure themselves against that impossible standard.

Findings from all these studies—regarding fear of males and "mental disorders"—indicate that women as a group show a particular psychology. Women are more likely than men to be fearful of males and to incur "mental-disorder" diagnoses that describe the characteristics of subordinates, and particularly the characteristics of subordinates so defined by their bodily characteristics. These aspects of the psychology of women as a group bear a striking resemblance to the array of symptoms associated with ongoing trauma, and may in fact function as survival strategies for coping with that trauma. We suggest that the first indicator of Stockholm Syndrome—showing symptoms of ongoing trauma—does seem to apply to women as a group.

2. Captive Is Bidirectionally Bonded to Her/His Captor

We will begin by showing that women bond with men, and we will briefly examine the bidirectional, romantic nature of that bond. Then we will explore how women's love of men may be made possible by the mental operation of splitting the terrorizing and kind sides of men.

Romantic, Bidirectional Bond between Men and Women

In this section we will examine the type of bond, called "love," that develops between men and women. Is this bond consistent with the type of bond that Stockholm Syndrome theory would lead us to expect?

There is absolutely no question that women bond with men. From adolescence on, most females in our culture put enormous energy into heterosexual dating relationships, with the ultimate goal of finding a male mate. By college age, more women than men are both married and engaged to be married, and more are "in love, but not engaged." More women than men report being in love. Although women and men begin dating at about the same age, women report that their first infatuation and their first love experience occur at younger ages (Kephart 1967). And college women report experiencing more intense feelings associated with love (for example, euphoria) than college males (Dion and Dion 1973). Marriage to men is almost universal among women.

When women captives bond to captors, the bond often takes on a romantic or erotic flavor. Recall that in the bank robbery in Stockholm (discussed in chapter 1), two of the women became engaged to their captors. In contrast, the bond that develops between male hostages and male captors is more likely to resemble friendship or a parental or filial bond (Moorehead 1980). Why might women's bonds to captors be experienced as romantic love or sexual attraction? Do the same forces that shape women hostages' bonding to male captors shape women's bonding in general to men? Rose (1985) says, "Desire and its expression are embedded in a social context that defines what constitutes a romantic or erotic event" (p. 250). Rose points out that one source of cultural-romance scripts aimed primarily at women and girls is popular fiction such as certain fairy tales, contemporary romance novels, and gothic novels. The heroines in the fairy tales that are most commonly anthologized are typically attractive, virtuous, and passive. At the beginning of the story the heroine may be captive or trapped in an evil spell or trance. Initially, the prince/rescuer may appear in the disguise of a disgusting frog or a loathsome beast.

Thus, women are reminded to be open to every male suitor, no matter how inappropriate he may appear at first. Rose maintains that, though the manifest themes are nonsexual, the latent theme in fairy tales is the sexual awakening of the female by the male. This tells women that our sexuality is controlled by men and that relationships with males promise passion and eroticism. Rose contends that similar themes also appear in romance novels.

The popularity of romance fiction is evident in its huge volume of sales to female readers. Ruggiero and Weston (1983) estimate that romance fiction accounts for 40 percent of paperback sales, suggesting that these novels appeal to a strong psychological need in women. Romantic fiction (like most well-known fairy tales) focuses on courtship and initiating relationships, or, put more precisely, creating heterosexual bonds between women and men. Rose (1985) notes that the males in romance novels are often initially described as "contemptuous or hostile to the heroine" (p. 255). She further notes that "readers are schooled overtly in the strange ability to completely reinterpret this behavior [so that] the hero's cruel and boorish behavior is really a sign of his intense attraction" (p. 255). Similarly, Modleski (1980) notes that "male brutality comes to be seen as a manifestation, not of contempt, but of love" (p. 439). By the end of the story, the female has conquered the originally aloof, brutal, cruel, and powerful male through "love." Women may be pulled to this type of fiction because it portrays the courtship period in male-female relationships—an emotionally intense phase, and the only one in which women experience some (sexual, erotic) power over men. Romance novels "serve to reinforce stereotypes about women: love, sex, violence and dependency go hand in hand" (Ruggiero and Weston 1983, p. 24). They also present the culture's intermixing of gender, sex, violence, and dependency in a way that normalizes the brew and helps women feel better about it. After all, in the end it is all about love.

The association of love and violence is not only a central motif in romantic fiction; it also is present in real-life heterosexual dating relationships. Studies of college students reveal that 21 percent of victims of violence in dating relationships felt the violence *improved* their relationship (O'Keeffe, Brockopp, and Chew 1986), and that 77 percent of dating couples who reported relationship violence planned to continue their relationship because they loved and enjoyed dating their partners (Lo and Sporakowski 1989). Research also indicates that individuals who planned to remain in violent dating relationships reported more commitment and love for their partners than those who planned to leave following violence (Lo and Sporakowski 1989). Similar findings were reported by another researcher (C. P. Flynn 1990): the amount of love women reported feeling for their partners increased both as the length of the relationship following the first episode of abuse increased ($r = .52$) and as the frequency of violence increased ($r = .38$). In fact, the number of days women stayed with their partners following the partners' first use of violence increased when violence was more frequent, when the women felt more love, and when the couple had been dating for a longer time before the violence occurred. The variable most predictive of length of stay following abuse was frequency of violence. Is it possible that violence creates both high arousal and confusion in the victim? Does the victim interpret the high arousal as evidence of love rather than terror, because interpreting the feelings as love is less fear-producing than interpreting them as terror? Are the reported commitment and "love" cognitive distortions, such that violent relationships are perceived as more intimate than nonviolent ones?

Studies of Stockholm Syndrome in a variety of subject populations suggest these questions might be answered affirmatively. Three Stockholm Syndrome factors have consistently emerged in our research (Graham, Ott, et al. 1990; Graham, Foliano, et al. 1990; Naber-Morris 1990). One factor measures extent of chronic interpersonal trauma (as in dating violence, child abuse), a second factor, lack of sense of self and, in part, confusion, and a third factor, the degree to which victims feel they cannot survive without their abuser's love. In all studies (except Naber-Morris 1990, but see Lipari 1993), a victim who was high on one factor tended to be high on all three factors, suggesting that, in the presence of chronic interpersonal trauma, victims lose their sense of self and become confused. The trauma would ensure that they also are experiencing a high degree of physiological arousal. If the victims are compliant and hypervigilant, and if the abuser shows some kindness, the confused victims may interpret their high arousal and hypervigilance as love, feeling that their survival is dependent on the abuser's loving them in return.[1]

Susan Sprecher (1985) found that, among college dating partners, the more love one felt, or the more involved one was in the relationship, the less power one perceived oneself as having within the relationship. Both males and females perceived themselves as having less power in relationships if they contributed more to the relationships than their partners. On the other hand, the more *absolute* contributions a man made, the more power he perceived himself having in the relationship. The opposite was true for women: the more absolute contributions a woman made, the less power she perceived herself having in the relationship.

Fairy tales and romance novels are prescriptions for pair bonding, but they give no blueprint for long-term relationships. Prescriptions for committed long-term relationships such as marriage are provided by experts (often male, or at least male-identified) who give women advice in "how to" books and women's magazines.

Cancian and Gordon (1988) analyzed the advice regarding love and anger given to women in women's magazines from 1900 to 1979 and found that it changed depending on women's economic situation. For example: "Before the 1960s, women were told that love was signified by suppressing their individual interests and feelings and attending to the needs of their husbands and their marriages. Unless they suppressed their autonomy, they were not experiencing or expressing true love. . . . In the late 1960s and 1970s, women's autonomy and assertion were encouraged" (pp. 320–321).

Cancian and Gordon question whether the messages of the articles they reviewed *reflected* the attitudes of their readers or whether the authors and publishers of the articles *manipulated* women to feel and behave in certain ways. Note that the messages women were given are consistent with Stockholm Syndrome dynamics, wherein victims look after the emotional needs of their abuser and increase their chances of economic survival by building a bond between themselves and the abuser. Before the 1960s, women were more dependent on marriage for survival. As more and more women began to work for pay outside the home and as divorce became more acceptable in the 1960s and 1970s, we were able to be more assertive in our relationships with men. Societal Stockholm Syndrome theory suggests that women are more likely to put men's interests, feelings, and needs before our own when our survival is dependent upon men's good will. The more dependent women are on men during any given period in history, the more likely we are to show these "selfless" behaviors. Whether the norms put forth in the magazines are traditional or liberal, the message that women are still responsible for the emotional climate of the relationship remains unchanged. The messages of these articles are simultaneously manipulative (they let women know what we must do to keep men happy) and reflective of women's interests (women seek to know what we must do to keep men happy so women can survive). In addition, the messages in the articles expose the power or lack of power of women at a given time.

Social scientists have identified a number of "love styles," and researchers have found differences in the styles of love espoused by males and females. Consistent findings are that males, more than females, espouse a style of love known as ludic (game-playing), while females more than males espouse pragmatic (practical, logical) and manic (possessive, dependent) love styles (Hendrick and Hendrick 1986, Studies 1 and 2; Bailey, Hendrick, and Hendrick 1987). People high in a game-playing style of love, such as male college students, don't mind deceiving their partners, don't make strong commitments, resist their partners' dependency on them, and are likely to have a number of partners at any given time. Thus, men's "style" of loving appears to be more exploitative than women's. Females, on the other hand, are more likely to love in ways that are more practical or logical and possessive or dependent. Hendrick, Hendrick, and Adler (1988) found that as possessive or dependent love increased, self-esteem decreased.

The only other style of love that men in some studies show more of than women is erotic love (Philbrick et al. 1988; Woll 1989), though at least one study has shown females espouse erotic love more than men do (Hendrick and Hendrick 1986, Study 2). Erotic love has a strong physical-attraction component to it. Woll (1989) found that those who scored high on erotic love also scored high in achievement, aggression, and dominance.

The gender differences reflected in love styles are what one would expect from love between dominant and subordinate group members, and one would expect erotic love to be more typical of a dominant group for which group membership is decided on the basis of sexual organs. The dominant group (men) disproportionately espouses love styles that are more exploitative and physically based. Other studies also indicate that, in considering dating and marriage partners, men attach greater importance to women's physical attractiveness than women attach to men's. (For a review, see Bar-Tal and Saxe 1976.) Thus, men's love styles bolster their dominant status (masculinity). On the other hand, women's more dependent love style suggests women feel a more desperate need for men than men feel for women. Women's more dependent love style, if acted upon, would serve to maintain women's subordinate status. And women's more practical love style may reflect our greater use of love as a practical tool of survival.

To summarize, the findings regarding love are consistent with Societal Stockholm Syndrome theory: men are more likely than women to initiate love; women are encouraged to remain psychologically and emotionally open to men of all types and are told, starting at a young age, that with love a grotesque frog will turn into a handsome, rich prince; men attach more importance to a woman's physical attractiveness than vice versa; young women are more likely than men both to be in love and to be infatuated; the more one loves another, the less power one has in the relationship; in dating relationships, many women cognitively distort men's violence, seeing it as a sign of love; the more violence women incur in dating relationships, the longer we are likely to stay in the relationship and the more love we are likely to report; and women are held responsible for the emotional climate of the relationship and for keeping the relationship together.

Victim Bonds to Positive Side of Abuser

Societal Stockholm Syndrome theory explains women's love of men as a form of bonding to an abuser, made possible in part by the mental-emotional operation of splitting. Because women's terror of male violence is so great and male kindnesses are so small by comparison, women engage in the psychic defense of splitting. Splitting means that one cannot simultaneously see both the good and the bad in another person or persons. Applied to male-female relations, splitting means that women see men as either all good or all bad, or that we see men as good and women as bad. As used here, splitting also refers to women's denial of men's violence and to our exaggerated perceptions of men's kindnesses. Splitting thus works to keep women's perceptions of the terrorizing side of men from overwhelming our perceptions of men's kind side and destroying women's hope for survival.

A result of this splitting is that women separate men into two classes, the predators (rapists, wife beaters, incest perpetrators) and the protectors. This compartmentalizing leaves women unable to recognize the ways in which all men are kind to women (in some ways) while also promoting and benefiting from their aggression against women. All women seem to engage in such splitting to one extent or another. Regarding antifeminists, Rowland (1984) comments: "There are . . . two groups of men: decent, loving husbands and fathers, and those unmarried, childless and irresponsible men" (p. 220). The husband who rapes and batters his wife and the father who sexually abuses his children are not recognized; nor is the kind, responsible bachelor. Any husband or father is, by definition, regarded as good; any bachelor as untrustworthy. While Rowland (1986) found feminists to "loathe . . . the violence and cruelty of men, . . . antifeminists seem either to ignore this [violence and cruelty], or [to] believe it only exists in the 'odd' case" (p. 687).

Having split apart the terrorizing and kind sides of men so that the hope created by male kindness is not overwhelmed by fear, and having denied the terrorizing side of men, women bond to the kind side of men. After all, why wouldn't a person bond to another person whom she saw as kind and whose threats of violence and actual violence she had denied? The result is that women "fall in love" with our oppressors even as we fear them. For instance, antifeminist women report that men are untrustworthy and are users of women, but they say they like men and find their husbands "wonderful" and "loving" (Rowland 1984). Women may "fall in love" with men because of our need to believe that the terror will end, that we can "tame" or "control" our terrorizers so that they will protect and nurture us (e.g., see Schlafly 1977, p. 17).

Splitting is manifested on a cultural level through societal demands that women love men no matter what they do to us and that women devalue women no matter how good we are. Dr. Edna Rawlings and I have asked students in our classes to describe characteristics of people whom they've heard called "man-haters" and "woman-haters." A man-hater is a woman who speaks her own mind, a feminist, or a lesbian: in other words, a woman who has her own voice and doesn't put men first is a man-hater. By contrast, students are unable to recall any situations in which they have heard someone being called a woman-hater. We ask, "Are rapists and wife batterers woman-haters?" They answer, "Just because a man rapes or batters women doesn't mean he hates women." The differential definitions ascribed to terms that should have equivalent meanings suggest an enormous collective need both to deny male hatred of women and to derogate independent female action (which might be used to expose expressions of that male hatred).

The bond between victim and abuser is not a healthy love, because the circumstances that produce it are not healthy. Because it emerges under conditions of terror against which women attempt to numb themselves, this bond has an addictive quality, in the sense that connection is desperately sought. (More will be said about this in chapter 5.) A healthy love does not have this desperate quality. Robin Norwood (1985) has argued that this type of relatedness is observed primarily among women. Her case-study descriptions make it clear that it is both unhealthy and psychologically debilitating to women. Unfortunately, Norwood does not relate love addiction in women to patriarchy nor portray it as a survival strategy.

Graham et al. (1993) found that a factor they call "love-dependence" was one of three factors emerging from their Stockholm Syndrome scale when the scale was completed by a normative sample of approximately 750 college women in heterosexual dating relationships. This love-dependence factor described the women as feeling their survival depended on their male partners' loving them. Statistical analysis involving multiple regression revealed that a woman's love-dependence regarding her partner was greater the less able she was to escape him, the more general kindness he showed her, the more emotional violence he directed at her, and the more hope (that the relationship would get better) that his kindness created in her.

Women's bonding with men may be an attempt to heal the wound created by male oppression (as well as an attempt to halt that oppression through love). It may be an attempt to find the comfort and self-assurance which have been denied to women by fear of male violence and by actual male violence. Such bonding may be an attempt to encourage men to stop their violence against women by promoting a seemingly incompatible response: their love of women. And it may be an attempt to gain indirect access to male power and privilege, since direct access is denied to the vast majority of women in patriarchy.

Do women, like the hostages that Frederick Hacker (1976) observed, see men, their abusers/captors, as "poor devils" who just need love to turn a life of violence into a life of doing good? Do we rationalize that it is because men have hard lives, or because they have not received enough love, that they are violent? For example, we may argue that the societal pressure on men to be masculine victimizes them by dehumanizing them, forcing them to deny their feelings and pain, including empathy. In the process of arguing this, we often forget that it is men who, as the dominant group in our society, are primarily responsible for defining social roles (and thus sex roles) and for enforcing sanctions against members who violate those roles (Polk 1976). Women may feel we can be men's saviors from the roles they have created if we can just love them enough. Women may even feel that as individuals we are the only ones who can help men out of the trap they have laid for themselves. But women need to remember that when we rationalize men's violence, we also excuse it—which helps keep men, as well as women, trapped in patriarchy.

The popular notions that "a woman's love can tame the most savage beast" and that "love conquers all" reveal an attempt to exercise control in a situation in which women otherwise feel powerless. A logical outcome of these notions is that, since it is women's love and influence that allegedly tames men, the failure of a relationship, even a brutal relationship, must be the woman's fault. The woman simply has not done a good enough job of taming her savage partner. And many people do draw that conclusion, as battered women's testimonies reveal.

If love of men arises from terror brought on by male threat to female survival, women have to defend against any feelings that might challenge our love for men. Is this one of the reasons that most women vehemently deny their own lesbian feelings? Could this denial occur because women experience their relationships with other women as *not* fraught with threats to survival but as respectful of their own needs, perspectives, and feelings (cf. Hite 1987; but see Lobel 1986 and Renzetti 1992)? The contrast between these relationships and those with men may be just too great for most women to deal with, so women's (psychologically healthy) feelings of attraction toward other women are simply denied. We propose that the greater women's fear of male violence, the greater will be our evangelisticlike support of heterosexism and male-female sex roles, and the greater will be our homophobia.[2] Stacked on the side of man-woman relationships is the need to survive. Stacked on the side of woman-woman relationships is the need for mutuality, respect, and one's own sense of self. As Maslow (1970) has argued, needs for mutuality, respect, and so forth take second place to the more basic need to survive. With such fundamentally important needs at stake, the issue of women's love for men (and women's heterosexuality) would be laden with considerable conflict and thus emotionality, as is the case.

Because of the coercive conditions under which heterosexual love arises, it has a regressive quality for women. Not being free to love as an equal, a woman relates to her male lover as a child relates to a parent. Thus it is not surprising that she is seen as childlike (Broverman et al. 1970). (At other times she relates to her lover like a "parentified" child who must be a parent to her parents, since she has less power than the person toward whom she is acting as parent.) However, as a survival strategy, heterosexual love may be safer for women *in the short run* than any other alternative short of collective action (such as that offered by the feminist movement) by women against male violence and tyranny.

3. Captive Is Intensely Grateful for Any Kindness, However Small, Shown by Captor

Do women as a group feel intensely grateful to men as a group for small kindnesses shown? Here we are looking for a gratitude that, on the surface, appears exaggerated. Unfortunately, this author knows of no empirical research designed to answer this question. If one were planning research in this area, one would have to define "intensely grateful." One would need a standard for determining a reasonable amount of gratitude. One standard would be the extent of women's gratitude for kindnesses shown under conditions of safety. The researcher would compare women's responses to kindness shown under conditions of safety versus under threat to survival. Men provide the researcher another standard. A researcher might evaluate whether women show more gratitude for kind acts in their behalf than do men. Lacking empirical support, we ask the reader to consider the following social facts and to contrast women's current responses with how one would expect women living in a safe environment to respond and with how one would expect men to respond if shown comparable kindnesses by women.

Many women have reasoned that we should not support the Equal Rights Amendment lest equality should cause men not to open doors for women. Women as a group thank men for the token kindnesses of male chivalry even while we deny that chivalry arises from—and strengthens—male-female sex roles of dominance and submission (Richardson 1983). Women thank men for putting us on a pedestal even while we deny that our need for the pedestal shows female dependence on male goodwill for women's individual and group survival. Women resist giving up the prestige and privilege (such as money) we derive from our associations with men—even when such resistance furthers our subordination within our individual relationships, and even when giving up indirect access to privilege is necessary if women are to gain direct access to power, fame, privilege, and the like. Women are grateful to men when they label us as "good women," for such women are the ones to whom men offer love, protection, and other kindnesses. Men bestow this label on women when we align ourselves with men, giving up alliances with other women and supporting male domination. This label is so valued by women that we compete with one another for this scarce resource, men's kindness. Many women consider men to be good husbands, good fathers, and "good catches" if they are "good providers," even if they beat their wives or molest their children. As Johnson (1989) points out, women feel overwhelmed with gratitude when men declare a U.N. "Decade of Women" or a U.S. "Year of the Woman"—as if men owned time.

Under conditions of safety, women would not be likely to express gratitude for these kindnesses from men. Nor is one likely to hear men express gratitude when denied equal rights in exchange for chivalrous acts of kindness shown to them, and so on. The fact that women *do* express gratitude reveals the profound power imbalance in male-female relationships and suggests that men constitute a threat to women's survival. Our ability to see men as kind enables us to bond with them and permits us to maintain the illusion that the bond between us lessens their abuse of us.

4. Captive Denies Captor's Violence against Her/ Him When Violence and/or Threats of Violence Are Actually Occurring, or Captive Rationalizes That Violence. The Captive Denies Her/His Own Anger at Captor, to Others and to Herself or Himself

If women as a group have Societal Stockholm Syndrome, we would expect women both to deny, minimize, or rationalize male violence and to deny our anger at men for their violence against women.

Denial, Minimization, or Rationalization of Violence

Finkelhor and Yllo (1985, p. 5) observed that many women who have been raped by their own husbands "do not see themselves as having been raped, . . . view the assault as part of a marital conflict for which they are to blame, . . . [and experience the rape as] part of a personal shame that they do not want others to know." The need to deny is so strong that even severely battered women will deny that battering occurred (Ferraro 1983). Hedda Nussbaum, former editor at Random House and common-law wife of New York attorney Joel Steinberg, had sixteen broken ribs, a broken nose, and legs ulcerated from repeated beatings at the time Steinberg killed their daughter, Lisa. Despite the extreme violence she experienced at Steinberg's hands, Hedda had reframed his abuse of her as a form of kindness. She reported at his trial that she had seen his violence as an attempt to help her overcome her faults and thus to become a better person ("He hit me to help me"; Ehrlich 1989). This reframing of abuse as kindness is simply an extreme form of everyday denial. Even severely battered women do not overemphasize the extent of abuse they have endured and minimize it instead (Kelly 1987; Okun 1986).

Do women in general respond to men's violence against women as a group in a manner similar to the raped wives and battered women described above? Do we deny, minimize, or rationalize men's violence against us?

Students in our Women's Studies courses protest the requirement to read and discuss articles about male violence against women. They report that they "don't want to go around being angry all the time." On the "Oprah" television show, female audience members complain about the "male-bashing" that, as Oprah points out in response, is not male-bashing, but truth-telling. Why would women protest the examination of male violence? Such responses are clearly not logical—after all, it would be only logical to call a hideous act a hideous act, and to demand that men stop. But even though such a response is not logical, there is a way in which it makes sense—it reflects the very violence it denies—it shows that women *do* feel afraid.

The reader may recall that women in our Psychology of Women classes, when asked to describe times they have heard the term "woman-hater" used, omit saying it is used to refer to rapists and batterers. In fact, asked if the term might refer to such groups, the women indicate that rapists and batterers do not necessarily hate women and reject use of the term for those groups. Many students say they have never heard the term "woman-hater" used. Do these "findings" suggest a cultural reluctance to talk about and even contemplate male violence?

Despite the criminal justice system's blindness when it comes to male violence against women (in rape, wife abuse, and sexual abuse) and its keen-sightedness in protecting men's rights (in divorce actions, right to pornography, and so on), many women believe social myths that flatter men. These myths state that men (having women's interests at heart) will protect women's rights; that not every man is a woman-hater (though every man profits from misogyny, and it is unheard-of for a man to decline a job he obtained because of male privilege or lack of equal access); and that violent men are sick and thus qualitatively different from other men (though rapists, for example, have not been found to differ psychologically from nonrapists; see Griffin 1979).

Women in general cling to the dream that men care about us and will protect us from violence. Denial is so strong that women believe that men *are* protecting us—we forget from whom—even as they oppress women.

Mae West captured this irony in her famous remark, "Funny, every man I meet wants to protect me. I can't figure out what from."

Females tend to deny that male intimates—the group most likely to physically violate women (M. D. Smith 1988)—are dangerous. In fact, women are likely to see male intimates as "loving" and "wonderful" while displacing our fear onto male strangers and our anger onto safer targets: ourselves, other women, and children. (See the discussion of splitting in the previous section.)

The fact that chance determines which individual woman is violated at any given time ("she just happened to be in the wrong place at the wrong time," as rapists remind us) is threatening to women, making us feel we have little control over whether and when we might be victimized. The theory of *defensive attributions* (Shaver 1970; Walster 1966) asserts that such threat of victimization is often defended against at an unconscious level, so that women (potential victims) need never consciously acknowledge the extent to which we are vulnerable. Research suggests such defensive attributions are especially likely if the consequences of victimization are severe (Burger 1981; Walster 1966). Women defend against such threats by telling ourselves that we are not like the victim ("I'm not young like her") and by blaming the victim for her or his victimization ("she shouldn't have dressed like that," "she shouldn't have been out so late by herself") (Shaver 1970; Walster 1966). The reader will recognize that such attributions suggest women *are* experiencing the threat of victimization ourselves.

It is aversive and demeaning to define oneself as a victim (Taylor, Wood, and Lichtman 1983). Blaming oneself for one's victimization may be one way to avoid defining oneself as a victim. Self-blame and other victim-coping strategies permit individuals to deny victimization and to preserve their self-esteem (Janoff-Bulman and Frieze 1983). One such strategy involves redefining the victimizing event so that its stressful or threatening qualities are minimized. Scheppele and Bart (1983) showed that women who were subjected to nonphallic sexual acts (e.g., cunnilingus, digital penetration of vagina) tended to label themselves as having escaped rape. Those who did not label themselves as victims of rape had less severe fear reactions.

When victimization cannot be denied, victims may reevaluate themselves in ways that are self-enhancing. Taylor, Wood, and Lichtman (1983) identified five such mechanisms of selective evaluation: (1) "downward comparisons," that is, comparing oneself with others who are less fortunate (e.g., minimizing the extent to which fear of male violence affects one's life by saying one has never been sexually abused or battered); (2) selective focusing on attributes that make one appear to be advantaged; (3) creating worse-case scenarios ("I may be a woman but at least I'm not a *[fill in the blank]* woman"); (4) identifying benefits from the victimizing experience ("Being a woman has made me more sensitive and empathic to others"); and (5) creating nonexistent normative standards that make one's own adjustment appear extraordinary ("Compared to most women, I have achieved a great deal"). At one time or another, probably all women have used one or more of these strategies to cope with victimization.

Denial of Anger

Societal Stockholm Syndrome theory asserts that, because we women fear male violence, we not only deny the violence but also do not express our anger at men, for to express anger might well make us the targets of male aggression. The more women fear retaliation, the less we are likely to express our anger. Rather, survival demands that women disguise our anger, even from ourselves.

Studying schoolchildren in the first, second, fifth, and sixth grades, Brody, Hay, and Venditor (1990) found that girls reported more intense feelings of anger toward males than toward females. The intensity of these feelings was greater than the intensity of boys' feelings toward either males or females. The more feminine the girls perceived themselves as being, the more intense their anger at males. The more masculine the girls perceived themselves as being, the more intense their anger at *females*. Further, girls with a strong sense of identity, as indicated by high self-reports of either femininity or masculinity, reported more intense feelings of anger than girls with less strong senses of identity. If girls feel such anger but women in general say we are not angry at men, how has the anger come to "disappear"? As females grow older and develop intimate bonds with men, do we increasingly deny our anger toward them?

How can we determine whether women as a group deny our anger toward men? In discussing Indicator 1 (evidence of ongoing trauma or PTSD) earlier in this chapter, we found that women are indeed fearful of men's violence. Is there evidence that we are also angry at men? If so, does that anger appear proportional to the injustice done to women? Is there evidence that women refrain from expressing our anger toward men out of fear of retaliation?

Unfortunately, there are several problems with the research literature on anger, so it is necessary to read this literature with extra care. One problem is that research studies focus predominantly on angry aggression (i.e., aggression aimed at harming the target person). Indeed, anger is sometimes treated synonymously with angry aggression. This may be because researchers (like other members of our culture) consider anger a male emotion and thus equate anger with angry aggression, or even with physical assaultiveness. Another problem with experimental studies of sex differences both in aggression and in responses to aggression is that findings obtained in such studies often have little relevance outside of the experimental laboratory setting. The experimental participants usually are aware that they are safe from retaliatory violence, particularly sexual violence, since an experimenter is present, since the ways in which aggression can be expressed are controlled, and since one can discontinue one's participation at any time. Also, the research literature does not include investigations of the types of violence to which women are routinely exposed, and to which we therefore might be expected to react, in the real world (cf. Eagly and Steffen 1986).

Women Inhibit Our Aggression Relative to Men. Studies consistently show that males are more aggressive than females (Eagly and Steffen 1986; Frodi, Macaulay, and Thome 1977).[3] Eagly and Steffen (1986) found that 89 percent of behavioral studies showed more male than female aggression. (If there were no sex differences, one would expect only 50 percent of the studies to show such a finding.) This sex difference was stronger for physical than for psychological aggression.

Frodi et al. (1977), looking for possible sex differences in the occurrence of aggression, surveyed a large body of psychological literature. They found that men are more aggressive than women. They also claimed that "fear of retaliation is unlikely to explain findings of less female than male aggression" (p. 644), yet they cited numerous research results suggesting otherwise. For example, they describe a study by Fischer, Kelm, and Rose (1969), who found that women who were angered because they had received negative evaluations described a neutral party *less* negatively if a knife was lying on the table than if no knife was present. On the other hand, presence of a table knife on the table stimulated angered men to *more* negatively evaluate a neutral party.

Eagly and Steffen (1986) found that, when presented with a range of aggressive acts frequently used in aggression research, women (as compared with men) thought that the acts would cause more harm, that they would experience more anxiety or guilt if they themselves committed the acts, and that they would "face more danger" (p. 315) of retaliation if they committed such acts of aggression. The tendency of women to perceive more guilt/anxiety and harm to others was most pronounced when the aggression was physical rather than psychological. And the sex difference in fear of danger for having aggressed tended to be larger in cases of physical than psychological aggression. These sex differences were obtained despite the fact that the acts of aggression used in the studies being reviewed were relatively benign (for example, honking at a person stopped at a green traffic light, administering mild shock to a subject in a psychological experiment). These findings led Eagly and Steffen to conclude "anticipated damage to oneself is an important mediator [and] raises questions about [Frodi et al.'s] conclusion that fear of retaliation, surely a major component of perceived danger, is an unimportant mediator" (p. 325).

Research, then, suggests that fear of retaliation leads women to inhibit acts of aggression, even (1) when the act is only mildly aggressive (like honking a car horn), (2) when the women are in the company of an experimenter (and thus relatively safe), (3) when women have no other modes of response except to aggress, (4) when the form of one's aggression (for example, shocking a person, honking a car horn) requires no gender-specific physical skills, and (5) when women know they are free to discontinue their participation in the studies at any time.

If women inhibit aggressive action out of fear of retaliation, then why do women inhibit aggression against female victims even more than against male victims? It is possible that—because women's role with respect to men is that of victim, while men's role is that of perpetrator—women identify with the female victim in aggression research and therefore inhibit aggression toward her more than against a male victim. It is also possible that, in the experimental situation, women do not have to deal with the real-life consequences of aggressing against men. Later, we will present some naturalistic studies indicating that, as in the real world, the victims of women's aggression tend to be other women (and children).

When women do express anger, there is evidence that we are likely to do so in nonphysical and nonaggressive ways. Studies by McCann et al. (1987) and by K. Smith et al. (1989) indicate that women prefer nonaggressive expressions of anger. McCann et al. factor-analyzed several self-report inventories and found that women scored higher than men on an Anger-Emotionality factor, and on Guilt, Resentment, and Irritability subscales. On the other hand, women scored lower than men on an Assaultiveness subscale. In K. Smith et al.'s (1989) study, male and female participants read ten vignettes in which anger was expressed by either male or female stimulus persons (SPs) in a variety of situations. Women gave more positive ratings to SPs exhibiting nonaggressive anger and more negative ratings to SPs exhibiting physical and aggressive anger. Males, on the other hand, did not discriminate between aggressive anger and nonaggressive anger—they only discriminated between degrees of anger expressed. The authors interpreted these findings to suggest that "women may perceive a narrower range of appropriate forms of anger expression (i.e., non-aggressive) than do men" (p. 497).

Not only does research suggest that women prefer nonaggressive responses over aggressive ones, but that when given a choice we prefer affectional responses. Shuntich and Shapiro (1991) found more affectional than aggressive responses between female dyads than between male and mixed-sex dyads. Further, the authors reported that "males seemed more likely to have lower levels of aggression when their [female] partner was more affectionate" (p. 296).

Women View the Expression of Anger, Especially Aggressive Expression, as More Costly to Ourselves. We believe the major reason women inhibit the expression of anger toward men is that women fear that acting aggressively will invite male retaliation. Recall Eagly and Steffen's (1986) finding that females feared more than did males that they would face risk of retaliation if they committed acts of aggression. Frodi, Macaulay, and Thome (1977) found that, when females acted aggressively, males were likely to loosen any inhibitions they had against aggressing against them.

Besides fearing physical retaliation, women also fear psychological retaliation from men. Here we will examine two forms of psychological retaliation: men's definition of women who express anger as deviant; and threats that women's anger will destroy our bonds with men.

Male culture ensures that women's anger is not taken seriously (and thus that women's anger will not lead to social change) by defining anger in women as pathological. Broverman et al. (1972) found that mental health professionals judged aggression to be a trait associated with a healthy man, but not a healthy woman. Feinblatt and Gold (1976) found that more girls than boys were referred to children's mental health centers for being defiant and verbally aggressive. Aggressive girls described in hypothetical case histories were rated both by graduate students in psychology and by parents as more disturbed, as being more in need of treatment, and as having poorer prognosis than boys described with identical problems. Hochschild (1983) found that males who displayed anger were thought to have deeply held convictions, while females were considered personally unstable.

Women are fearful of expressing anger at men because we fear such expressions will disrupt our bonds with men—bonds we see as life jackets in a sea of male aggression. Egerton (1988) reported that although both men and women in her study saw the expression of anger as equally appropriate, women associated angry expression with greater costs. These costs included loss of relationships. Bernardez-Bonesatti (1978) argues that anger is threatening to women's communal goals because it may involve interpersonal conflicts. Likewise, Eagly and Steffen (1986) point out that the female gender role (which is conceptualized as the role of subordinate, or victim) gives primacy to "caring and other communal qualities" which "may favor behaviors incompatible with aggressiveness toward other people" (p. 310). When Tannen (1990) analyzed gender-related patterns of 2d, 6th, and 10th-grade same-sex best friends talking to each other for 20 minutes about something serious or intimate, she found that males occasionally made reference to violence in their conversations, but females never did. Tannen also found that the girls (unlike the boys) showed great concern with anger, fights, and disagreements, which they believed to result in the destruction of intimacy. Similarly, in a study by Davis, LaRosa, and Foshee (1992), in which females and males were required to imagine themselves in the role of a supervisor expressing justifiable anger at a subordinate, females judged the angry display as having greater relationship and personal costs. These studies indicate that women associate our own expression of anger with the threat of damaging or destroying interpersonal relationships, and we see this as a price too high to pay.[4]

Given women's concern for the effects of violence on relationships, why do many researchers find women and men reporting that women are *more* violent than men in dating and marital relationships? After reviewing a number of studies of physical abuse in dating relationships, Sugarman and Hotaling (1989) concluded, "These studies suggest that women have higher levels of both inflicting and sustaining violence in contrast to men" (p. 104). Also, in a study of conjugal violence, Straus, Gelles, and Steinmetz (1980) reported that women and men were equally likely to be violent, with women committing more severely violent acts.

Several factors must be kept in mind when looking at these research reports. First, the finding that women both inflict and sustain more violence is inherently contradictory. In addition, the studies tend to count acts of self-reported violence (number of slaps, kicks, hits, etc.) *without regard to the differential strength of men and women*. (This may explain why participants in experimental studies rate male aggression less positively than female aggression [Harris 1991].) Also, there is evidence that men underreport and women overreport their own violent acts. Okun (1986) cited an unpublished paper by Bulcroft and Straus in which the researchers found that children report more father-to-mother violence than the father reported; furthermore, children report less mother-to-father violence than mothers report. Okun confirmed this pattern of male underreporting and female overreporting in his clinical experience with couples. Research by Harris (1991) offers an explanation for why males might be more likely than females to underreport their violence: "Aggression against female victims tends to be [viewed] ... more negatively than aggression against males" (p. 183).

Another factor to keep in mind is that, in most studies of intimate, heterosexual violence, the context of the violence is generally not described; thus, violence initiation and self-defense against an attack are counted equally as partner violence. Okun suggests that preemptive violence may be a protective reaction against impending violence for women who have been through the cycle of violence more than once. In these cases, women predict from the mate's behavioral cues that a blow is coming, and they therefore attack first. Battered women who are in the tension-building phase of the violence cycle may attempt to provoke what they believe is an inevitable attack—in the hope of getting the attack over quickly, before their male partners' anger builds any higher, resulting in even greater violence (L. Walker 1979, 1984). When women threaten violence it may be to scare the partner into stopping the violence; when men threaten violence it may be for the purpose of frightening women into not leaving because of the violence. Women probably use weapons in self-defense to equalize the threat of violence from the male partner. In a study by Kirkpatrick and associates, reported in a newspaper article by Collins (1986), Kirkpatrick is quoted as saying that "in order for women to kill [a male partner], it had to be perceived by them as a life-threatening situation." In contrast, he portrayed homicidal men as "on the edge of violence most of the time," often killing over trivial slights. (For a more detailed critique of research finding that women inflict more violence than men, see Okun 1986.)

Women May Deny Anger toward Men by Blaming Ourselves for Being Abused, Thereby Directing Aggression Inward. If women inhibit our aggression relative to men, seeing the expression of such aggression as very likely to be costly to ourselves, where does women's anger go? Hochschild (1983) found that women report crying (and feeling hurt) as an anger response. Obviously, these differ from the aggressive responses typically expressed by men. Women's responses suggest that we tend to hurt ourselves rather than others when we feel angry. Studies show that women blame ourselves and turn our anger against ourselves more than men do (McCann et al. 1987). Keeping in mind that anger turned inward is associated with depression, twice as many women as men have been found to suffer from unipolar depression. This female pattern of anger turned inward (also referred to as "anger in") was found in a severe form in a study of hospitalized abuse victims. In examining psychiatric hospital records, Mills, Rieker, and Carmen (1984) discovered that, for males and females who were abused, males became more aggressive against others, while females became more actively suicidal and self-destructive. This self-destructiveness was more pronounced among females who had been sexually abused and was more severe if the sexual abuse had been perpetrated by a family member.

Self-blame is one way of coping with victimization so that one does not have to experience anger at powerful perpetrators of abuse. If the blame is attributed to one's character, it can lead to depression and lowered self-esteem. However, if the blame is directed at one's behavior, self-esteem is preserved and one can believe that by changing one's behavior, one can avoid future victimization (see Janoff-Bulman 1979).

Women May Displace Anger toward Men onto Safer Targets, such as Other Women and Children. Examples of women's displaced aggression include lesbian battering (women battering our female partners), rapes of women by women, women's crimes against other women, and child abuse (of both male and female children). Because few researchers have examined female aggression toward females, the data are sketchy and in some cases the findings are confusing or contradictory.

Statistics on the extent of lesbian battering are not readily available. In a questionnaire study of seventy-five heterosexual women and fifty-five homosexual women, Brand and Kidd (1986) found that, in committed relationships, there was no statistically significant difference between the amount of physical abuse by partners reported by heterosexual women (27 percent) and homosexual women (25 percent); however, the physical abuse in dating relationships reported by heterosexual women (19 percent) was statistically significantly higher than the amount reported by homosexual women (5 percent). Brand and Kidd report that "male aggressors accounted for a higher percentage of all categories of incidents except one, the infliction of pain beyond that which was consensual when practicing sadomasochism [S/M]" (p. 1310). However, the difference between the percentages of heterosexual and homosexual women reporting abuse from S/M was not statistically significant, and the number of women reporting abuse in the S/M category was extremely small: only one (of seventy-five) heterosexual woman and four (of fifty-five) homosexual women.

With respect to reported rapes of females, Brand and Kidd found that 29 percent were committed by women. This is a considerable increase over the .7 percent of women raped by women reported by Russell (1984, p. 67). Russell identified only five female rapists in her study and in only two cases did the females act alone without male accomplices. Differences in methodology used by the researchers may account for the differences in findings.[5]

Studies of child sexual abuse reveal that perpetrators are predominantly men and victims are predominantly female. Retrospective studies that attempt to assess prevalence rates in society (e.g., Finkelhor 1979; Russell 1986) and studies which draw their subjects from agency clientele (e.g., Milner and Robertson 1990; Kercher and McShane 1984) both have limitations and biases. Milner and Robertson had no female sexual offenders in their sample of child abusers from several social services agencies and from a parent-child program. Kercher and McShane reported that perpetrators in their large multiagency sample were seldom female (only 3.2 percent). Over half of the female offenders were mothers or stepmothers of victims. Male offenders were equally likely to be fathers, stepfathers or acquaintances of the victims. For both male and female offenders, the victims tended to be female; 83.6 percent of victims of male offenders were female and 74.3 percent of the victims of female offenders were female.

Using data from the Second National Family Violence Survey, involving 6,002 households, Gelles (1989) compared reported child physical abuse by mothers and fathers in two-parent homes with child abuse in both mother-headed and father-headed single-parent homes. No sex differences in violence rates were reported by mothers and fathers in two-parent homes. However, the reported rate of very severe violence was 71 percent higher for single mothers than for mothers in two-parent homes. Severe violence by single fathers was 420 percent higher than it was for fathers in two-parent households. The study further indicated that poverty accounted for the greater abuse by single-parent females but not for the greater abuse by single-parent males.

Neglect is one form of child abuse in which women appear to be the chief offenders. Eighty-three percent of the agency-confirmed child neglectors in Milner and Robertson's (1990) study were women. This finding is not surprising since most child caretakers in this society are women, and since neglect is a passive form of abuse and one which sometimes (as in leaving children unattended) may stem from desperate economic straits. For example, single mothers who lack a support system and cannot afford child care are blamed for child endangerment when they leave their children at home unattended to go to the grocery store, to the bank, and so on. The finding also is not surprising because mothers are more likely than fathers to be blamed for cases of child neglect, for absent fathers are not viewed as neglectful.

Other types of maternal behavior may be emotionally destructive (e.g., verbal and psychological abuse), but they do not result in societal intervention. Statistics on their frequency are therefore not available.[6]

Homicide is the most severe form of child abuse. Silverman and Kennedy (1988) report that women's homicide rates in Canada were only 10–12 percent of all homicides committed. Crittenden and Craig (1990) report that, except for neonatal murders, most murders of children are committed by men: "Mothers accounted for 86% of neonatal deaths,[7] 39% of infant deaths, 22% of toddler deaths, 23% of preschooler deaths, and 8% of child deaths" (p. 208). While acknowledging that noninfant murders of children by mothers results from child battering, Silverman and Kennedy (1988) link women's killing of their male partners and nonneonatal children to wife abuse: "If uncontained violence is directed against females, they may eventually strike out against their spouses or they turn their frustration, anger, and hurt on their children. . . . In a sense, they may transfer their feelings to a convenient and perhaps frustrating target" (p. 124).

To determine whom female offenders victimize, V. Young (1979) used victim surveys and limited her study to personal victimization crimes. Two thirds of the victims of female assaults were women. When women committed homicide, their victims were usually family members; only 10 percent of women's homicide victims were strangers (Mann 1990). In terms of the displacement of anger hypothesis, it is interesting to note that Mann found that the victims of black women's homicides were more often (abusive) male partners, while nonblack women were more likely to kill other females and children.

Overall, research indicates that women commit less violence than do men in most categories of interpersonal violence (for example, homicide, battering, rape, and child sexual abuse). Child physical abuse by women and men does not differ; however, women spend enormously more time in the company of children than do men. Women's rates of child neglect are higher than those of men, probably because women are responsible for most of the children in our culture and are more likely to be economically disadvantaged than men. However, we feel it would be a grave mistake to brush aside the evidence that women can, and do, commit violence—and that women's violence tends to descend on "safer" targets than men. No violence should be excused. Instead, violence should be understood and stopped. And female violence is not likely to end unless we comprehend the context of denied anger that gives rise to it. Stockholm Syndrome theory leads this author to hypothesize that female violence is a response to anger, generated by massive violence from dominants (men), that is denied and often displaced. When pushed to their limits, some women either explode in murderous rage at their abusers or displace their anger onto more vulnerable targets.

When women deny men's violence against us, it is impossible for us to recognize that violence is an effort to maintain male domination, female submissiveness, and possibly even female love of men. Denial of male violence makes it impossible for women to recognize, much less understand, that our love of men and our (adopted) femininity may be attempts to limit men's abuse of women. Denial of male violence also precludes the taking of steps to end violence.

5. Captive Is Hypervigilant Regarding the Captor's Needs and Seeks to Keep the Captor Happy. In the Service of Keeping the Captor Happy, Captive Tries to "Get Inside the Captor's Head"

Once men show women any kindness, however small, women do whatever we can to have the kindness continue. If men feel warmth toward women, they might not do violence to us, so women do what we can to encourage feelings of warmth. If men feel warmth toward women, they also might not let other men hurt us. If women can arouse the kindness of any one man, maybe other men also will think we are valuable and therefore won't hurt us because they will respect that man's property or fear his wrath if they show us disrespect. (Such thinking, of course, rarely occurs at a conscious level.)

Desperately wanting to keep men kind, women try to get inside men's heads, so to speak, so that we can know what makes them happy, sad, angry, depressed, or appreciative. We try to decipher every nuance of men's verbal and nonverbal behavior. For example, females more than males look at the person with whom we are talking. Rubin (1970) suggested that women's greater gazing "may allow women to obtain cues from [our] male partners concerning the appropriateness of [our] behavior" (p. 272). Laboratory studies repeatedly show females to be better decoders of others' nonverbal cues than males at all ages (Hall 1987).[8] Women are more sensitive to the feelings and thoughts of males than of females. More particularly, a woman engaging in a task in which she is subordinate to a man is much more sensitive to the man's thoughts and feelings than one engaging in a task in which she is dominant (Snodgrass 1985). Weitz (1976) found that women were "nonverbally more submissive with more dominant male partners" (p. 179) and nonverbally more cold with more affiliable male partners. She found, on the other hand, that female nonverbal behaviors were not associated with the dominance or affiliableness of their female partners, nor were male nonverbal behaviors associated with their female partners' dominance or warmth. These findings led Weitz to propose that females use a "monitoring mechanism . . . [to] adjust their nonverbal communications to fit the male in the interaction" (p. 175), thereby helping to ensure that women's interactions with men go smoothly.

Additional evidence exists indicating that women use any available information to alter our behavior in ways that make interactions with men go smoothly. For instance, college women in a mock-interview situation presented themselves as more traditional (in appearance, verbal and nonverbal behavior, and view presented) when meeting with a man whom they believed to have traditional values and presented themselves as more nontraditional when meeting with a man believed to have nontraditional values (von Baeyer, Sherk, and Zanna 1981). Similarly, Zanna and

Pack (1975) found that women college students portrayed themselves as more or less traditional, depending on the "attractiveness" of the man with whom they were to interact in an experiment.

It may be easier for women to recognize how we change our bodies than how we change our personalities for the purpose of winning over men. Consider, for instance, some of the many physical ways women change ourselves to make ourselves more attractive to men: dieting, exercising, using laxatives, vomiting, lying out in the sun or under sun lamps to get a tan, wearing makeup (which makes us look continually sexually aroused), plucking eyebrows, sleeping in curlers, having our nose fixed, using bust developers, having breast-reduction or enlargement operations, having silicone treatments, undergoing liposuction and facelifts, having our stomachs tied and thighs and bottoms tucked, shaving and waxing body hair, having electrolysis, straightening hair, getting permanents, dyeing hair, using hot curlers and irons, wearing perfume, douching, polishing nails, sculpturing nails, wearing fake finger nails, piercing ears and noses, wearing contact lenses rather than glasses, giving ourselves facials, using mud packs, wearing fake eyelashes, and wearing girdles, bras, jewelry, high-heeled shoes, and restrictive clothes (cf. Dworkin 1974).

Might it be that men are attracted to women who do these things because these actions communicate the lengths to which women will go to change ourselves in order to win men's approval and love? Are men attracted to women who do these things because such acts communicate to men that women don't think much of our (female) bodies? Recall that male dominance is created and maintained by men convincing women of the superiority of the penis and of the inferiority of the "castrated" female body. The extent to which women change ourselves to make ourselves attractive to men reflects (1) the extent to which women seek to make ourselves acceptable to men, (2) the extent to which women seek to connect to men, and thus (3) the extent to which women feel the need for men's affection and approval and (4) the extent to which women feel unworthy of men's affection and approval *just as we are* (unchanged).

Given that women's primary need is to survive, all needs other than keeping men happy assume secondary importance. To the extent that these secondary needs diminish women's ability to keep men happy, they are denied. For this reason, women as a group are less conscious of our own needs, wants, and perspectives than we are of those of men. Women may not even know what our own needs, wants, and perspectives are (J. Miller 1976), though we can articulate men's feelings with hardly a hesitation. Women's survival depends both on taking care of men's needs and on men *knowing* women are doing this, so that men will (continue to) feel kindly toward women.[9]

Sociologists have reported on the widespread and unreciprocated domestic, sexual, glamor, reproductive, and emotional buffering services which women provide to men as wives (Bernard 1971; Hartmann 1987; Hite 1987). The advantages to men wrought by women's "wifely duties" are so apparent that it is now commonly recognized that everyone (including women) needs a wife. By doing the wash, taking care of the children, fixing dinner, cleaning the house, taking the clothes to the cleaners, buying the groceries, ironing the clothes, staying home for deliveries, ad infinitum, wives look after men's day-to-day needs. In addition, many women bring home a paycheck. For these reasons, men have more leisure time than women (Hartmann 1987).

Oakley (1974) notes that "a study of housework is . . . a study of women's situation" (p. 9). Housewives spend between 3,000 and 4,000 hours a year doing housework. In a review of studies on housework, Hartmann (1987) concluded that 70 percent of housework is done by wives, 15 percent by the children, and 15 percent by husbands. The percentage of housework done by husbands remains approximately the same whether or not the wife is gainfully employed. In addition to engaging in paid employment and in addition to doing the vast majority of the housework, wives do most of the child care, particularly when the children are young or when there are many children. A husband creates an average of 8 hours more housework per week for his wife than he performs. An unemployed wife spends a minimum of 40 hours per week on housework and husband, whereas an employed wife spends a minimum of 30 hours per week. Women of different races, classes, and ethnicities appeared equally responsible for the housework and child care performed.

In addition to all these things which women do to make men's lives more pleasant, all women are expected to "stroke" men, that is, to provide emotional support (Bernard 1971). Women stroke men by continually letting them know women consider them intrinsically better, more expert, stronger, and so on. This keeps men from feeling challenged by us. If men feel competitive with us, they may feel compelled to assert their dominance in violent ways. Women know this, and so, even when a woman is more competent than a man, she strokes him by, for example, putting herself down, building him up, or never mentioning her accomplishments. After all, a threatened man spells D-A-N-G-E-R to a woman.

Looking after men's needs to the neglect of our own occurs even in the most seemingly benign circumstances. If beating him in a game of tennis makes him unhappy, women will often let the man win. If appearing too smart threatens him, women often act dumb. If he wants to show women how to do something, we often let him, even if we already know how to do it. Bernard (1971), citing Mintz (1967), describes a professional woman who went to an annual sociology conference and ran into a male colleague whom she hadn't seen since the last annual conference. The male colleague bought the woman a cocktail and spent their entire time together telling her about his many accomplishments during the previous year. Although she had many accomplishments of her own about which she could have told him, he never asked her about them, and she never offered to tell him about them. It was mutually understood that, because he was a male and she a female, the two of them would spend their time together talking about only his accomplishments, stroking his ego. Bernard (1971, pp. 93–94) asks at what cost to women this stroking is done:

> Her own achievements of the year—papers, research proposal, and book manuscript—now seemed inconsequential. In one brief encounter he had cut her down way below size and built himself up at her expense. Unlike a male peer, she could not elicit the same support from him. Her achievements were not rewarded by appreciative listening on his part. Now they seemed trivial even to her.

Bernard notes another cost as well: "If women must perform the stroking function they are ipso facto disqualified from jobs that require fighting and competing and challenging. It is difficult to be supportive to a competitor or opponent" (p. 94). But Bernard may have missed the point. We propose that it is precisely because women seek to communicate to men the message, "We are not your competitors," that we do this stroking.

A concept known as "the altruistic other orientation" (AOO) was created by Joyce Walstedt (1977) to capture this phenomenon. She developed the construct "to reflect a life-long orientation of self-sacrifice in women, a generalized personality disposition that involves putting men (husbands, lovers, bosses, sons, etc.), but not women, ahead day after day, year after year" (p. 163). Walstedt described the AOO as "a central concept in the psychology of women" (p. 165) and as "a powerful shaper and restrictor of female personality development" (p. 174). She found that women who adopted AOO were less likely to be self-supporting or to have attained as many academic degrees as women who had not adopted it. Still, even those women who did not report an AOO disagreed with the statements, "I rarely perform personal services for my husband such as ironing his shirts, packing his suitcase, folding his socks or sewing on buttons" (73 percent), and "I think a wife should put herself and her job, educational or volunteer work goals first and her husband second" (70 percent).[10]

When men get angry, we assume it is because we have done something wrong, just as abused children feel they were abused because they were bad. Our belief that we, not men, are responsible for men's feelings and behaviors helps us feel we have some control over a situation in which we would otherwise feel powerless. We would rather feel at fault and remain vigilant than acknowledge our powerlessness.

6. Captive Sees the World from the Captor's Perspective. She or He May Not Have Her or His Own Perspective. Captive Experiences Own Sense of Self through the Captor's Eyes

It [is] men alone who could convince women that women are a politically oppressed group.

(Atkinson 1974, p. 39)

Because women's survival depends on knowing how things affect men's moods, we come to experience the world from men's perspectives. Eventually, we are no longer aware of our own feelings, thoughts, and moods; we are only aware of theirs. Several factors facilitate this process. One is that it is advantageous for women to deny our own feelings because they only get in the way of looking after men's feelings, which women must attend to in order to reduce male violence against us. Another factor is women's physical isolation from other women, in large part due to the one-on-one pairing of men and women in physically separate domiciles. Still another factor is women's ideological isolation from any perspective other than that of men, due to male control of communication media such as television, radio, and newspapers. Women's physical and ideological isolation means that we have few reminders of our own perspectives or even of the fact that there might be such a thing. Women's adoption of a male perspective takes many forms, such as the wish to be male/masculine, a preference for male babies, negative feelings about our bodies, lowered expectations of and for women, and lack of feelings of entitlement.

The Wish to Be Male/Masculine

As captives of male violence, we come to see ourselves and other women as men see us (and for this we are labeled narcissistic). For example, most women devalue womanness, even in ourselves, and some even hate it. Although most people prefer being their own sex, females are more likely to want to be males than vice versa (Parsons 1976, cited by Frieze et al. 1978). D. Brown (1957) cites three studies in which adults were asked which sex they would rather have been born as, or whether they ever wished they had been born as the other sex. Brown indicates that only 2½–4 percent of adult males in these polls were aware of ever having wanted to be female, whereas 20–31 percent of adult females were aware of having wished to be male. Another source of evidence about people's identification with their biological sex is the draw-a-person test. In a meta-analysis of nineteen studies using the draw-a-person test, Heinrich and Triebe (1972) found that boys showed a greater tendency than girls to draw a same-sex picture first, beginning around 11 years of age and continuing until 18 years, the last age studied.

Sex-role preference refers to "behavior associated with one sex or the other that the individual would like to adopt, or that he [sic] perceives as the preferred or more desirable behavior" (D. Brown 1956, p. 3). Tests, primarily involving the "It Scale," indicate that boys have a stronger

masculine sex-role preference than girls have a feminine sex-role preference (Brown 1956, 1957; Domash and Balter 1976; Goldman, Smith, and
Keller 1982; Hartup and Zook 1960; Rabban 1950; Ward 1973).[11]

Females' internalization of males' devaluation of femaleness is demonstrated in other ways as well. Girls are more likely to report having
friendships with boys than boys are with girls (Parsons 1976, cited by
Frieze et al. 1978). Boys develop a preference for toys associated with boys
at an earlier age than girls develop a preference for toys associated with
girls (Rabban 1950).[12]

Ambivalence about being feminine is also shown in a study by Bailey,
Hendrick, and Hendrick (1987). Using the Bem Sex Role Inventory (Bem
1974), these researchers found that college students (both male and female) felt its positive masculine traits described them more than its positive feminine traits did. They also found that women are more likely to
perceive themselves as masculine than men are to perceive themselves as
feminine. These findings suggest that females, as well as males, would
rather see themselves as masculine than as feminine.

In one sense, the ambivalence women may feel about being female
reveals an attempt by females to maintain feelings of self-worth by denying our membership in the less valued group (females). Unfortunately,
when expressed in the form of a desire to be male, women's ambivalence
reveals a hatred of our own selves. If women identified men—and not
women's own femaleness—as the source of our oppression, we would
feel ambivalent toward men, not toward women's femaleness. The ambivalence females express about being feminine has the *potential* to become a
form of resistance against patriarchy. To the extent that females resist
being feminine *while still embracing our femaleness,* we challenge cultural
norms of female subordination.

The female "gender-blenders" interviewed by Devor (1989) can help us
see how women's ambivalence about being female usually tends to reinforce patriarchy. These women clearly identified with men. They dressed
like men, and they viewed women as most men view women—inferior.
They showed strong devaluation of femaleness and of the *subordinate
behaviors* assigned to women by the male-dominant culture. Their strong
rejection of the feminine role for themselves was related to their strong
acceptance of the message, presented to them by older family members,

that females are sexual objects, are subordinate, and are deficient in comparison to men.

It is probably impossible for women not to internalize men's denigration of femaleness and femininity to some extent. For example, both the women who adopt the feminine role for themselves and the gender-blenders described by Devor have internalized the notion that females are subordinate. Neither group questions male culture's definition of femaleness and femininity. The gender-blender challenges the belief that *she* is a subordinate but not the belief that women as a group are subordinate (though her dress, if it is known that she is female, *may* challenge the belief that women are feminine). The strongly feminine woman challenges neither. Some research suggests that women with nontraditional sex-role attitudes have internalized negative attitudes toward women more than have women with conventional sex-role attitudes (Nguyen 1993; Weitz 1976). In the same way, lesbian couples who are into butch/femme roles have adopted male notions that every couple should have a dominant and a subordinate (while challenging the notions that the dominant in a couple has to be male and that only men and women can be couples).

Do We Prefer Male or Female Babies?

Do women value other women less than we value men? American women's sex preference ratio of ideal number of sons to daughters is 110, indicating a preference for sons (Westoff and Rindfuss 1974). Do women buy the idea that men should be dominant over us, and that women should learn to play a subordinate role? One way a "yes" to such questions is communicated is in women's preference for a male child as the firstborn. Although women's preference for a firstborn male child is less strong than men's, women as a group very clearly favor a male over a female firstborn child (Dinitz, Dynes, and Clarke 1954; Largey 1972; Markle 1974; Markle and Nam 1971; Matteson and Terranova 1977; Rent and Rent 1977; Teitelbaum 1970; Westoff and Rindfuss 1974; Wood and Bean 1977; see Williamson 1976, for a cross-cultural review of these findings). Women in support of the women's movement have shown less of a preference, however (Calway-Fagen, Wallston, and Gabel 1979; Fidell,

Hoffman, and Keith-Spiegel 1979; Rent and Rent 1977; but see Gilroy and Steinbacher 1983).

Women's Feelings about Our Bodies

Because men threaten women with physical violence *because we are women*, that is, because we have female bodies, women devalue our bodies, and some women even hate them. Ninety percent of individuals suffering from either anorexia nervosa or bulimia are women (Bemis 1978; Druss and Henifin 1979; Halmi, Falk, and Schwartz 1981). Even if a woman does not become anorexic or bulimic, she is still likely to experience negative feelings toward her body. Koff, Rierdan, and Stubbs (1990) found that women, relative to men, were less satisfied with their bodies overall and experienced their bodies less positively. Yet women had more differentiated body images than men, for women's feelings were more variable than men's regarding different parts of their bodies. Mintz and Betz (1986) found that women felt less satisfied than men about their height, weight, breast/chest, hips, thighs, calves, and body build. (It is probably no accident that erogenous areas such as the breasts/chests, hips, and thighs are areas about which women show more dissatisfaction than men.)

Mintz and Betz found that "women reported being on the average 10 pounds *over* their ideal weight while men reported being 3 pounds *under* their ideal weight" (p. 193). These findings are consistent with Societal Stockholm Syndrome theory. Dominants want to be viewed as larger than they are because largeness is associated with power within patriarchy. Subordinates want to be viewed as smaller than they are, because they do not want to threaten dominants and in fact want dominants to find them attractive. Being found attractive by dominants enhances the likelihood of a bond developing with dominants.

Fallon and Rozin (1985) found that, among male college students, their current size (figure) did not differ from the size they most wanted to be, nor did their current size differ from the size the men thought would be most attractive to females. The women college students, on the other hand, perceived their current size as being larger than the size they would like to be, and they rated their current size as larger than the size they thought would be most attractive to men. In fact, on the average, women wanted to be a size that was even thinner than the size they thought men would most find attractive. By comparison, men thought that the size women would find most attractive for them was *heavier* (or less thin) than women's ratings of the size women found most attractive for men.

These findings suggest that women do not feel good about our bodies—that we do not physically want to be who we are. In some cases, the dissatisfaction is so strong as to be life-threatening, as with anorexia nervosa.

Lowered Expectations of and for Women

Women (as well as men) have lower expectations for women than for men. Deaux and Farris (1977) asked male and female research participants to solve either difficult or easy anagrams and told the participants either that males typically perform better at the task or that females typically perform better at the task. Participants were then asked to estimate the number of anagrams they expected to solve. After working to solve the anagrams, participants were asked to rate their success or failure at the task, their ability, the extent to which luck and skill were involved in their solving the anagrams, and their expectations regarding their future performance.

Deaux and Farris found that, before actually working on the anagrams, males predicted that they would do better than the females thought they would do. On the other hand, females more than males felt that it was important for them to perform well. After performing the anagram task, males evaluated their own performance more positively than did females, even though the two sexes performed equally well. Besides perceiving themselves as more successful than the females perceived themselves, the males also perceived themselves as having more ability than the females perceived themselves as having. Females in the failure condition (the condition with the more difficult anagrams to solve) rated their own performance more negatively than males rated the males' performance. Males in the failure condition continued to predict greater success in future performance for themselves than did females. Even though the tasks were actually performed equally well by both sexes, women generally attributed their performance to good or bad luck, men generally attributed their performance to skill, and the tasks were rated as easier by males than by females.

Deaux and Farris note that "the patterns of attributions found in the present studies are quite parallel to those explanations offered by judges of male and female performers in other contexts" (p. 70). More specifically, Deaux and Emswiller (1974) found that other people attribute men's successful performance to ability and women's successful performance to luck.

Research findings such as these indicate that women have bought male culture's message that women are not as competent as men. Women see ourselves as less successful than men when we are actually equally successful; we are more likely than men to attribute our successes to luck, not skill; we believe we must work harder in order to succeed than men believe they have to work; we (more than men) believe that it is more *important* that we succeed; and we believe that we have performed less well than men when in fact we have performed equally well. Having internalized negative cultural messages about the relative worth and capabilities of women and men, women have a steep psychological hurdle to climb before we ever set out to do a task, even when we may perform tasks as well as or better than men.

Lack of Feelings of Entitlement

In general, women are no less satisfied than men are with their jobs and pay, despite the fact that women earn less than men for "objectively similar performance inputs" (Major 1987, p. 125). Also, despite the fact that women know other women are paid less than they deserve, women think that they personally are not underpaid. Similarly, women express no less satisfaction than men do with their marriages, despite the fact that women do more of the household chores, do more child care, and have less say in important decisions than men, even when both husband and wife work full time (Major 1987). Do women believe we *deserve* less than men?

Numerous studies have been carried out in an attempt to understand women's paradoxical responses to employment and pay injustices. The studies typically use an experimental situation in which male and female subjects are asked to do a task in same- or mixed-sex groups. At the end of the task, the subjects are asked to pay either themselves or their partner any amount up to a maximum. In two such studies, Callahan-Levy and Messe (1979) found that females paid themselves less than did male subjects. This sex difference in self-pay occurred at all age levels, from first graders to undergraduate college students. In fact, the older the girls, the less they paid themselves relative to what boys their same age paid themselves![13] The sex difference in self-pay was not due to females feeling they had done a poorer job than males, for there was no difference in the two sexes' self-reported evaluations of their performance (Callahan-Levy and Messe 1979).

Major et al. (1984) asked subjects to count sets of dots in various spatial configurations. Subjects were told, "Our only requirement is that you do as much work as you think is fair for the amount of money we have been able to pay you. The $4.00 is yours to keep regardless of how long you work on the task or how many sets of dots you count" (p. 1406). Females worked longer than males for the $4.00. They also counted more dot sets, counted dot sets correctly more often, and worked more efficiently than men. Despite the fact that women outperformed men on every measure, men and women did not differ in the performance evaluations they gave themselves!

These findings regarding women's feelings of entitlement indicate that, as females, we do not believe our labor is worth as much as men believe theirs is worth. The results therefore suggest that women have internalized male culture's view that women's labor is worth less than men's. Surely this reflects some kind of diminished self-worth in women.

Reviewing the evidence regarding women's lack of feeling of entitlement, women's lowered expectations of and for women, our feelings about our bodies, our preference for male firstborn babies, and our wishes to be male/masculine, we must conclude that women tend to see ourselves and the world from men's perspective. Several writers have noted the tendency of members of oppressed groups to take on an oppressor's perspective. This phenomenon in general is called "false consciousness." In a woman, when the oppressor is male, it is called "male-identification." In women it is also referred to as "not having a voice." "Not having a voice" can mean one has a male perspective or it can mean one doesn't know one's own perspective. The former is evidence of a greater degree of Stockholm Syndrome than the latter. Either is evidence of a lack of sense of self. Because, in a patriarchy, a woman must remain vigilant to men's needs and wants, and because this requires that she look at the world from the male perspective, a woman intent upon surviving is at high risk of losing her sense of self. The sense of self she is most likely to develop is one that is experienced through men's eyes, not her own eyes. The research of Belenky et al. (1986), Gilligan (1982), and Jack (1991) documents the loss of sense of self which many women show in relationships with men in the roles of partner, father, and teacher. On a more positive note, Rowland (1984) found that feminists, unlike antifeminists, wanted to relate to men only if it did not cost them their selfhood and their equality. Still, most women describe feeling empty when we go through periods of not having men in our lives. The depth of this emptiness reveals the extent of women's loss of sense of self.

When members of an oppressed group have their own perspectives, they are said to have a "raised consciousness." When a women has her own perspective, she is said to be "woman-identified." Woman-identification is not the perspective internalized by most women because it is not the perspective of men. Understandably, men are highly critical of woman-identification and of woman-identified women. So are many women. As women work to help ourselves and other women find our own perspectives, it is important that women's taking on of men's perspective not be viewed as a deficit but as an understandable survival strategy.

7. Captive Sees Outside Authorities Trying to Win Her/His Release as "Bad Guys" and Sees Captor as "Good Guy." Captive Sees Captor as Protecting Him/Her

The need to keep men happy, along with women's need to deny the survival-dependent aspects of this need, leads to the apparently strange fact that women take on men's perspective even when it appears counter to our interest to do so. Just as hostages come to feel that the police trying to win their release are the "bad guys" and that their captors are the "good guys," many women paradoxically believe and feel that men, not feminists, have our best interests at heart. This fact has led Alison Jaggar (1983) to argue that "any theory that claims to express the standpoint of women must be able to explain why it is itself rejected by the vast majority of women" (p. 382). Many women side with men against feminists, and many women side with men against lesbians. In fact, women who are antifeminist tend also be antigay (cf. Minnigerode 1976). Thus, many women believe and feel that those persons trying to win our release from male domination and trying to end male violence against women—feminists and lesbians—are the "bad guys" and men are the "good guys."

Most Women's Rejection of Feminism

Feminism is a movement and theory about women, by women, and for women's rights and liberation. A woman's rejection of feminism is a rejection of her own rights. Such a rejection is tantamount to a slave wanting forever to be a slave. Women's rejection of feminism is therefore an example of women taking men's perspective. Korman (1983) found that approximately one-third of single, undergraduate women at a large, southeastern university espoused traditional values, one-third espoused a moderate ideology, and one-third embraced feminist values. But of the women espousing feminist values, only 35 percent saw themselves as a "feminist." Korman conjectured that these findings may indicate women's reluctance to "vocally defend the feminist movement," thereby "smoothing interpersonal relations, particularly male-female relations." She also speculated that "women may be reluctant to call themselves feminists because this might then open them to purposive harassment and abuse concerning their politics and values, from other women as well as men" (p. 438). A study by Jacobson (1979) provides support for this notion. She found that undergraduate women "have mixed feelings about the concept [of women's rights]. On the one hand, they tend to perceive it as somewhat right, rational, feminine, good, and beautiful, while on the other hand, they tend to perceive it as somewhat radical, hostile, biased, argumentative and cold" (p. 368). Jacobson found that college women viewed the term "Equal Rights for Women" most favorably, the terms "Women's Lib" and "Feminism" intermediately, and "Women's Liberation" least favorably. Women viewed these terms as more positive than men did, but also as more argumentative.

Smith and Self (1981) found that even undergraduate women identifying themselves as feminists were unlikely to question male/female relationship issues, such as women asking men for dates, men opening doors for women, and husbands being the heads of households. Still, women college students expressed more positive attitudes toward feminism in 1975 than they did in 1936 (Doyle 1976). In a 1990 national sample, 30 percent of adult American women reported seeing themselves as more feminist than not; 43 percent of adult men saw themselves as more supportive of the women's movement than not (Times Mirror Center for the People and the Press 1990).

Consistent with Stockholm Syndrome theory, most women are not strongly supportive of "feminist issues." For example, women and men are approximately equally supportive of the Equal Rights Amendment (ERA), some polls finding women slightly more supportive and others showing men to be slightly more supportive. Furthermore, there is no evidence that attitudes concerning the ERA affected women's voting behavior more than men's (Mansbridge 1985). And women are no more likely to support female candidates for office than are men (Zipp and Plutzer 1985). Also, men as a group are more likely than women to support abortions for women who do not want children (Shapiro and Mahajan 1986). The so-called "gender gap" has been strongest as regards government policy issues involving the use of violence. Women have been found to hold more negative opinions regarding violent policies than do men (T. Smith 1984).

McGoldrick, Anderson, and Walsh (1989) provide an example of the ways in which women publicly express their lack of support for women's issues. Invitations to attend a 1984 meeting on family therapy were responded to negatively by professional women because only women were invited and the meeting was focused on women's issues. One "leading woman" responded to the invitation by saying there was no need for such a meeting and that "there are no women out there I would be interested in meeting" (p. 3). A second woman rejected the invitation, saying she was not concerned with issues of gender. A third "said she had no 'legitimate excuse' to go off for three days 'with just women'" (p. 3) because she had already been away from her husband too much. Some women were concerned "their male colleagues would be upset with them for attending" (p. 3). Upon attending the meeting, participants realized that, out of a need to protect and defer to men, they had not dealt with gender issues in their professional work. The meeting motivated the women to begin dealing with these issues.

Except with regard to issues of violence and abortion, women's and men's attitudes concerning women's issues are similar. Women are more negative than men about government actions involving violence and, to a lesser extent, women are more negative than men about abortion. Although a sizable minority of women express profeminist attitudes, even they are reluctant to adopt the label of "feminist," apparently because its adoption is viewed as creating unnecessary conflict in relations with men. Even women daring to wear the label of "feminist" have been reluctant to question male-female relations in their own lives. All this strongly suggests evidence of Societal Stockholm Syndrome.

Women's Homophobia

Men benefit from homophobia because heterosexism strengthens the male power structure. Heterosexism says that every man can and should have a woman to take care of him (sexually, domestically, emotionally, etc.). But why do women go along with heterosexism and homophobia?

Heterosexism gives women a stake in patriarchy by giving special privileges (for example, prestige and financial support) to women who put men first, women who appear to be men's willing servants. Because heterosexual relations are one of the few avenues to power available to women within patriarchy, such relations are embraced by most women (Bunch 1983). For many white, middle- and upper-class women, heterosexual relations are "the golden cage"—a prison, but a pleasant prison. For lower-class and/or African-American women, heterosexism provides a group (homosexuals) to whom to feel superior in a world in which they usually feel inferior.

To whom does homosexuality pose a threat? To straight men, male homosexuality represents the threat of men treating other men the way men treat women. Male homosexuality communicates that men can be seen and treated the way women are seen and treated—as rapable. Male homosexuality challenges the notions that persons with a penis should be dominant in relationships and that every man should have a woman to serve him personally and whose personal life he controls.

Lesbianism is threatening to men when lesbians don't put men first; lesbians are not men's domestic, emotional, sexual, or reproductive slaves; lesbians are competitors for women's love, sex, and loyalty; lesbians offer women an alternative to men; lesbians are proof that women don't need men to survive; lesbians model strong, independent women who can do anything a man can do except provide their own sperm to impregnate a woman.

Duley (1986) has noted that, historically and cross-culturally, lesbianism is "morbidified" only when women are sufficiently well off within a culture to be able to actually live apart from men. That is, lesbianism is derogated only when women as a group are sufficiently well off that a woman is able to choose to live with a woman as opposed to a man. Such is the case in current-day American culture. Even now, though, lesbianism is acceptable to men when men believe lesbian sex exists for their titillation (as in pornography and as in forcing women into a *ménage à trois*). Thus, lesbianism is acceptable to men when it doesn't threaten their domination of women and unacceptable to men when it does threaten that domination.

Women's antilesbianism, heterosexism, and homophobia exemplify women taking men's perspective. For women, antilesbianism is self-hating. A woman who is antilesbian is working against her own best interests: she hates women who love and care about other women. She hates women (and probably men) whose lifestyle threatens male domination.

The question for all women, then, is whether we choose to buy into the cultural "morbidification" of lesbianism, further strengthening patriarchy, or whether we choose to support lesbianism as a needed challenge to patriarchy. There are any number of answers we may live in our personal lives, one of which concerns our heterosexual/homosexual practices, and another the extent or degree of our homophobia and heterosexism.

Because women are told our sexuality does not belong to us, but rather to men, most women have not even experimented with non-male-centered forms of sex. For example, Kinsey et al.'s (1953) findings indicated that only a small minority of women aged 20 to 35 years had refrained from sexual intercourse and still fewer had experienced even incidental sexual relations with other women. The findings suggest that only a small proportion of women are challenging male right of access to women's bodies, whether through celibacy or lesbianism.

Strong adherence to sex roles is associated with low levels of same-sex intimacy and with high homophobia among women (and men; Stark 1991). Further, it appears that women's attitudes toward lesbians are as negative as men's (Kite 1984). To the extent that women harbor negative attitudes toward lesbians and lesbianism, we demonstrate identification with men. To the extent that women express negative attitudes toward lesbians in our words and deeds, we strengthen patriarchy. The hesitation of women as a group to endorse feminism and to accept lesbianism and celibacy as valid sexual choices strongly suggests that women have taken on men's perspective to such an extent that we see our oppressors as friends and our actual allies as enemies. These attitudes on the part of women as a group strongly suggest the presence of Societal Stockholm Syndrome.

8. Captive Finds It Psychologically Difficult to Leave Captor Even After Her/His Physical Release Has Been Won

Women's release from male domination and threats of male violence has not been negotiated—unlike many hostages, women do not have outside authorities to bargain for our release. Nor have women yet found a way to prevent or avoid male violence. Nevertheless, if the psychology described in the previous seven sections has developed culturally for women as a group, we propose that women *would* find it extremely psychologically difficult to leave or disengage from men even if we could escape men and their violence forever by doing so.[14] We see six reasons for this.

First, like newly released hostages, women would fear showing any disloyalty to men because, if we did and men later caught up with us, men might not be so kind to women as they were before (that is, this time men might not let women live, or they might show even greater violence toward women). It is easy for women to believe men *would* catch up with us because men's violence has happened in the past and that's proof enough that it could happen again. Women might live the rest of our lives fearful of showing any disloyalty, preparing for the time when men might catch up with us again. If men in the future want women living with them and looking after them, women will feel that living apart from men and not looking after men are forms of disloyalty.

Second, because women have denied our terror, the danger we are in, and our anger, we see no reason to leave men or to psychologically disengage from them. Third, because men have successfully kept women isolated from one another (through male-female pairing, separate domiciles, woman-woman competition, antifeminism, homophobia, and devaluing women), women will find it psychologically difficult to leave or disengage from those to whom we have bonded (men). The more effort women have put into building and maintaining relationships with men, the less likely we will be to walk away from those relationships. Because of the long-term nature of women's isolation, women feel that, without men, we will be alone and further isolated. We feel we will have no one. We do not see relations with other women as an alternative.

Fourth, because women, as a group and as individuals, experience our sense of self through men's eyes, without men we would not know who we are. Without men, what would it mean to be female? Feminine? Attractive? Living apart from men is likely to be experienced as a threat to women's psychic survival. Threats by men to disengage from women would be experienced as threats to our psychic and physical survival. Women might feel that, without men, life isn't worth living. This response itself would reveal the extent to which women experience ourselves through men's eyes. The more lost women feel without men, the more we have defined ourselves through our relationships with men and in relation to men.

Fifth, people resist taking on a new worldview, which a choice to leave or psychologically disengage from men would require of women. Though current conditions are difficult, at least women know what it takes to survive under male domination, whereas new conditions would be unknown and therefore more scary. And sixth, given that male dominance has been held in place through terror, women will have a need to "master" the psychological effects of male domination before being psychologically free of men and of the threat men have created for women. That is, we have an unconscious need to figure out how we got into this mess with men, how we can prevent it happening again, and how we can stop it if it does happen again—whether we choose to be with men or not.

Because of the presence of the four Stockholm Syndrome precursor conditions in most extant cultures, few women have sought to psychologically and/or physically separate from men. (Those who have—for example, separatist lesbian feminists—should be studied to determine how Stockholm Syndrome conditions and psychodynamics differ for them.) As long as these four conditions are in effect, the possibility of separation from men will remain remote for most women.

9. Captive Fears Captor Will Come Back to Get Her/Him Even After Captor Is Dead or in Prison. She or He Fears Thinking Disloyal Thoughts about Captor for Fear of Retaliation

As stated earlier, women as a group have not yet won release from male domination and violence. However, like the released hostage who fears that the captor will return to get him or her—even if that captor is dead or in prison—once release is accomplished, whether by force or diplomacy, women are likely to still fear men's returning to "get us." This fear will ensure that most women, even after our "release" is won, will remain loyal to men. Our loyalty will be manifest as a continuing male-identification. But, as time goes on, and women's feelings of safety increase, women's male-identification is likely to subside, though it probably will never vanish entirely. It is noteworthy that even science fiction writers attempting to imagine women's lives after separation from men have shown how rare and fragile is the absence of such fears (for example, Gearhart 1979; Gilman 1979; Russ 1977).

Conclusion

We have proposed that, to the extent that Graham's nine indicators of Stockholm Syndrome accurately reflect women's psychology, women as a group show evidence of Societal Stockholm Syndrome in our relations with men as a group. The research findings reviewed in this chapter indicate that women as a group show symptoms of ongoing trauma, as reflected in women's fear of males and "mental disorders" (for example, anxiety, depression, eating disorders, borderline personality disorder). Research and everyday observations show that women are bonded to their oppressor group (men)—as revealed in the responses of women to dating violence, the fiction and the "expert" advice provided for women, the contrast between women's and men's love styles, and women's splitting of men into "good men" and "bad men." Women as a group feel too grateful for men's small "kindnesses" and "chivalric" responses. As a group, women deny men's violence toward us and we deny our own anger at men: women's minimization of male violence, our defensive attributions in response to instances of victimization, the "disappearance" of our anger as we grow from girls to women, our inhibition of aggression toward men, our view of anger as dangerously disruptive of relationships, and our directing of aggression onto ourselves, other women, and children—all these point to a pattern of denial. Women show hypervigilance regarding the abuser group's needs in that we are highly alert to nonverbal cues; we unconsciously shape our behavior and opinions to agree with the men with whom we interact; we modify our bodies to suit men's preferences; and we routinely take care of men's domestic needs. Research findings from many sources converge to indicate that women as a group see the world from a male perspective and often lack a female perspective—as revealed by the wish to be male/masculine, a preference for male children, dissatisfaction with the female body, reduced expectations regarding women's competence, and a lack of feelings of entitlement. The degree to which women as a group have taken men's perspective—so that women see men as "the good guys" and those who oppose male domination as "the bad guys"—appears in women's rejection of feminism and women's homophobia. Though women have not yet won release from male domination, there are multiple reasons to believe that women as a group, like hostages and victims of abuse, would find it psychologically difficult to leave our abusers even after release had been won. And, were women to win release from male domination, it appears likely that we, like hostages and victims of abuse, would fear the return of our abusers. The evidence presented here strongly suggests that women's psychology *is* well described by Graham's nine indicators. We suggest, therefore, that Stockholm Syndrome psychodynamics describe women's responses to male violence and structure much of what is referred to as women's psychology, which is a particular psychology of the oppressed. A word of caution is in order, however. The research cited in this chapter was conducted on predominantly white samples. Often the sample was comprised entirely of college students. It is therefore unclear whether the findings generalize to nonwhites and people who are not college students.

In the next chapter we will examine three features of women's psychology that are shaped by the Stockholm Syndrome–conducive conditions to which women are exposed in patriarchy. These three features—femininity, love of men, and heterosexuality—define what it means to be female in patriarchy.

The Beauties and the Beasts: Women's Femininity, Love of Men, and Heterosexuality

In this chapter we ask whether societywide Stockholm Syndrome might account for women's femininity, heterosexuality, and love of (or affection for) men. If Stockholm Syndrome does account for these characteristics in women, the pervasiveness of the four Stockholm Syndrome-conducive conditions in women's lives could account for these characteristics being viewed as "normal" in women. "Expert opinion" (men's opinion) would have us believe that females are inherently feminine, that women are heterosexual because of a genetic command to mate with men and thereby preserve the species or because we lack a penis (Freud 1925), and that therefore it is only "natural" that women love men. Thousands of scientific studies have been carried out for the purpose of proving or disproving that femininity in women and masculinity in men are genetically determined. The fact of most women's heterosexuality and love of men is so taken for granted that few have bothered even to question it. Sigmund Freud is frequently credited as an exception because he attempted to understand how these qualities developed in women, questioning their inevitability.

Recent feminist theoreticians (for example, Benjamin 1988; Chodorow 1978; Dinnerstein 1976) have followed Freud in attempting to account for these otherwise taken-for-granted aspects of women's psychology, though their conclusions differ from his. Freud (1931) saw the development of women's love for men and of heterosexuality as developmental challenges because females as a rule spend their early lives bonded to a female (mother) figure. The development of heterosexuality and love of men requires, then, that females subsequently transfer their affections to a male figure. Freud's answer to this developmental dilemma lay in the penis.

Freud thought that a woman's femininity, love of men, and heterosexuality resulted from her early discovery that she (and other women) lacked a penis. This discovery, he thought, led women to renounce active sexual striving, to turn our affections toward men (away from our mothers), and to wish to have children (and especially sons) in an effort to indirectly gain a penis. Feminist scholars have reinterpreted Freud's theory, arguing that it is not the penis which women long for, but the power of those who have penises (see, for example, Herman, with Hirschman, 1981). Like these earlier feminist scholars, this author recognizes the power differential between men and women as crucial in accounting for women's characteristics, but I take a different route from them, examining the possibility that femininity, heterosexuality, and love of men are women's responses to male threats against female survival. Thus, I do not see women's femininity, love of men, and heterosexuality as biologically determined and thus inevitable. Rather, I see them as the consequences of social conditions characterized by male violence against women, and particularly against women's (physical and psychic) sexual beings.

While these three characteristics of women (femininity, love of men, and heterosexuality) are separable, there is a sense in which all three are essential aspects of women's identity within patriarchal culture. That is, in patriarchy, these three characteristics form the essence of what it means to be female. The behaviors and personality traits we commonly have in mind when speaking about "femininity" clearly are central to feminine identity. But so are heterosexuality and women's love for men. For instance, Bem (1981) has noted that "many societies, including our own, treat an exclusively heterosexual orientation as the *sine qua non* of adequate masculinity and femininity" (p. 361). I would add that love (affection) for men is also an essential ingredient of women's identity as culturally defined (feminine identity). Therefore I will refer to the composite of femininity, women's love for men, and heterosexuality as "feminine identity." This overarching term has the advantage of reminding women that we are bound to feel threatened when the naturalness of any of these three characteristics for women is questioned. We feel threatened because these three characteristics are central to how we see ourselves as individuals.[1] Questioning the naturalness of the three characteristics leads women to question our identities as individuals. As readers proceed through this chapter, I ask you to keep in mind both the reasonableness of the anger and fear that our ideas may arouse, for in fact we are calling the inevitability and the desirability of feminine identity into question.

At this time, psychology as a discipline cannot tell us what a psychology of women would look like under conditions of safety and mutuality between the sexes. Women's behavior, like that of all people, is a function of the context in which it occurs, limited only by the biological parameters of what is possible for the organism. Under conditions of domination, one can expect to see defensive behaviors (cf. Allport 1954; Rawlings and Carter 1977). Under conditions of safety, one would expect to see a very different set of behaviors (for example, authenticity, playfulness, creativity; cf. Hampden-Turner 1971). One of these sets of behaviors should not be considered more "natural" or biologically based than the other. Women are genetically capable of behaving in ways appropriate either for an environment of safety or for an environment of domination. We also are genetically capable of discriminating between different social contexts and of adapting our behavior accordingly. A psychology of women constructed under conditions of safety and mutuality very likely would look very different than the psychology we see in our current culture (cf. Hampden-Turner 1971; Maslow 1966). Ultimately, of course, a comprehensive psychology of women would have to incorporate women's responses to all types of social conditions and cultures. Traditional psychology of (white, middle-class) women provides an extremely narrow picture of women, since it is constructed only under conditions of domination. Also, because these conditions of domination are seen as inevitable (rather than as just one possible set of conditions), the resulting psychology of women makes sex roles look biologically determined rather than socially created.

Currently, while conditions of domination still prevail, we are faced with the task of constructing an *accurate* psychology of women. Women's responses to men's violence against us may be better understood than they have been in the past if we examine the theoretical application of Stockholm Syndrome psychodynamics to women in our relations with men. Examining the influence of male violence on the cornerstones of women's identity—femininity, love of men, and heterosexuality—may also lead to a better understanding of women's psychology. In providing such an examination here, I hope to further the understanding of women's psychology as a psychology of victimization that is socially created, survival-oriented, and changeable.

Femininity

> When a woman uses feminine means she can command a loyalty that no amount of aggression ever could. The experience of women is that the violence men often seek out is terrifying and overpowering, but that by using the feminine means that nature gave her woman can deal with the most powerful man as an equal.
>
> (Goldberg 1974, p. 328)

> Under patriarchal order women are oppressed in [our] very psychologies of femininity.
>
> (Mitchell 1974, p. 414)

> While many claim that there is a feminine principle which must exert itself to counterbalance masculinism pervading world cultures, what they seem to ignore is that the feminine has its origin in masculinist ideology and does not represent a break from it.
>
> (Hoagland 1989, p. 85)

> There is nothing like femininity to dignify one's indignity as one's identity. (MacKinnon 1987, p. 56)

Citizens of countries we view as weaker than us are thought of as feminine. A man who is raped (victimized) by another man is viewed by others as having been made feminine. The more we perceive the raped man as submitting as opposed to actively resisting throughout the rape ordeal, the more femininity we attribute to him. Femininity, then, is attributed to those who are weaker, those who are victims, and those who submit.

Femininity represents the survival strategy of a victim of threatened or actual violence, who, because she or he sees no way to escape or to successfully win in a violent showdown, assumes the role of subordinate. Femininity is also attributed to one who attempts to win over an enemy by inducing that foe to stop its violence and threats of violence. Here I argue that femininity is a blueprint for how to get along with one's enemy by trying to win over the enemy.[2] Femininity is a Stockholm Syndrome response.

At the core of Stockholm Syndrome are terror and the cognitive distortions that serve to aid victims in dealing with terror. Such distortions are associated with Stockholm Syndrome and perhaps give rise to the syndrome or permit it to develop (see chapter two). Having adopted femininity, and thus Societal Stockholm Syndrome, as our survival strategy, women are actively denying the facts of our subordination: the danger that men pose to women, the fact that femininity *is* a survival strategy for us within the context of terror created by that male violence, the fact that we *are* subordinates of men and victims of male violence. Our denials of these facts constitute cognitive distortions. These cognitive distortions help women manage our terror and help us hang on to the hope that, if we can just love men enough, men will bond with us, stop terrorizing us, and treat us with love, not violence and threats of violence.

In the remainder of this section, we examine evidence bearing on the above conceptualization of femininity: that the term "femininity" refers to personality traits associated with subordinates and to personality traits of individuals who have taken on behaviors pleasing to dominants.

In 1951 Helen M. Hacker compared the castelike status of women to that of African-Americans ("Negroes"). (See table 5.1.) She argued that characteristics ascribed to both African-Americans and to women (for example, childlike behaviors, inferiority, acting helpless or weak) were due to oppression rather than being innate traits. Thirty years later, Hacker (1981) reviewed her 1951 paper and decided that her earlier observations were still applicable to women.

Both women and "Negroes" were identified by Hacker as having *adopted* behaviors such as acting weak and helpless, appearing to have inferior intelligence,[3] behaving more emotional and childlike, appearing as inferior or weaker, and having a deferential or flattering manner. Examining this composite of behaviors leads one to realize that people who adopt such behaviors are considered feminine. Hacker's observations

TABLE 5.1
Castelike Status of Women and Negroes

Negroes	Women
I. HIGH SOCIAL VISIBILITY	
a. Skin color, other "racial" characteristics.	a. Secondary sex characteristics.
b. (Sometimes) distinctive dress—bandana, flashy clothes	b. Distinctive dress—skirts, etc.
2. ASCRIBED ATTRIBUTES	
a. Inferior intelligence, smaller brain, less convoluted, scarcity of geniuses.	a. Ditto
b. More free in instinctual gratifications. More emotional, "primitive" and childlike. Imagined sexual prowess envied.	b. Irresponsible, inconsistent, emotionally unstable. Lacking strong super-ego. Women as "temptresses."
c. Common stereotype: "inferior."	c. "Weaker."
3. RATIONALIZATIONS OF STATUS	
a. Thought all right in his place.	a. Woman's place is in the home.
b. Myth of contented Negro.	b. Myth of contented woman; "feminine" woman is happy in subordinate role.
4. ACCOMMODATION ATTITUDES	
a. Supplicatory whining, intonation of voice.	a. Rising inflection, smiles, laughs, downward glances.
b. Deferential manner.	b. Flattering manner.
c. Concealment of real feelings.	c. "Feminine wiles."
d. Outwit "white folks."	d. Outwit "menfolk."
e. Careful study of points at which dominant group is susceptible to influence.	e. Ditto
f. Fake appeals for directives.	f. Appearance of helplessness
5. DISCRIMINATIONS	
a. Limitations on education—should fit "place" in society.	a. Ditto.
b. Confined to traditional jobs—barred from supervisory positions. Their competition feared. No family precedents for new aspirations.	b. Ditto.
c. Deprived of political importance.	c. Ditto.

Negroes	Women
d. Social and professional segregation.	d. Ditto.
e. More vulnerable to criticism.	e. E.g., conduct in bars.

6. SIMILAR PROBLEMS

a. Roles not clearly defined, but in flux as result of social change.	a. Ditto.

Reprinted from *Social Forces*, 30 (October 1951). "Women as a minority group" by H. M. Hacker. Copyright © The University of North Carolina Press.

suggest that the concepts of oppression and femininity have a great deal in common.

Hacker is not the only writer who has observed similarities between the psychology of women and that of other oppressed groups. Characteristics of dominants and subordinates are identified by Miller (1976) in her book about the effects of subordination on women's psychology. Also, characteristics of the more and less powerful are identified by sociologist Jean Lipman-Blumen (1984). Parallels between psychological characteristics of the oppressed and women's psychology are apparent in these writers' works, indicating that women's psychology *is* a psychology of the oppressed. They also make apparent that those behaviors which male culture classifies as "feminine" are behaviors that one would expect to characterize any oppressed group.

Besides being associated with femininity, the behaviors, feelings, and perceptions that Miller and Lipman-Blumen view as characterizing the less powerful are also aspects of Stockholm Syndrome. For instance, Lipman-Blumen (1984) points out that the less powerful, of necessity, resort to indirect influence attempts such as use of intelligence, canniness, intuition, interpersonal skill, charm, sexuality, deception, and avoidance. Howard, Blumstein, and Schwartz (1986) found that indirect influence tactics were more often used by persons who had less power in a relationship. Similarly, Miller (1976) argues that subordinates become highly attuned to dominants, learning what pleases and displeases them. "Feminine intuition" and "feminine wiles" are skills developed for these purposes. (The reader may recognize these characteristics as "captive denies own anger at captor" and "captive is hypervigilant to captor's needs, wants, and desires" within a Stockholm Syndrome conceptualization.) Miller goes on to point out that, because subordinates need to please dominants in order to survive, subordinates know more about dominants than they know about themselves. A result of this discrepancy between subordinates' self-knowledge and other-knowledge is that subordinates come to believe the dominants' claim that subordinates are incapable, and to believe other "untruths" created by the dominants that help the dominants maintain power. (The reader will recognize these characteristics as one of the nine major indicators of Graham's Stockholm Syndrome: "captive takes captor's perspective.")

Each year we ask half the students in our Psychology of Women classes (most of whom are women) to provide word associations to the words "masculine" and "feminine" and ask the other half, working independently, to provide associations to the words "dominant" and "subordinate." (We invite the reader to do this too before reading any further. A word association is the first word that comes to mind when one thinks of, say, "masculine." You should not stop to analyze your associations as you write them down. Nor should you censor or revise terms. Rather, you should write down as many words as you can think of in as short a time as possible. Now, write down all the associations you have for each of the four terms: masculine, feminine, dominant, and subordinate. Generate all the word associations you can for the first term before moving on to the second term. Keep separate the associations for each of the four terms.)

Students are consistently surprised by the outcome. Students' word associations to "masculine" and "dominant" are often identical ("strong," "powerful," "in control," "courageous," "has money and status," "leader," "aggressive," "competitive," "strong-minded"). Likewise, word associations to "feminine" and "subordinate" are often identical ("weak," "small," "dependent," "insecure," "non-assertive"). However, the students notice that, when the associations are similar but not identical, they tend to be more positive for the word "feminine" than for the word "subordinate." For example, associations to "feminine" but not to "subordinate" include "nice," "caring," "intuitive," "sensitive," and "flexible." Word associations to "subordinate" but not to "feminine" include "indecisive," "passive," "handicapped," "fearful," "captive," "intimidated," "oppressed," "suppressed," and "puppet."

Interestingly, when we have varied this task and asked students to generate word associations for the terms "feminine" and "victim," we have obtained similar findings. In many instances, common terms are associated with both words. When word associations differ for the two terms, the associations to the word "feminine" tend to be more positive than those to the word "victim."

We view the positive associations to the word "feminine" to refer to (Societal) Stockholm Syndrome strategies for interacting with dominants. Being nice, caring, intuitive, sensitive, and flexible help ensure that interactions of subordinates with dominants go smoothly. As discussed in chapter 4, we propose that oppressed group members adopt such behaviors in order not to threaten dominant group members.

The negative associations to the word "subordinate" emphasize lack of power and the negative effects on subordinates of such lack of power (e.g., passive, handicapped, fearful, captive). The differences in word associations to "feminine" and "subordinate" suggest that the students do not view positive traits such as caring and sensitivity as responses to being, for example, fearful and captive. Thus, this observed difference in word associations suggests that the students deny that hostile conditions producing subordination may generate positive, feminine, Stockholm Syndrome characteristics. Such denial would be consistent with Societal Stockholm Syndrome.

The relevance to women of the negative words associated with the word "subordinate" was uncovered in chapter 4, where it was shown that women as a group are more depressed, anxious, and fearful than men. Moreover, women were found to act less aggressively and both to be more likely to deny anger at others and attribute our successes to luck, not skill, than men. These findings suggest that the negative terms students associate with the term "subordinate" do in fact apply to women as a group. That is, women *are* more fearful, intimidated, and handicapped compared to men, feeling, for example, that we must do more than men for the same amount of pay yet feeling that we are unable to express our anger for fear of men's retaliation.[4] If women as a group are subordinate to (captives of) men as a group, we would expect women to have such a psychology. The work of Jeanne Block (1976) sheds further light on the fact that, for females, the psychology of subordination is similar to the psychology of femininity in its positive (Societal Stockholm Syndrome) aspects. In particular, Block's summary of research on sex differences suggests that the behavior of females *is* described by both the negative characteristics attributed to subordinates by students and the positive characteristics attributed to femininity. Viewed more broadly, Block's findings offer additional support for the conclusion that masculinity and femininity are code words for male domination and female subordination.

In an article criticizing Maccoby and Jacklin's (1974) interpretation of sex-difference findings, Block summarized the existing psychological literature on sex differences. In the studies analyzed by Block, the subjects' ages spanned from childhood to adulthood. In 55 percent of 94 studies, males showed significantly more aggressiveness than females (vs. 5 percent in which females showed more aggressiveness), and in 39 percent of 89 studies, males showed more dominance (vs. 5 percent for females). These findings support the contention that males play the role of abuser, aggressor, or captor (since victims do not stick around to be aggressed against unless they cannot escape). Given this greater show of dominance and aggressiveness, it is not surprising that males also showed more strength and potency of self-concept, greater confidence on task performance, and more curiosity and exploration. More specifically, in 88 percent of eight studies males showed significantly more strength and potency of self-concept than females. In none of the eight studies did females show more. Also, in 76 percent of 33 studies, males showed significantly greater confidence on task performance than females. Again, in none of the studies did females show greater confidence than males. Finally, in 55 percent of 94 studies, males showed significantly more curiosity and exploration, whereas in only 16 percent of these studies did females show more. To sum up, females were found to be less dominant and aggressive than males and to show poorer self-concept, less confidence, and less curiosity and exploration. Besides being characteristics of females, these are also *feminine* characteristics. The reader may notice that these female-typical findings are consistent with the word associations students in our classes made to both the terms "feminine" and "subordinate."

The *social* characteristics which were more prevalent in females were those expected of a hostage, captive, or victim: fear, timidity, and anxiety, social desirability, compliance and rule following, dependency, suggestibility, and sociability. Block discovered that in 46 percent of 79 studies females demonstrated significantly more fear, timidity, or anxiety; in none of the studies did males show significantly more of these characteristics. In 78 percent of 9 studies females were significantly more concerned than males with social desirability; again, in none of these studies did males show significantly more concern. In 51 percent of 51 studies females showed significantly more compliance and rule following than males, who showed significantly more in only 2 percent of these studies. Females showed more dependency (32 percent vs. 11 percent in 88 studies), suggestibility (28 percent vs. 17 percent in 215 studies), and sociability (28 percent vs. 17 percent in 215 studies) than males. These social characteristics are similar to word associations made by students to the term "subordinate" but not to the term "feminine," suggesting that such characteristics are culturally *denied* aspects of feminine behavior. Is there a cultural need to obscure the relationship between femininity and negative traits attributed to subordinates?

A sex difference in "nurturance, maternal behavior, helping, donating, and sharing" was also found: females demonstrated more of these qualities in 17 percent of 58 studies while males showed more in 12 percent of the 58. Although the latter finding is in the expected direction, it is not as great a difference as might be as expected in light of the other differences. The reader may notice that these behaviors are similar to the more positive words that students associated with the term "feminine" but not with the term "subordinate."

These sex-typical characteristics identified by Block suggest that there is much more commonality between the words "feminine" and "subordinate" than students' words associations would suggest. Consistent with this notion, Howard et al. (1986) found femininity was associated with having less power in a relationship. To the extent that feminine, subordinate, and oppressed group characteristics are similar, we feel compelled to ask whether conditions of hostility, oppression, and subordination produce feminine behaviors in subordinates. Stockholm Syndrome theory argues affirmatively and specifies the conditions under which femininity is engendered. These conditions are the four Stockholm Syndrome-conducive conditions of perceived threat to survival, perceived inability to escape, perceived kindness, and isolation. Societal Stockholm Syndrome theory further suggests that such feminine behaviors constitute survival strategies designed to improve the chances of hostage (female) survival.

Sara Hoagland (1989, pp. 69–70), feminist philosopher, has taken a similar position, noting that

> when people begin to talk about the importance of altruism and self-sacrifice, it indicates they perceive an inherent conflict of interests among those involved. . . . Further, to resolve the conflict of interests, those with lesser institutional power will be expected to be altruistic. In this respect, altruism and self-sacrifice are considered "feminine virtues." 'Femininity' is a concept which makes female submission to male domination seem natural and normal. A such, the "feminine virtues" function to preserve the relationship of dominance and subordination, facilitating the access of those with greater institutional power to the resources of those with lesser institutional power.

Empirical support for the position that the more positive traits associated with femininity (e.g., sensitivity, caring) are responses to subordination and oppression is provided by a study by Snodgrass (1985). Using mixed sex and same-sex dyads, Snodgrass found that whether one played a dominant (teacher) versus subordinate (learner) role in a teacher/student task determined how sensitive one was to the other's feelings. The task involved one student (the dominant) teaching another student (the subordinate) sign language. The student who was the learner would later be tested on what she or he had learned. Snodgrass found that subordinates, whether male or female, were more sensitive than dominants to the other's feelings and thoughts. Further, subordinates' sensitivity was to how dominants were perceiving them as subordinates. The more the subordinate saw himself or herself as a subordinate, the stronger was this effect. This finding led Snodgrass to conclude that "it is the subordinate role (especially when the subordinates perceive themselves as subordinate) that leads to greater sensitivity to the feelings and thoughts of the other person" (p. 152). Although males were not differentially affected by the gender of the person with whom they were interacting, females were. Whether the female functioned as dominant or as subordinate, she was most sensitive when interacting with a male and least sensitive when interacting with a female. Of all the dyad combinations examined (male-male, female-female, or mixed sex), the most sensitivity to dominants' feelings and thoughts were obtained in the female subordinate/male dominant condition. The least sensitivity was observed in the female subordinate/female dominant condition. Snodgrass notes, "This finding casts doubt on the existence of 'women's intuition'" (p. 151). Women's intuition is actually subordinate's intuition or feminine intuition, since femininity is associated with subordinate status.

Snodgrass's study involves a seemingly innocuous situation in which one college student teaches another college student, a stranger, sign language, a skill on which the learner will later be tested. Still, one sees the feminine trait of sensitivity to another's feelings and thoughts change in ways consistent with Stockholm Syndrome theory. More to the point, the amount of sensitivity (hypervigilance) shown by the learner, as subordinate, was directly proportional to the degree of subordination the person perceived herself or himself to be experiencing. These findings provide support for the proposition made here that the more positive feminine traits of sensitivity, caring, and so on, are caused by (perceived) conditions of subordination or oppression.

Recall that in chapter 1, Symonds (1982) was reported to have found that hostages, feeling overwhelmed during their captivity, automatically respond to captors with appeasement, submission, ingratiation, cooperation, and empathy. That is, under conditions of threat to survival, and seeing no way to escape, captives use these feminine behaviors in an effort to win over their captors and thus survive. Recall also that, in the same chapter, Turner (1990) advised potential hostages to help their captors both maintain hope and stay calm. Also, McClure (1978) advised potential hostages to neutralize the captor's hostility, try to come across as a person (as opposed to, say, a representative of an enemy nation), draw out the captor about his/her personal life, point out to captor parallels between the captor's life and one's own life, control the extent of one's identification with the captor, and then let the captor know you take him or her seriously but don't be too submissive. Essentially, Turner's and McClure's advice to hostages is to take responsibility for both the captor's feelings and the smooth functioning of the captor-captive relationship. These experts were advising hostages, then, to behave in a (prosocial) feminine manner without overdoing it and without becoming an emotional satellite of the captor.

In general, then, the psychological sequelae (behavior, emotions, attitudes, perceptions) associated with Stockholm Syndrome, femininity, and oppression are quite similar. This is because, we would argue, the psychologies associated with Stockholm Syndrome and femininity are products of oppression. And, we would argue, they are constructed by similar environmental conditions: perceived threat to survival, perceived inability to escape, some show of kindness, and isolation.

While the psychology of *any* oppressed group shares many of the features described above by Hacker, Lipman-Blumen, and Miller (assuming the presence of the four Stockholm Syndrome-conducive conditions), variations can be expected. That is, particular aspects of men's oppression of women lead to peculiar forms of domination. The fact that inclusion in the oppressed group "women" is based on anatomical sex characteristics ensures that the oppression of women takes the form of sexual violence, (obsessive) concern with women as sexual objects, and (compulsive) male-female sexual relations that emphasize men's domination of women. Therefore, because the term "femininity" has been used prototypically by male culture to refer to the (submissive) behaviors of females, and because the oppression of women but not generally other groups has taken a sexualized form, the concept of "femininity" is imbued with sexual connotations which the concepts of "oppression" and Stockholm Syndrome generally lack.

The peculiar forms of this oppression in turn shape the character of women's response to their victimization. Like the female child who is raped by her father and then becomes promiscuous as an adult—feeling that she has worth only as a body capable of giving men pleasure—women as a group believe we must win men's favor through our bodies and that our primary worth is as physical beings who bring men pleasure. Women whose actions are consistent with these beliefs are viewed by male culture as feminine. Therefore, while the psychology of women generally resembles the psychology of other oppressed groups, in many ways it also is, as is the psychology of femininity, idiosyncratic to an oppression that is sexually and anatomically based.

To the extent that femininity is a psychology of the oppressed, or an indication of Societal Stockholm Syndrome, we are forced to ask whether women should support our culture's glorification of "feminine qualities."

It is one thing to be feminine in order to survive when you know why you are doing what you are doing; it's another thing to celebrate femininity as proof of one's womanhood.

However, we do recommend that women understand femininity's function and the role that it plays in our survival in a patriarchy. Contempt is publicly expressed for battered women who stay with their partners and each day use every ounce of ingenuity they possess to keep their abusers from becoming (emotionally and physically) violent. Perhaps we would see the similarities between battered women and women in general if we understood the *function* that femininity plays in subordinates. Could it be that all women in a patriarchy are battered women and that our femininity is both our strategy for surviving and the proof of our oppression (if proof other than men's violence against us were needed)? Perhaps there is no difference in kind—only in degree—between the behavior of women who are feminine in their relations with men and the behavior of battered women who defer to their abusive partners and protect their partners from prosecution for violence against them. Members of both groups generally experience their behaviors as internally motivated. Most women believe we are inherently feminine by virtue of our biology (forgetting all the times our mothers had to remind us to "act like a lady"), or we believe that we would choose to wear makeup, curl our hair, and wear high heels even if men didn't find women who dressed this way more attractive. Similarly, most battered women who cannot find a way to leave their partners believe that they stay because they choose to (forgetting the impact of their partners' threats to kill them if they leave). For members of either group to believe differently, we would need to acknowledge the external variables controlling our behavior—and thus would need to acknowledge our terror. Public opinion (which reflects the male perspective) strengthens these female beliefs, for it is publicly thought that both women in general and battered women *desire* to relate to men as we do, submitting to men and looking after them even to the point of neglecting our own needs.

Just as we do not recommend that women merely glorify femininity, so we do not recommend that femininity merely be rejected. Societal Stockholm Syndrome theory explains how femininity is socially constructed. Simply because femininity is a response to abuse does not mean that some of the traits labeled as feminine are not sources of strength or desirable qualities. After all, femininity has helped women to survive, and this is proof enough of its desirability. However, women need critically to examine feminine qualities in terms of their costs and benefits and, on the basis of the findings, consciously decide which ones we want to retain, which we want to modify, and which we want to discard. Because the costs and benefits of behaviors change as social conditions change, we also need to identify the social conditions (for example, safety versus threat) under which we desire to retain, modify, or discard various feminine qualities. A feminine quality such as nurturance might be more beneficial than costly under conditions of mutuality but more costly than beneficial under conditions of subordination.

Another thing women need to consider in making decisions about retaining, modifying, or discarding feminine qualities is that feminine behaviors may have qualitatively different characters when expressed in coercive versus noncoercive environments. For example, if social conditions changed from male domination to equality, women might continue to be more concerned about personal appearance than men but might dress to please ourselves rather than men.

A reevaluation of femininity also would cast nonfeminine ("masculine" or nontraditional) women in a different light. Why have mental health professionals chosen to see masculine women as less mentally healthy than feminine women (Broverman et al. 1970; Waisberg and Page 1988) even though research indicates the opposite (Bem 1975) and even though the same masculine characteristics are viewed as healthy when they occur in men (Broverman et al. 1970)? That is, why are the same characteristics psychologically healthy for one sex but not for the other?

Why have men found unfeminine women unattractive? Why are men attracted to feminine women? What fears, if any, do we have about men seeing us as unfeminine? Do we fear they will reject or abandon us? Why do men's accusations that unfeminine women are lesbian strike fear into our hearts? Coming at the issue from another direction—how are strong, nonfeminine women able to emerge in patriarchy? What is the impact of these women's behavior on men's treatment of women in general? Are the negative attitudes many women express toward these strong women the result of their fears that men may treat all women badly if men are threatened by strong, nonfeminine women? Or are the negative attitudes toward these women an example of women adopting men's perspectives as our own? What is the impact of these women's behavior on women? Do they stir up repressed feelings of rebelliousness against male tyranny? Do they remind women of our strength?

While it is understandable why men would extol femininity as next to godliness in women, it is more difficult to understand why women play the role of "sex-role gatekeepers," so that in a thousand different ways we encourage or even chide one another to be feminine. Have women so bought the abuser's line that we are doing his dirty work for him, ensuring women's continued submission—or are women benevolently teaching one another how to survive in a patriarchal culture—or both? And if we are teaching other women how to survive in a patriarchy, could we teach ourselves and one another a different way of surviving, a way that would not strengthen our oppression?

Analysis of the role played by femininity in patriarchy arouses fear and raises questions generated by those fears. For example, if male violence is ended, is femininity likely to disappear? And would that mean the disappearance of feminine qualities such as sensitivity, empathy, and nurturance? If women stopped being feminine, would men love us even less than they do now? If men stopped loving women, would we be left all alone? And wouldn't women lose access to men's money, power, and prestige? If men no longer loved women, would women be able to survive? Would we even want to? If women stopped being feminine, would we be giving away a source of power (for example, "feminine wiles") without getting another source of power to replace our femininity? Wouldn't we then be truly powerless? If women stopped being feminine, would men be more likely to abuse us? Once men *did* begin abusing us, how might women convince them to stop if we no longer used our feminine wiles? If women stopped being feminine, would we know who we were (since femininity is a central aspect of most women's identity) or even know how to interact with the world? And would the world respond to women in a way that is better or worse than the way it responds now? Would women start acting like men? If male violence stopped and/or women stopped being feminine, would women victimize others as we have been victimized?

It is scary for women to contemplate no longer being feminine. However, it need not remain scary. Therapists know that when a person examines her *feelings* about an issue, the course of action she needs to take for herself becomes readily clear to her. That clarity appears to come without effort once people know what it is that is scaring them and why. There is every reason to believe that if women examine what it is about giving up our femininity that scares us and *why* it scares us, we will know whether we need to keep our femininity, change it in some way so that it might be more useful, or give it up. Furthermore, the forces that are controlling women's feelings and behaviors through fear will no longer have their power, giving women more control of our lives than we now have.

Women's Love of Men

Two major themes appear to organize women's lives: the theme of violence against us (through pornography, rape, incest, wife abuse, etc.; Daly 1978; Dworkin 1974), and the theme of the need for connection (Jordan et al. 1991; Miller 1976). In reviewing the treatment of women by men, Atkinson (1974) observed: "Perhaps the most damning characteristic of the class of women is that, in the face of horrifying evidence of [our] situation, [we] stubbornly claim that, in spite of everything, [we] 'love' [our] Oppressor" (p. 105). Without the explanation provided by an account of Stockholm Syndrome psychodynamics, it is hard to understand why women want to be feminine and even harder to see why we insist that we love men, the gender that is more violent toward us.

We propose that women's need for connection and our love for men grow out of needs for protection and safety resulting from a deep-seated fear of male violence. By this, we do not mean that women would not love men or want to connect with others if male violence against women did not exist. But, in a world that is safer for women, would not desire (vs. need) for connection and love quite possibly have psychologically healthier and less desperate qualities?

Women's Need for Connection

In this section we will address the following questions: Do women seek to connect with others more than do men? If so, is this need to connect a response to male violence?

Do Women Seek to Connect with Others More Than Do Men?

Throughout chapter 4 we can find numerous examples that confirm that women's need for connection is greater than men's. In the section on "captive denies own anger," for example, we observed that women, compared to men, expressed more concern for the disruptive effects of anger and aggression on relationships. In the section on "captive bidirectionally bonds to captor," we noted that women's love styles are more communal while men's are more exploitative. We also pointed out in that section that women are held primarily responsible for the maintenance of relationships. In the section "captive is hypervigilant to the needs, wants, and desires of the captor," we discovered that women are willing to drastically change their self-presentations to make social interactions go more smoothly. We also learned that although women are better at decoding others' expressions than are men (Hall 1987), in real-life interactions we use this skill primarily when interacting with men (Snodgrass 1985).

While many other examples appear in chapter 4, we hope that our brief allusion to a few of them will suffice to remind the reader, who has followed the threads of our argument to this point, that need for connection is indeed a prominent feature of women's psychology. Women's need for connection, in contrast to men's need for separation and autonomy, is the cardinal theme of some of the most well-known writings on the psychology of women (e.g., Belenky et al. 1986; Chodorow 1978; Gilligan 1982; Jordan et al. 1991).

The works of Gilligan (1982), of Belenky et al. (1986), and of the Stone Center group (e.g., Jordan et al. 1991) point out the extent to which women, but not usually men, define ourselves through relationships. The reader is encouraged to listen closely to these scholars, for although their language implies that women seek connection with *people,* close observation reveals that it is actually connection to men and men's approval that the women they describe so desperately seek. This is important because it exposes that need for connection and approval are not general female traits. Rather, women look to men in particular as the source from which we hope to gain satisfaction of these needs. This specificity suggests that there is something about male-female relations (and possibly male violence against women in particular) that creates women's need for connection and approval. In fact, the descriptions of woman-woman interactions described by the Stone Center group and by Belenky et al., like those by Hite (1987), reveal that women actually *find* connection and support in our relations with other women (though we *look for* such connection and support from men), and that woman-woman relations differ dramatically from women's relations with men, where the needs for connection and approval are rarely satisfied (cf. Chodorow 1978). Confirming these observations, Wheeler, Reis, and Nezlek (1983) found that, among both sexes, loneliness decreased as one spent more time with females, but *increased* as one spent more time with males.

The Stone Center group uses insights from psychoanalysis, psychotherapy, and research on women's psychology in their ongoing efforts to construct a theory of women's self-identity from a positive, female-centered perspective. Reaffirming traditional female values of empathy, nurturance, and connection, the Stone Center writings contrast with male-oriented theories of development that correlate maturity with separation and autonomy (i.e., masculinity) and, thus, portray women as deficient. Women's sense of self is characterized as "self-in-relation," which can be described as a sense of self "organized around being able to make and then maintain affiliation and relationships" (Miller 1976, p. 83). While being sympathetic with the Stone Center's efforts to create a psychology of women based on women's experiences and while impressed with the richness of many of their clinical case examples, the current author finds problems with their analysis. My main quarrel with the Stone Center theorists is that, in articulating the self-in-relation theory, they ignore the broader social context of violence in which women's psychological development takes place. This seems strange since one of the leading theorists in the group, Miller (1976), has produced an insightful analysis of the psychological consequences of oppression in dominants and subordinates.

While Gilligan, Belenky et al., and the Stone Center group have not examined women's relationships within the framework of Stockholm Syndrome, their findings nevertheless support such a conceptualization. The theory of Societal Stockholm Syndrome not only provides a social context for viewing the findings of these clinicians and researchers but also provides a set of psychodynamics for conceptualizing women's attachments with men.

Is Women's Greater Need to Connect a Response to Male Violence?

In this section we will try to answer this question. Evidence for this thesis comes from a variety of sources. The reader is once again reminded of the observations of Symonds (1982) regarding hostage's responses to captors and how the behaviors appear to be in the service of creating a bond with the captor and thus for the sake of surviving. The reader will also recall that McClure (1978) advises potential hostages to present themselves to captors as people and to ask captors questions about their lives, their families, and so on. Obviously, these recommendations are in the service of creating a bond with the captor and are directed toward that end. McClure makes these recommendations because the creation of such a bond increases the likelihood of captors permitting hostages to survive. It is easy to see that hostages or victims have a greater need to connect to, and thus create a bond with, persons (captors or abusers) who hold the victims' lives in their hands than to connect to persons who do not. We propose that the same is true for women: women bond with men for the purpose of inhibiting men's aggression against us.

In reviewing research findings regarding the effects of observing violence, Franzblau (1979) uncovered evidence that girls respond differently to observed violence than boys. While males more readily imitated the violence they observed, the girls more often cried, leading researchers to drop them from studies, and, when given the opportunity, they more often responded in prosocial ways. Franzblau proposes that this tendency for girls to react prosocially in response to observed violence may increase with age.

The above findings support the thesis that women's need to connect to men is a response to male violence against women as a group. How might women's continuing efforts to connect with others and to promote positive relations with others help us to avert male violence? Aries (1987) notes, "The interactions of men can be characterized as more task-oriented, dominant, directive, hierarchical; and women's as more social-emotional, expressive, supportive, facilitative, cooperative, personal, and egalitarian" (p. 170). That women's discourse style encourages men not to view us as their competitors is made apparent by the finding that men in mixed-sex groups alter their own discourse style to be more like women's and thereby increase "the frequency of supportive, personal interaction" and decrease "combativeness" (p. 160). Thus, women's communication style appears to decrease the combativeness and threat to dominance which men apparently experience when interacting with other men.

Societal Stockholm Syndrome theory helps us to understand gender differences in discourse style. Men's discourse style helps to maintain a dominance hierarchy and to provide men status within that hierarchy. Women's discourse style functions both to communicate to men that women are not in battle with men for dominance and to build a bridge to men—a bridge whose purpose is to eliminate violence from male/female interactions and to encourage the men with whom women are interacting to protect those women from other men's violence as men strive for dominance.[5]

Like me, Shuntich and Shapiro (1991) question whether "affection can be used as an aggression control strategy" (p. 283). The authors found that when one member of a dyad expressed affection, the receiver of this communication was less likely to respond with an aggressive message. This relation was stronger for female-female dyads than for male-male dyads. However, "when the data from the male-female dyads [*sic*] examined separately, males seemed more likely to have lower levels of aggression when their partner was more affectionate" (p. 296). Thus it appears that female expressions of affection tend to reduce the frequency of aggressive communications by male partners in a dyad. However, this strategy, if it is a strategy of females, works more effectively with other females than with males.

Miller and others in the Stone Center group believe that women's desire for connection is a quality that women would want to keep, whether under conditions of subordination or of mutuality. But much of women's desire for connection, as described by Miller and others of this group, appears to be rooted in male-female relationships that lack reciprocity, respect for the woman's needs and feelings, and positive valuation of the woman.

For example, observations by Belenky et al. (1986) and Stiver (1991) both suggest girls develop such a Stockholm Syndrome response to their fathers and provide indications of why this occurs. Belenky et al. report that fathers are more likely than mothers to reject the daughter if she holds an alternative viewpoint. Rejection of a child because her viewpoint differs from those of the parents *is* a form of psychic violence, inhibiting the growth of an independent sense of self.[6] Stiver argues that fathers' psychic violence leads daughters to attach earlier and more intensely to fathers than do boys, even though fathers prefer sons and are more responsive to boys earlier. Stiver proposes, "This observation may account in part for the little girls' yearning and struggles to capture the interest and attention of their fathers in order to feel loved by them" (p. 111).

Miller (1991) observes that developmentally girls develop "a sense of self who must defer to others' needs or desires" (p. 20) and that the Stockholm Syndrome psychodynamics (to use our language) continue as the girl reaches adolescence and becomes involved in heterosexual relationships. Although, Miller proposes, women may yearn for an identity of "being-in-relation," which means "developing all of one's self in increasingly complex ways, in increasingly complex relationships," she acknowledges, "In the current situation, however, it still tends to mean for women the old kind of relationship [with men], with the suppression of the full participation of the woman's way of seeing and acting" (p. 22).

If women's need for connection is indeed rooted in male violence, it seems questionable, then, whether a desperate, obsessive need for connection, of the type currently seen in women's relations with men (see Belenky et al. 1986 and Gilligan 1982), would be present in women in an egalitarian, nonviolent culture. An analogy may be helpful here: a person who shows a strong need for liquids when thirsty does not show this need when she or he has already consumed enough. The present author does not believe that, in an egalitarian culture, women's need for connection would take precedence over the need for sense of self or self-esteem, for example. I believe women would refuse to settle for anything less than mutually empowering relationships. Women would not be desperate for connection at any price. I am proposing, then, that women's currently strong need for connection, particularly with men, is a product of men's violence against women in present society.

Unfortunately, the self-in-relation model and Gilligan's (1982) and others' writings on women's special capacity for empathy and connection have had the effect of glorifying these traditionally feminine values, whether or not this was the intention of the authors. The readiness with which these theories of female development have been embraced, especially by women in the social sciences and clinical professions, may reflect the difficulty women have in acknowledging our victim status.

In summary, the application of Societal Stockholm Syndrome theory to women as a group, as well as our review of self-in-relation theory, lead us to ask if women's need for connection with men follows from the omnipresent threat of male violence against women. Considering that women experience lifelong trauma within patriarchal cultures as a result of the threat to survival posed by male violence, I ask whether a need for connection with men could be part of a Societal Stockholm Syndrome response to this threat. I ask if the threat to survival perceived by women as a consequence of men's violence creates enormous pressure for women to bond with men (our captors and abusers) and to seek safety through intimacy in relationships with men. Are connection and love safety nets for women? Is this the same attempt at survival observed in battered women and abused children? Conventionally, women's love of men has been viewed in extremes (a form of splitting that operates at the cultural level): battered women bond to their abusers and are blamed for doing so; women bond to men generally and this is glorified and celebrated. In fact, does the one not deserve the same celebration—or lack of celebration—as the other? After all, both may be survival strategies.

Love

Radical feminists are to be credited with exposing male domination and the terroristic violence against women that functions to keep this domination in place (e.g., Barry 1979; Brownmiller 1975; Daly 1978; Dworkin 1974; MacKinnon 1979). Having exposed male domination of women and the violence and threats of violence that underlie that domination, radical feminists then have been forced to ask why most women love men. Many radical feminists have come to an understanding, both of women's love for men and of heterosexuality, that is compatible with that provided by Societal Stockholm Syndrom·: theory.

Asking why women would love men under conditions of servitude, Atkinson (1974) argues that men's "love" for women exists only where there is a power imbalance: "Magnetism (or attraction) depends upon inequity . . . if the inequity changes, the fusion and the magnetism fall with the inequity. A woman can unite with a man as long as she is a woman, i.e., subordinate, and no longer" (p. 290). Atkinson's argument reminds one of many men's needs to degrade, humiliate, and inflict pain on women in their sexual fantasies and in their sexual behavior in order to have an erotic sexual experience. And one is reminded that many of these same men relate to women in seemingly intimate, caring ways.

The fact that divorce rates increase as the wife's salary increases, providing her with increased power relative to her husband, supports this aspect of Atkinson's argument (though other interpretations also exist; Starkey 1991). For Atkinson, love is also numerous other things: (1) It is "a kind of hysterical state, a mindless state therefore a painless state, into which women retreat when the contradiction between the last shreds of their human survival and the everyday contingencies of being a woman becomes most acute" (p. 291). (2) Love is "a euphoric state of fantasy in which the victim transforms her oppressor into her redeemer. She turns her natural hostility toward the aggressor against the remnants of herself—her Consciousness—and sees her counterpart in contrast to herself as all-powerful (as he is by now at her expense)" (1974, p. 62). And (3), love is an attempt on the part of a woman to fuse with her oppressor in order to "recoup her definitional and political losses." Atkinson thus sees women's love as arising from a need to disguise for ourselves the fact of our domination by men and by the need to improve women's status by aligning ourselves with one is who is more powerful than ourselves.

Atkinson's perspective fits well with a Societal Stockholm Syndrome explanation of women's love of men. However, a Stockholm Syndrome explanation emphasizes the threat to survival created by men's violence, whereas Atkinson emphasizes men's dominance over women. Ultimately, of course, male domination and the threat to women's survival are inseparable, since that domination is maintained by violence and the threat of violence (cf. Clark and Lewis 1977; Griffin 1979; Polk 1976).

If we are right that love develops under conditions of terror, how do we account for the fact that many women view their relationships with their male partners as egalitarian? In fact, within intimate heterosexual relationships, both women and men generate the fantasy of the egalitarian relationship. Studies by Elizabeth Grauerholz (1987) and Zanna and Pack (1975) help us to understand this phenomenon. Grauerholz asked if "men possess greater power than women, [why is] there a tendency for both men and women in heterosexual dating and marital relationships to report an equal distribution of power in their relationships" (p. 563)? She found that, for both sexes, perceived egalitarianism within the relationship increased as perceived likelihood of finding another partner who was as good or better than their present partner decreased! This finding suggests that, when people feel they lack relational alternatives, they improve their evaluations of their current relationship.[7]

The study by Zanna and Pack (1975) bears only indirectly on this issue. They found that college-age females were more likely to distort information given them about a man partner in an experiment, seeing him as holding less conventional views regarding women, when the man was described to them as having more "desirable" traits. One usually associates nontraditionality with more egalitarian male-female relationships. This distortion occurred in cases where women were given information that the male partner held traditional views of women as well as in cases where women were led to believe their male partners' views were nontraditional. Because the women reported more positive feelings about the nontraditional than the traditional male partner, these findings suggest the women distorted their perceptions of their male partners in the direction of misperceiving the partners as more like the person the women wanted the men to be (namely, nontraditional). Together, these two studies suggest that, if the male partner is viewed as desirable, and as women's perceptions of getting a partner who is any better decrease, women's perceptions of being in an egalitarian relationship with a male partner are prone to distortion in the direction of misperceiving the relation as more egalitarian than it is.

Men benefit from women's repression of our terror and the psychic distortions underlying our love for men, since slaves who love their masters are easier to dominate. Probably for this reason, Atkinson seems to think women are a little crazy for loving their oppressors—just as battered women are thought crazy for loving their abusers, or hostages for sympathizing with their captors. Although men have a stake in furthering the myth that loving men is something "ecstatic, noble, fulfilling, and even redemptive" (Frye 1983, p. 72), it is important that women too have a stake, given our captive status and the fact of male violence.

From our perspective, informed by the concept of Societal Stockholm Syndrome, love does more than enable women to recoup our losses and deny our terror. Through love, which has been women's answer to our need for connection, we hope to persuade men to stop their violence against us ("love conquers all") or at least protect us from other men's violence. This is undoubtedly one of the more important functions of love under conditions of terror: people love in an attempt to survive.

Of course, a Stockholm Syndrome–type love is not the only type of love that a person may feel toward another. Love can also exist under conditions of mutual empowerment, but this latter type of love is qualitatively different from that seen in persons showing Stockholm Syndrome. A Stockholm Syndrome–type love is desperate because it is a survival response to terror. In fact, the phrase "emotional *binding*" may communicate more about the nature of this love than the phrase "emotional bonding."

Although women love men in an attempt to survive, paradoxically, through our love of men women provide them with services (domestic, emotional, reproductive, sexual) that enable them to keep up the oppression. And because of women's needs to deny our terror and to see the world from our abusers' perspective, we begin to believe that we provide these services because we want to keep things the way they are. And of course a part of us does want to keep things as they are, simply because the life we know feels safer than the life we don't know. Because the stakes are so great, change feels life threatening.

The concept of Societal Stockholm Syndrome enables us to go beyond previous conceptualizations of women's love for men by explaining why most women sacrifice so much of ourselves in relationships with men. It also offers an explanation for why love grows in face of the threat of violence. The framework provided by Societal Stockholm Syndrome theory allows us to see the unhealthiness of patriarchal male-female relationships, yet not fall into blaming women (as "sick" or pitiful for loving our abusers) for our victimization.

Societal Stockholm Syndrome, and the conditions of captivity and terror underlying it, helps us put women's love of men in perspective. Isn't love an instrument for women in our attempts to gain male protection? Is women's love of men an instrument for turning men's anger and hatred of all that is subordinate (female) into reciprocated love? Is women's love of men a psychological defense against realizing our situation, the terror involved in that situation, and the costs of trying to guarantee our physical survival?

Yet, even seeing the "reasonableness" of women's love for men (given women's captive status), we must ask ourselves if love is working. Is it accomplishing all that women need it to accomplish? Does it stop or reduce male violence against women? Apparently not. Russell (1984) found that a woman was more likely to be the victim of rape by her husband than by anyone else. Walker (1979) reported that battering increased after marriage. Does love help to equalize the male-female relationship? Sprecher's (1985) findings suggest that it does not. Hacker (1981) observed, "The presence of love does not in itself argue for either equality of status nor fullness of communication" (p. 172). Although men's love of their women partners may help reduce the power imbalance for some couples, particularly during the courtship stage of the relationship, it does not equalize it. Also, to the extent that love means women provide unreciprocated services to men, it does not even *help* to equalize the relationship. Does love help to equalize relations *between men and women generally?* Love *may help* within marriage, but it does not equalize relations. As Hacker notes, "Since inequalities of status are preserved in marriage, a dominant group member may be willing to marry a member of a group which, in general, he would not wish admitted to his club" (p. 172). And Hoagland (1989), paraphrasing and quoting Claudia Card, notes, "Intimacy has not cured the violence in women's lives; instead, it 'has given the violent greater access to their victims'" (p. 84). Logic would lead us to believe that love within marriage may not even *help* equalize male-female relations in society generally. It is within the family that most men learn that women are there to serve them, whether as mother, wife, or daughter. Many women have questioned how men can discriminate against women when they have mothers, wives, and daughters. In fact, it is in just these intimate relationships that men have the greatest interest in maintaining male domination.[8] And it is through these relationships that people learn the social reality that women are second-class citizens.

Loving one's abuser makes sense if one cannot escape and if one's love *does* cause one's abuser to stop or decrease his abuse (thus improving one's chances of survival). But women's love for men apparently has not reduced men's abuse of women. Even if it had, isn't love still just a temporary solution? Wouldn't loving one's enemy be a long-term solution to domination only if it led to equality and freedom, and wouldn't this include the freedom to love whom one pleased? Would not anything less be only a partial or temporary solution? Under conditions of freedom, wouldn't women be as free to love women as men? (Whether or not one feels one would still want men as primary love objects, the issue is that one now does not have such freedom of choice.) Our love of men does not seem to have won us freedom from domination or abuse.

We are not arguing that if given a real choice—a choice made in a context where men did not threaten women with violence or isolate us from other women—women would not choose to love men. However, we feel that under conditions of freedom women's love of men would be similar to women's love of women (and therefore more healthy). Women's love of men would be no more desperate than our love of other women. Neither love would be possessive or addictive. Also, under such conditions men would be considerably more lovable than they are now. But until societal conditions conducive to a real choice exist, there is no way of knowing that women's love of men is not simply a sign of Societal Stockholm Syndrome and a product of men's threat to women's survival.

If women were safe from male violence, would the degree and nature of intimacy between women and men differ from what it is now? If yes, how would it differ? In particular, to what extent does the power imbalance currently permeating male-female relations limit the amount of intimacy possible between the sexes? How does this power imbalance limit the ways in which intimacy can be communicated? How does it affect the aspects of our lives about which we can be intimate with one another?

Casting women's love of men within the framework of Societal Stockholm Syndrome leads us to ask if women should stop providing men with our love, unless and until male violence against women stops. Simply asking such a question may arouse considerable fear. The source of this fear may be revealed in questions such as the following: If women were to stop loving men, would we be giving up one of our primary sources of power and control in our relationships with men? If women stopped loving men, would we lose what heterosexual privileges we now have? If women stopped loving men, would they stop loving women? If women stopped loving men, would men make us continue to do all the things for them that we now do, but without the belief that we do these things out of love and with only the awareness that we are indeed their servants? If women stopped loving men, would they stop protecting us from other men's violence? If women stopped loving men, would those who had been nonabusive become violent with us? These questions reveal the fear that both underlies women's love of men and gives impetus (passion) to that love. The extent of women's fear reveals both the extent of our Societal Stockholm Syndrome and the severity of the Stockholm Syndrome-conducive conditions that generate the fear. These fears also identify the issues with which women need to come to terms if we are to break out of Stockholm Syndrome.

Women's Heterosexuality

Like women's femininity and love of men, our heterosexuality has largely been taken for granted, yet, when addressed as an issue to be explained, it has been a very difficult phenomenon for which to account. Heterosexuality and sexuality more generally, as social constructions, differ at different times in history and in disparate cultures. Our genetic heritage as humans provides us the *potential* to practice sexuality through a wide range of behaviors and to conceptualize our sexualities in a variety of forms. It is our social environment, though, that determines what sexual practices we select to express from our genetic repertoire and what concepts we use to think about ourselves as sexual beings (cf. Foucault 1976/78). Although we differentiate between *identification* with a sexual orientation (homosexual, bisexual, or heterosexual) and sexual *practice*, we view both as socially determined. In particular, we propose that both are determined by societywide Stockholm Syndrome–conducive conditions.

Most women derive their primary sexual enjoyment from relations with men. Why? As Freud (1925) pointed out, women's first and primary love object is female. Why then would most women transfer their love to male objects in adulthood? Psychiatrist Judith Herman (with Hirschman 1981) summarizes the current feminist psychoanalytic explanation of heterosexuality. Grounded in Freud's Oedipus complex, this explanation takes into account the social context in which most children grow up. For feminist psychoanalytic theorists such as Juliet Mitchell, Helen Block Lewis, and Nancy Chodorow, the Oedipal crisis comes when "girls [discover] . . . that the object of their first love [their mother] is socially regarded as an inferior being, as the possession of a powerful father" (Herman, with Hirschman, 1981, p. 55). As a consequence of this discovery, the girl, seeing the father as the only parent having the power to confer dominant status, attempts to develop a special relationship with him so as to achieve equality with him and other men:

> The girl's eroticized interest in her father does not develop out of an earlier bond with the father as caretaker. Rather, it is a reaction to the girl's discovery that males are everywhere preferred to females, and that even her mother, the object of her first love, chooses men above women, her father and brother above herself. She turns to her father in the hope that he will make her into an honorary boy. In her imagination, her father has the power to confer the emblem of maleness (penis or phallus) upon her. It is for this reason that she wishes to seduce or be seduced by him. *By establishing a special and privileged relationship with her father,* she seeks to be elevated into the superior company of men. (Herman, with Hirschman, 1981, p. 57; emphasis added)

In adulthood, the special relationship which the girl earlier sought with the father for the purpose of attaining equality with men is transferred to other males for the same purpose:

> Even when the girl does give up her erotic attachment to her father, she is encouraged to persist in the fantasy that some other man, like her father, will some day take possession of her, raising her above the common lot of womankind. The successful attainment of conventional adult heterosexuality in fact requires an incomplete resolution of the female Oedipus complex and a channeling of female sexuality into submissive relationships with

older, stronger, richer, more powerful men. (Herman, with Hirschman, 1981, p. 57)

Thus, for these psychoanalytic writers, the heterosexuality of most women is born of women's inferior status. However, I would add that this inferior status is maintained through threat of force and therefore threat to survival (cf. Clark and Lewis 1977). Therefore I do not see most women's identification of themselves as heterosexual as a truly free choice.

In "Compulsory Heterosexuality and Lesbian Existence," Adrienne Rich (1980) rejects the portrayal of heterosexuality as a choice or preference of women. She views heterosexuality as a political institution or ideology created and maintained through male domination of women. Rich describes in detail the myriad ways in which male power, ranging from brute force to consciousness control, is used to enforce women's heterosexuality and, from that, concludes "that an enormous potential counterforce is having to be restrained" (p. 222). Like Catherine MacKinnon (1979), Rich rejects Brownmiller's distinction between rape as violence and intercourse as sexuality, since this distinction obscures similarities between the two in male-dominated cultures. MacKinnon contends that, under conditions of male domination, female consent is not a meaningful concept.

Rich's account does not explain why men's oppression of women, more so than oppression of other groups, takes a sexualized form. I believe that the framework provided by Societal Stockholm Syndrome theory can do much to account for why men's oppression of women, as compared to their oppression of other groups, takes a sexualized form. The theory can also do much to account for most women's practice of heterosexuality and most women's identification of themselves as heterosexual. I propose that compulsory heterosexuality is one of the primary vehicles through which men keep sex differences and thus their dominance salient. Frye (1983) has argued that, for acceptance into the group of dominants, men are required to have sex with women *often*. Gay men, she argues, are castigated by other men because they do not do this. Men are required to establish male dominance through sex. The goal for men is to "make" as many women as possible.

To "make" a woman in sex is seen by men as putting a woman in her place, that is, as using her for the purpose for which she was intended (by men). Making a woman is seen to cheapen the woman, making her less valuable, and to make the man more macho or powerful. Not coincidentally, then, heterosexual sex is viewed as making a man a man and making a woman a woman. In other words, sex is defined and practiced by men in ways that further both male dominance and female submission. We propose that *there is no time when bonding to one's abuser is more likely to arise than at the quintessential moment when her subordination and his domination is revealed most clearly—in the heterosexual act.*

Because people are sorted into dominants and subordinates on the basis of our anatomical sex differences, much of men's violence against women is against our bodies and our sexual organs in particular, so that the superiority of the penis (and thus maleness) is made clear to all. The biggest threat for most women, and one that is always present, is the threat of rape—the threat of violence directed toward women's sexual organs and women as sexual beings. Men affirm male superiority through use of the penis as a weapon against the female. Consider, for example, that many batterers force sex upon their female partner immediately after beating her, suggesting that sex for them is the penultimate act of aggression (cf. Okun 1986, p. 55). (This is the aspect of the battering episode that women most hate.) Cultural myths, most blatantly portrayed in pornography, portray female-male sex as an act of aggression. These myths tell us that the power and size of the penis are what give women sexual pleasure, that pain and humiliation are sexual turn-ons for women, and that when a man forces sex on an uncooperative female, she ends up loving it and begging for more (cf. Efron 1985).

How does Societal Stockholm Syndrome explain women's practice of heterosexuality and women's identification of themselves as heterosexual? And why would threat of violence against one's physical body, and particularly against one's sexual body parts, encourage heterosexuality? It is at the moment and place of greatest threat or abuse that a victim works hardest to establish or maintain a bond with her aggressor. If it is at our sexual organs that women are most vulnerable to male abuse, it will be through our sexual organs that women will most try to forge an attachment or union (bond) with men. Thus, women's efforts to create or maintain a bond with men will be greatest during sexual interactions. In other words, *because men's abuse of women is sexualized, women's bonds with men are sexualized.* And because men's abuse of women is sexualized, the primary way women establish and maintain bonds with men is through sex or sexualized interactions.

If men want women's sexual and reproductive services, and women's safety and survival depend on men's feelings toward women, women who seek to survive and who see no other means of escaping men's violence will provide men sexual and reproductive services. Sixty-one to 72 percent of women report having "entirely heterosexual experiences" (Kinsey et al. 1953). Men force women, at a cultural level, to be sexual with them (i.e., to practice heterosexuality), either through social pressure (a woman is disparagingly dubbed as "frigid" or a "prick tease" if she doesn't have sex with a man when *he* wants it), rape, or laws regarding the rights of men in marriage (cf. Rich 1980). But men's forcing women to be sexual with them does not in itself explain most women's identification as heterosexual. A woman may experience herself as heterosexual even if she has never had sex with a male. Most women, prior to their first sexual encounter, do experience themselves as heterosexual. Alternatively, a woman may be sexual with women but consider herself heterosexual. It is most women's experience of themselves as heterosexual that we are concerned with here. Experiencing oneself as heterosexual means that one's primary sexual and emotional enjoyment occurs when having sex with members of the other sex.[9]

If providing sexual and reproductive services to men pleases men, women will provide the services in the (unconscious) hope of welding a bond between us and men—a bond that might be used to prevent or thwart (further) sexual violence. If this analysis is correct, women will most desire men to express love to us during the sexual act. The need for such expressions of love will be greatest during sex because it is during sex that the nature of the relationship of a particular man to a particular woman is established.

To have sex with a man, a woman needs to feel the man is sufficiently bonded with her that either he would not be violent with her or she would be able to persuade him to stop being violent if he became so. This is a reason that male expressions of love during sex are highly sought by women.

Interestingly, many women report that sex is the only time or the primary time that their male partners are sensitive or loving toward them. As victims of male terror, most women will do whatever we can do, or have to do, to keep men being kind to us. If male kindness occurs primarily during sex, most women will want sex with men and want it often. In fact, because survival depends on men's kindness, when men's kindness is expressed "in bed," women will be strongly drawn to have sex with men despite the many ways in which "normal sex" resembles rape (cf. MacKinnon 1983). When done lovingly and nonviolently, sex with a man can provide adult females feelings of mastery over sexual exploitation. When sex is not accompanied by kindness, it is likely to be experienced by women as simply another form of male violation.

Recall that, under conditions of terror, victims are intensely grateful for small demonstrations of kindness shown to them by the abuser. If a man expresses love to a woman during sex, when exactly those parts of a woman's body most responsible for her membership in the subordinate group (female) and subjected to male violence are exposed to him, and she feels most vulnerable, the woman is likely to feel intensely grateful and to bond. Women are thus less likely than men to separate love and sex. And, expressions of love in the context of sex are likely to create more intense bonds in women than in men.

If a man shows a woman kindness *during* sex, the woman will bond to the positive side of the man and deny his violent side. (Consider here women's denial of their anger at men regarding pornography, rape, incest, and sexual harassment.) In other words, she will view him as different from other men, incapable of being violent toward her or other women. Or she will view men as a group as "not really all that violent." (Such cognitive distortions help the woman feel more in control and less helpless.) Women deny our anger at men and bond to men's positive or gentle sides, which are experienced when men are being sexual or romantic (which includes being sexual).

In our zeal to find a man who will not violate us sexually and who will protect us from other men who might violate us, women who have found such a man will work to keep him a protector rather than a violator. We do this by remaining hypervigilant to men's needs, particularly their sexual needs.

Much of the message that a woman tries to communicate to the man is that *he* is special. *He* is the *only* man that she will permit to share these moments with ("have his way with") her. *He* is the *only* man with whom she *chooses* to have sex. Even if their sex is marked by violence or innuendos of violence, she tries to communicate to him that he is special—she only chooses to do this with him. In this way she seeks to have him treat her as special, to see her as valuable, despite his feelings regarding women in general. In this way she also solicits his aid in helping to ensure that she will not be violated by any other man.

The rank of this man among men is important to the woman's safety. If the man has the (physical, financial, intellectual, etc.) means to prevent other men from doing violence to her or to ensure that they never do violence to her again, her feelings of safety and her actual safety are increased. This is why it is important to women, as victims of terror, to align ourselves with men who have power of some sort.

Because men perceive women as existing for men's sexual gratification, and because subordinates (women) take on dominants' (men's) perspectives, women in time come to see ourselves as existing for men's sexual pleasure. We lose any former sense that our bodies exist for us, that is, for our own pleasure.[10] To please men, women wear tight skirts or other "provocative" clothes, pose for magazines such as *Playboy,* compete in "beauty" contests which mostly men judge, "sleep around," or even have sex with a husband on occasions when we do not desire sex, etc. The titillation for men is that they experience such women as wanting to be *their* sexual subordinate ("I'm so good [or such a man] that she *wants* me to [sexually] dominate her. She wants me to use my maleness to dominate her femaleness.") In doing these things women learn we can have power over men, because men yearn to have women who want to be dominated by them. This is when men feel most like men, that is, when they most feel dominant.[11] Furthermore, because men enjoy women doing these things, women report we enjoy doing them. (Exceptions are women who see the violence or threat of violence inherent in such activities.)

Because men want women's sexual services for themselves only, seeing female-female sexuality as taking something from them, men make women's heterosexuality compulsory. As a result, females view male sexual partners as "good" and female sexual partners as "bad" *for women*. But compulsory heterosexuality for women means more than that women should simply have sex with men rather than with women. It means also that women should have sex with men no matter how badly we have been treated by men. Consider, for example, the rape victim who is pressured to "return" to men sexually and affectionally through such remarks as "Are you angry at all men now?" with the implication that being angry at men as a group, or at any man other than the rapist, is not acceptable. Consider also the many ways it is communicated to women that we must have sex with our husbands, whether by priests, sex therapists, the family doctor, or one's own mother. Choosing to give up sex with men or to withdraw from men *because men are physically violent toward women* is not considered a legitimate option for women. Imagine the responses you would get if you told others you were giving up sex with men or disengaging from men because men are violent toward women. Choosing to withdraw from men simply because men do not relate to us in mutually empowering ways is treated as heresy.

Recall from chapter 3 that, as court trials involving allegations of rape demonstrate, it is often difficult for people to discriminate rape from sex. And women and men frequently view sex and rape differently. More specifically, men often see sex where women see rape. And often, members of the same sex do not agree on whether rape or merely sex occurred. Individuals may themselves oscillate back and forth between their understanding of what transpired between them and other persons. In other words, there is a great deal of confusion about sex—when it is simply sex and when it is more than simply sex (rape)—in male-dominated cultures. This confusion exists because men in such cultures have defined sex as an act in which male dominance is normatively expressed. This confusion exists because sex occurs within a context of male sexual violence against women.

Because sex occurs within this violent context, elements of rape can be found in sex occurring between even the most trusting and loving partners. As MacKinnon (1987) has observed, rape is a part of sex and sex is a part of rape. Female subordination and vulnerability have been eroticized by males. The reverse—the eroticization of male power and dominance over women—seems also to be true.[12] In fact it may be that women collude with men in keeping elements of rape present in sex. More specifically, a woman may help preserve elements of rape in sex relationships with a trusted, loving partner because of her need to "master" sexual violence. That is, a woman may gain some sense of mastery over the threats of sexual violence that she encounters daily by, in a sense, "taming the savage beast" when sex with a trusted, loving partner (the beast) is mixed with elements of rape.

I wish to be clear about this—in contradistinction to Freud, I am not saying that heterosexual intercourse is *intrinsically* aggressive but that it is *made so* by patriarchy. However, we live within patriarchy, where sex is equated with the subjugation of women, so, for all practical purposes, heterosexual intercourse is a form of aggression.[13] In addition, I would argue that, in an egalitarian culture, because aggressive heterosexual sex would not be needed to maintain "proof" of male (penile) superiority, heterosexuality would not be compulsory. Cross-cultural, historical evidence for a relationship between female subordination and heterosexuality is provided by Blackwood (1984): in a number of Native American tribes in western North America, cross-dressing by females and marriage to other women were socially supported. Gender was not defined in terms of a person's anatomical sex characteristics but rather in terms of the person's performance of a social role. Egalitarian modes of production and relations between men and women existed. As the tribes' contact with westward-moving white settlers increased, and as men, but not women, grew wealthy through trade and warfare, females came to be seen as inferior within the tribes and their heterosexuality became compulsory. The only male rape of a woman that Blackwood discusses occurred at this time in history, and the rapist's purpose was to punish the woman for whom his wife had left him.

As with love, we are not arguing that if given a real choice—a choice made in a culture free of the threat of male violence against women—women would not develop a heterosexual identity. But we do believe that women would feel equally free to practice homosexuality and to develop a homosexual identity. However, until women are free from the threat of male violence, there is no way of knowing if women's heterosexual practice and identity are anything other than Societal Stockholm Syndrome responses.

Several questions emerge from this conceptualization of women's heterosexuality. Would "normal" intercourse, as experienced by a subordinate *conscious* of her position and of her need to "tame the savage beast" in order to win better treatment, feel like rape? Is women's eroticization of dominance an attempt to deny our subordinate status and the terror associated with it? Is women's eroticization of dominance an attempt to "master" male sexual violence against us? Does women's eroticization of male dominance stem from the need to find hope in terror? Is women's eroticization of male dominance accomplished by viewing the sex act through the eyes of the (male) aggressor? Diiorio (1989) has observed that "the social processes that mold the sexuality of individuals remain poorly understood and research has focused almost exclusively on the family context. . . . Questions concerning the relationship between sexuality and masculinity and the sexual socialization process in contexts beyond childhood and the family remain poorly investigated" (p. 261). The theory of Societal Stockholm Syndrome provides a framework for generating testable hypotheses regarding the role that male-female power dynamics play in constructing women's sexuality and sexual identity. We offer this theory in the hope that it will generate research designed to answer this question and others about the impact of male-female power relations on female sexuality.

As with our "reevaluation" of femininity in general and women's love of men in particular, this analysis of the relation between women's heterosexuality (identity and practice) and Societal Stockholm Syndrome is certain to raise fears. For example, if we women gave up our heterosexuality (identity and practice), could we continue to use sex as a source of power in our relationships with men, since sex is one of the few sources of power we now have in dealing with men? If women gave up our heterosexual identity, would we come to define our present heterosexual practices as acts of prostitution wherein we exchange sex for survival, for protection, and for whatever crumbs of warmth and caring we can get? If women gave up our heterosexual identity, would we experience all sex with men as rape and no longer be able to obtain reassurance and comfort from men's expressions of tenderness during "love-making?" If women gave up our heterosexual identity, would men dispense with these demonstrations of tenderness? If women gave up our heterosexual identity and the eroticism we derive from male dominance, might we be giving up our only source of eroticism? If women took on a homosexual identity, would we regard each other as targets for our domination, such that there might no longer be anyone with whom we would be safe? If women gave up our heterosexual practice or identity, would men see us as disloyal? Would men call us disparaging names ("lezzie," "man-hater, "bull dyke") and target us for *more* harassment? Would women lose the crumbs of approval from men that we have worked so hard to get? Would we be seen as perverted? Would our friends no longer want to be with us? If women gave up our practice of heterosexuality, might men force themselves on women sexually even more than they do now (in an effort to break women's resistance and demonstrate power)? And would women then be forced to acknowledge that men's use of compulsory heterosexuality constitutes the foundation on which male domination is built? If women gave up our heterosexual identity, would we be forced to acknowledge the ways we feel betrayed by our bodies (which sometimes respond with "pleasure" to sexual violence committed against us) and thus the extent of our alienation from our bodies? Would women be forced to see how this alienation has been used by men to help maintain female subordination? Looking at this area from a different vantage point, if women were safe from male violence, how would our experience of what we consider erotic change? If women were safe from male violence, how would our experience with and attitudes toward our bodies change? As before, the fears and concerns underlying these questions serve as guideposts for women's journey out of Societal Stockholm Syndrome.

Conclusion

In this chapter we have asked if women's feminine identity (composed of femininity, love for men, and heterosexual identity and practice) is indicative of Societal Stockholm Syndrome. Clearly, we found sufficient evidence to warrant continued questioning, investigation, and research. We also proposed a theory about the nature of the relationship between feminine identity, Societal Stockholm Syndrome, and the four Stockholm Syndrome-conducive conditions. In summary, we proposed that women's femininity, love for men, and heterosexual identity and practice are survival strategies observed under conditions of terror—conditions that are described by the four Stockholm Syndrome precursors (threat to survival, inability to escape, isolation, and kindness). In addition, we asked questions prompted by women's fears about giving up our femininity, love of men, and heterosexual identity and practice—questions we must address if women ever are to break out of Societal Stockholm Syndrome in our relations with men. These questions expose the forces which maintain feminine identity in women and thus maintain male domination. Because they expose these forces, our questions serve as guideposts for women's liberation.

The concept of Societal Stockholm Syndrome casts women's relations with men in a new light. Rather than celebrating femininity and thus glorifying women's responses to oppression, this concept allows us to see femininity as the posturing of an oppressed group intent on survival. Rather than presenting women's love of men as some rapturous state that all women should strive to attain, the concept of Societal Stockholm Syndrome illuminates the social context within which this love develops and illuminates love's function within that context. Rather than accepting most women's heterosexuality as biologically determined, the concept of Societal Stockholm Syndrome presents women's sexuality as a primary battleground for the establishment and maintenance of male domination. The concept of Societal Stockholm Syndrome leads us to see that women as a group must find a way to escape this life predicament on our own, just as battered women are forced to do. Men will not "save" women from men's tyranny.

There are four central questions women in a patriarchal society need to ask: Is survival enough? Are femininity, love of men, and heterosexuality accomplishing for us all that we need to accomplish? Do their benefits outweigh their costs? If we decide that they are the direction we want to continue to take, what are the advantages and disadvantages of our being conscious of their function in our lives?

I, the author, have several additional questions: If men did not do violence to women (or threaten violence) and patriarchy did not exist for us, would we women so badly need to be liked by men? Would we work so hard to win men's favor? Would the way we love men (the nature of that love) differ from the way we love them now? Would we love women differently if our love of women didn't threaten men? How would we see ourselves if we no longer took femininity, love for men, and heterosexuality for granted? Would our feelings about our bodies be as they are now? What would it feel like to see ourselves and one another through our own—not men's—eyes?

Until male violence toward women stops and women feel safe with (and safe from) men, it is impossible to say whether women's femininity, love for men, and heterosexual identity are anything other than survival responses. (Recall that feminine identity is not synonymous with women's identity except under conditions of male terrorization of women.) Looking at the issue from another angle, women's femininity, love of men, and heterosexuality are attempts at *individual* solutions to oppression, even though they are individual solutions adopted by massive numbers of women. Might women end oppression by uniting rather than employing these individual solutions? And what form might *group* solutions take? Should women join Eleanor Smeal in her efforts to get women politicians elected so that women will have a legislative voice in running this country and thus in running our own lives? Or should women follow Sonia Johnson's (1987, 1989) recommendation to exorcise patriarchy (or internalized oppression) from our minds, and stop strengthening patriarchy by resisting it? Or do we seek other alternatives? In the next chapter we use our understanding of Stockholm Syndrome and the conditions conducive to it to seek solutions to the ultimate question emerging from our considerations thus far: How can women break out of Societal Stockholm Syndrome?

Moving from Surviving to Thriving: Breaking Out of Societal Stockholm Syndrome

We are all, women, connected to or in relationship with a battering culture. . . .

As women in a battering culture, where can we go to escape? Camus said somewhere that in order to critique this world, it is necessary to find another world to stand on. Where is that other world, that world outside the battering environment?

Where are our safe houses?

How can we break that connection?

(Swift 1987, p. 20)

Recognizing the inseparability of the individual and society, we look in this chapter to several sources of information on how women can escape Societal Stockholm Syndrome. Those sources are feminist science fiction, women's groups, and feminist methods of resistance. Under four headings, four themes drawn from feminist science fiction—distrust, women as warriors, powers of connection, and language—we first will discuss ways that feminist science fiction and women's groups can nurture women's imagination and courage so that social action is undertaken from a position of strength rather than despair. Then, in the second part of the chapter, we will examine four methods of resistance—four methods for generating social action tactics to advance women's reshaping of the world.

Before discussing the first four themes, the authors will comment on the importance of the imagination and our use of feminist science fiction.

The quotation we placed at the beginning of this chapter asks where women can find the perspective outside our battering culture that will allow us to critique, and therefore start to transform, that culture. One answer is that through our imaginations, we can create that other world. Such creation is not fabrication but invention: *invenire,* to come upon, which is to dis-cover, to un-cover, to re-member, to re-collect. The new perspective women need is a rediscovery of a perspective we may have possessed but have forgotten. As Wittig (1971, p. 89) reminds us: "There was a time when you were not a slave, remember that. You walked alone, full of laughter, you bathed bare-bellied. You say you have lost all recollection of it, remember. . . . You say there are no words to describe this time, you say it does not exist. But remember. Make an effort to remember. Or, failing that, invent."

Our reliance on imaginative literature here is not arbitrary; it corresponds to the problem confronting us. The imagination has to be freed for hope to appear. In therapy we often see that those who have been abused are unable to know what they want, because imagination has been denied them. Even to imagine that one *could* want seems to abuse victims to be impossible or somehow wrong. And this is just how the abuser wants it to be—for to imagine things being other than they are is to be disloyal to the abuser. In multiple forms, every day, abusers give victims the message that *they,* the abusers, will decide what is to be and what should be: they, not the victims, will do any wanting; the victims' role is simply to want to please the abusers, to want only what *they* want. Is it any wonder, then, that victims of abuse come to feel not only unable to imagine but also convinced that it is wrong, wasteful, and self-indulgent to imagine?

Because the abuser correctly fears the victim's imagination, women's encouragement of that imagination here is a subversive act. Just as political tyrannies censor communications and religious tyrannies condemn fiction, the abuser feels threatened by any reading or daydreaming in which the victim may engage and will oppose these forms of communication with the self just as he moves to isolate the victim from other people. However, for those of us not under 24-hour surveillance, reading work (such as feminist science fiction) that nourishes the imagination and therefore moves us toward change, is possible.

There is much more in feminist science fiction relevant to our concern of escape from Societal Stockholm Syndrome than the authors can discuss here; we will limit ourselves to a handful of themes. Four themes—distrust, women as warriors, powers of connection, and language—will guide our consideration of what feminist science fiction can reveal of ways available to ordinary women, every day, as women seek the world's release from patriarchal bondage. Feminist science fiction, together with women's groups, can show women how to move into social action in ways that retain the energy and validity of each woman's determination to live and prosper.

Themes That Move Us from Surviving to Thriving

Distrust/Holding Men Accountable

In showing us women who hold others, as well as themselves, account-able, feminist science fiction enlarges the chink in the wall of isolation that imprisons women. Gilman's (1979) *Herland* and two stories by Tiptree (Alice Sheldon) make explicit this theme of accountability, which occurs in less overt ways in many other works of feminist science fiction.

In *Herland,* three early-twentieth-century men from the United States find a land inhabited solely by women and are allowed to learn its history and ways. They are treated well—and are carefully watched—by the women. Since the three men (in varying degrees) show themselves able to learn and follow the land's code of conduct and since they are strongly attracted to three young women of the country, who also care for them, they are permitted to marry. For each of the three men, marriage intensifies his struggle with the deep differences between the women's culture and his own patriarchal beliefs, and each responds in his own way. The women of Herland have been as observant of characterological differences as of the men's common need for firm guidance and gentle restraint, and they respond decisively when Terry, one of the men, attempts to force himself on his wife. She defends herself, temporarily subdues him, calls for aid, and is assisted by the other women in overpowering and binding him. Terry then is tried and banished forever from their land, and he is prevented from pursuing his furious wife during the short time before he is escorted out of the country.

In Tiptree's (1975) "The Women Men Don't See," similar decisiveness is displayed by Ruth Parsons, an apparently mousey librarian, in her dealings with Don Fenton when the two are stranded in a Mexican mangrove swamp. Ruth calmly anticipates and skillfully deflects the many aggressive and stupid moves Don makes against her privacy, her body, and her plans for the escape of herself and her daughter to an alien planet. What Don first sees as her "paranoia" emerges as a highly intelligent distrust of him and his kind. Don, befuddled with patriarchy as well as tequila, is left at the end of the story to contemplate the puzzle of why a woman could wish to leave his world for another. Ruth's decisiveness in reaching for freedom, like that of the women of Herland in maintaining their freedom, reflects her preexisting mental stance. Neither ignoring male aggression nor excusing it, she does not make the mistake of questioning only her own perceptions or rejecting only her own actions when things go wrong. She remembers that others, too, have the obligation to think and behave in responsible ways.

Ruth's story is played out on the societal level in Tiptree's (1978) novella, "Houston, Houston, Do You Read?" Here, as in *Herland,* three men from this culture contact a women-only world. In this case, that world is our future Earth and the men encounter it when a solar flare disrupts their space mission, kicking them out in time. Rescued before the life-support on their own craft runs out, they are taken on board a spaceship operated by five women from Earth's future. While the men are treated well and are not distrusted out of hand, the women have not forgotten history, and they unobtrusively keep an eye on the men's behavior. When, under the influence of a relaxing recreational drug, two of the three men act on their aggressive fantasies by attempting rape and a takeover of the ship, the women immobilize them and indicate they will not be allowed loose on Earth. Though the fantasy of Lorimer, the most "enlightened" of the three, is that the women will kill them, it is not clear just what the women will decide to do. However, it is evident that they do not plan on allowing the men free run of Earth.

In both Gilman's and Tiptree's stories, women neither gratuitously devalue men nor excuse inexcusable behavior. Responsible themselves, they hold others responsible for those others' actions. They therefore are able to acknowledge their fear of men and to be angry as well as self-searching. In trusting themselves, the women in these stories are able to mistrust others when appropriate and therefore are not powerless to effect change.

Distrust of males and holding men accountable for their behavior are important strategies for women's survival while we are still living in a patriarchy but working toward some other type of world. According to Janeway (1980), one of the powers of the weak is disbelief—distrust of the motives and actions of dominants. Subordinates need to develop a healthy mistrust of the motives of dominants and not assume that dominants, who are generally self-serving, will act in the subordinates' best interests (even if dominants knew what subordinates' best interests were, which they do not). Many wise women, including Miller (1986) and Johnson (1987), advise women to attend to, and begin trusting, our own experiences and inner feelings, from which we have become alienated as a consequence of patriarchal violence.

Johnson (1987) warns us that patriarchy is always lying to women and, since patriarchal thinking is dichotomous, truth can be discovered by reversing patriarchal beliefs. For example, patriarchy tells us that women depend on men. The illusion that women are dependent is maintained by erecting barriers such as male violence and economic constraints to prevent women from becoming independent. If women were naturally dependent, no barriers to prevent us from leaving men would be necessary.

Women also need to distrust men by giving up the expectation that men will be kind and "give us our rights." When a woman proudly says that her husband lets her do something (like work), she is admitting that he controls her. He can always decide not to let her work. Recent history provides an example of the same phenomenon at a societal level in the United States: the Supreme Court, which had ruled that women could legally obtain abortions, presumably due to the right to privacy, then compromised that right by giving states the legal power to control women's access to abortion. Women need to take the position that our rights are our rights and men cannot give women what is already ours. This may mean that women will have to engage in civil disobedience to protest unjust laws that men make with respect to women's rights.

Women must hold men accountable for their behavior. Women do men no favors in terms of their growth as responsible, caring human beings if women allow men to abuse us. It is not genuine love that causes women to put up with men's destructive behavior; it is the fear-induced love produced by Stockholm Syndrome. Stockholm Syndrome hurts men's development as well as women's. Remembering that in chapter 5 we called heterosexuality and love of men into question as *essential* qualities of women, it is worth reframing here these aspects of women's psychology in light of what feminist science fiction shows us: if men are people toward whom women feel sexual attraction, do women have sufficient self-respect to demand that men be human beings worthy of women's sexual interaction with them? If women feel affection for men, do we love them, and ourselves, sufficiently to demand that they become responsible for their actions?

Leghorn and Parker (1981) insist that men and their institutions need to be held accountable on a collective level as well as an individual level. They suggest that every time men or men's institutions exploit women, men's actions be made to have clear consequences for them. Women need to ask ourselves what men are most afraid of and then use men's fears to disrupt the dominance-relation between men and women. Two examples provided by Leghorn and Parker of holding men accountable on an individual level are publishing the names of known rapists in newspapers and showing up in a group at a rapist's place of employment to inform the employer of the man's crime. French (1992) gives several examples of women all over the globe holding men accountable. In India, for instance, "women bang pots and pans outside the houses of men most abusive to their wives. Feminist groups like Saheli agitate against widespread 'dowry deaths,' and have forced passage of a law requiring any 'accidental death' or 'suicide' of a woman in the first seven years of her marriage to be investigated for possible foul play" (p. 204). An example of holding institutions accountable is consumer boycotts, and women may think of additional creative ways to accomplish this goal. The networks of women that provide corroboration and affirmation of individual women's distrust of men should help women remember that mistrust is a collective as well as a deeply personal phenomenon.

Women's groups provide the basis for much of women's strength to hold men accountable on both the individual and the collective level. In a group where women openly discuss their everyday experiences, a woman can see that other women have an extensive basis for their distrust of men and are far from arbitrary or ill-considered in their judgments. This, as well as the support of the other women, helps make a woman more likely to respect her own observations and less likely to yield to the external and internalized pressure to "just give him one more chance" when the man in question clearly has already blown multiple chances.

Whenever women hold men accountable, we invoke a reality that stands outside the artificial, though powerful, dominance-relation of men as a group to women as a group. Whenever a woman holds a man responsible for his behavior, she defies patriarchy's claim to define reality, she calls the universe to witness, she says, "Power is power, but it is not truth. You are as human as I—no less, and no more. You cannot escape the work of being human even if you punish me or kill me for reminding you of that work."

Distrust of men and holding men accountable start a woman off on a journey, inner or outer, to find her true self. But initially, because this search is precipitated by a recognition of the untrustworthiness of men as a group (that is, by a shattering of Societal Stockholm Syndrome's protective denial), women may experience real despair, feeling empty and lacking any sense of self. Since bonding with our captors has eroded women's sense of self, we need to discover who we are apart from our captors.

As part of creating or reclaiming ourselves, women need to learn what we want, and we need to assert our needs and wishes. In doing this we not only hold men responsible for their actions, but we also hold ourselves responsible for our own behavior. Women should not take responsibility for having been victims, but once we develop awareness of our victimization, we must take responsibility for our choices and actions with respect to our oppression. We must decide what values are worth living for and, if necessary, dying for, and we must choose to let those values guide our actions. In doing this, we connect with the meaning of the perennial theme of women as warriors.

Women as Warriors/Honoring Our Anger

Women's individual and collective power to bring about change is perhaps most evident in the feminist science fiction that shows us armed women, violent women, women able to fight back physically. Feminist science fiction such as Piercy's (1976) *Woman on the Edge of Time,* Charnas's (1978) *Motherlines,* and McIntyre's (1978) *Dreamsnake* show us women exercising such power.

For the reader of *Motherlines,* Sheel Torrinor, the Riding Woman who enjoys killing men roaming in the borderlands, may stand out in memory as the only violent woman in the novel. Yet the other Riding Women, who recognize the crippling of spirit caused by too much killing, also kill men—but without pleasure. They recognize killing as a needed act of self-defense. All the Riding Women are warriors, claiming as their own the skills of fighting, horse-handling, and desert survival as surely as they claim motherhood.

Similarly, in *Dreamsnake,* Snake, though a peaceful healer, readily defends herself when attacked by a crazy man trying to steal her medicinal serpents, and she does not see this ability as anything extraordinary. In *Woman on the Edge of Time,* Connie, too, is a peaceful woman. Yet she chooses murder, even at the cost of any hope for her own freedom, when murder is the only way she can defend a future struggling to be born, a future threatened by the mind-control schemes of powerful psychiatrists. Her anger toward a corrupt system does not contradict, but reflects, her care for a still-unborn human future; she is able to fight back only because she has come to see and honor herself as nurturing and loving.

These women all show themselves able and willing to fight back; they all show us that this power, too, belongs to women. In imagining the extreme of physical violence in self-defense—if only as a last resort—the reader of feminist science fiction can begin to imagine herself as able to bring about change in her own situation. This message of readerly identification—"You can fight back, and you can win"—is the true force of the woman-warrior theme in feminist science fiction.

Perhaps because women create and nurture life and because violence has been used against us, women, as a group, abhor violence and tend to use it only in self-defense or in defense of helpless others, such as children or the elderly. (Patriarchy tells women that we are not supposed to resort to violence even in self-defense when threatened with rape or battering, but violence on behalf of defenseless others is allowed.) Also, many women believe that means and ends are not separate and that it is a contradiction to attempt to create a peaceful world through violence (for example, see Johnson 1987, 1989).

Nonviolent protest suits women more than the use of violence or terrorism. Engaging in nonviolent protests requires people to put their lives on the line and therefore requires the extraordinary courage of the warrior. When the military or the police attack peaceful protesters, the oppressive nature of the establishment's power is exposed. However, Janeway (1980, pp. 301–302) cautions that it is just because nonviolence is "typically feminine" that it may lose its power when women use it. She does not advocate that women give up this tactic, but she warns that it may become less effective unless we take care to counter misunderstandings of our use of it. Janeway gives an example from the English suffragette movement to show that violence may work when nonviolent means are ineffective: The sitting Liberal Government had agreed to introduce a "Votes for Women" bill in Parliament but then stalled on it. Though imprisoned suffragettes continued to protest by refusing to eat, force feeding had become common, so their nonviolent protest was silenced. The suffragettes then threw rocks through the plate-glass windows of Bond Street shops. This outburst of women's violence against property shook the country and prodded the politicians into action.

If we accept the self-interested patriarchal version of women as all sweetness and light, as *only* loving and tender, we are giving up our human strength, our anger and power—and this simply reinforces the status quo. The Amazon or woman warrior is an archetype that reminds us of the strength, power, and anger which are necessary for action, even for nonviolent action. Women need to learn to feel and claim their anger, just as men need to verbally express their anger rather than translate it into misdirected aggression (Miller 1983). The male fantasy of a man-hating Amazon nation[1] reveals men's (unconscious) awareness of the depth of women's (repressed) anger, and it reveals men's fear that women some day may act on that anger and seek retribution for patriarchal atrocities against women. Rather than being guilt-tripped by our awareness of this male fantasy, we could let it remind us of the just cause for women's collective anger.

As Piercy (1982) tells us, good anger acted on is fiercely beautiful, but swallowed anger corrupts and destroys our strength. Women must recognize and accept our own and other women's capacity for anger if we are to escape the hold of Societal Stockholm Syndrome. Connecting with our bodies and with women collectively—both of which contain a knowledge of anger as valid—can free women to resist patriarchy. Learning self-defense, though it will not eradicate violence against women, can connect a woman with her own vitality, her psychological as well as physical will to survive and prosper. Physical exercise can do this as well. Taking control of her own body greatly assists a woman in taking control of her life as her own (which, of course, is why the patriarchal definition of femininity so effectively cripples women's resistance).

Personal defense training and assertiveness training have been found to be forms of consciousness raising for women. By practicing self-defense and assertiveness in situations in which they previously had experienced fear or had felt they had no right to resist, the women in studies by Kidder, Boell, and Moyer (1983) began to develop a sense of certain rights, especially the right to say no to men. Self-defense and assertiveness activities also increased the women's awareness of men's intrusions, potential assaults, and violations. Heightened awareness of when men were intruding upon their space increased these women's ability to sense danger at earlier stages in their interactions with men. As a result of their new consciousness and skills, the women in these studies became less likely to blame themselves for their victimization (for instance, by sexual harassment or coercion) but became more willing to take responsibility for their responses to these violations.

What does it do to your sense of bodily self to think of yourself as a warrior? How do we begin to see other women differently if we imagine them as warriors? Telling our own experiences and bearing witness to other women's experiences—whether in reading self-defense success stories (Caignon and Groves 1987), taking part in a rape survivors' therapy group, or attending a speakout—allows women to locate our cause for anger, contact our determination to bring about change, and begin to develop strategies in cooperation with other women to make such change.

Anger is a matter of saying no, of drawing a line, of saying "this is not acceptable." And if we cannot say no, we cannot say an honest yes either. In patriarchy, women are taught to make connection with others *at the expense of* asserting our own needs, wishes, and boundaries. Feminists, though, see that women can arrive at connection with others *through* respect for our own limits.

We begin to exit from Societal Stockholm Syndrome by identifying the strengths of women in society. Miller (1986) notes that the affiliative qualities patriarchy has declared to be women's weaknesses, qualities which make us "unfit for power," are actually strengths that women can reclaim and use for our own purposes. The context in which women's strengths have developed is the patriarchal system. To question any one of the components of the patriarchal system—that women's qualities are weaknesses, that the relation between women and men should not be one of mutuality, and that women should not attend to our own develop-ment—is to question the entire system. It is worth asking what might open up now if women withdrew the support we give to patriarchy and instead began valuing our own qualities, engaging with other women in using our qualities for the sake of women's own development, while demanding mutuality in our relationships with men.

Janeway (1980) identifies building community among subordinates as one of the powers of the weak. It is true that women's affiliation has been directed toward dominants. However, women can reclaim our affiliative skills for ourselves by building networks and support systems among women. In the process, we will reduce the strength of a major Societal Stockholm Syndrome precursor condition: isolation. And, because the four precursor conditions are so intertwined, reducing isolation can sig-nificantly weaken the other three.

Powers of Connection

A third theme in feminist science fiction, which at first glance may seem sheer escapist self-indulgence, can bring women as readers to a realization of our own power as our own. This is the theme of supernatu-ral powers, which appears in nonfeminist as well as feminist science fiction, but in feminist works it is treated in a way more inviting of the symbolic reading offered here.

While the implications of authorial concern with supernatural powers can be traced through many works of feminist science fiction, here we will focus on one work, Gearhart's (1979) *The Wanderground: Stories of the Hill*

Women. This novel/collection of related stories refers to many "unusual mental powers" found among the women of the Wanderground, who have chosen to live outside the male-controlled City in order to escape male violence and exploitation. These women can "mind-stretch," extending outward their abilities to hear, to see, to pick up emotions, and to communicate with human and nonhuman beings. For instance, one of the women, Jacqua, is able to hear in her head the slow, clanking sound, some miles away, of a woman walking in armor, a woman who has been raped and has fled the City (pp. 1–6). They can shift control from their consciousness to their "lonth," a deep part of awareness that can guide their movements in involuntary fashion when they are in danger or under great pressure. They can enfold each other mentally/emotionally to provide help. For instance, in the "remember rooms," where the young women allow themselves to mentally re-live the atrocities of women's shared past, from the time before women began to leave the City in significant numbers, the rememberers are mentally "enwrapped" by guides, adult women, so that they can experience history without being psychologically destroyed (pp. 138–166). The women of the Wanderground also can ride on the wind and raise objects, toting them along. They can shield themselves and each other against intruding thoughts and emotions spilling out from others. In one case, Betha, a woman serving on observation duty in the City where, disguised as a man, she can monitor male activities, is shown shielding herself carefully as she negotiates the numerous I.D. checkpoints and displaying male behavior where her identity might be detected (pp. 110–117). The women also can "gather-stretch" many minds together, when bodies are widely scattered, to share knowledge simultaneously.

Such an extravagant list of powers may suggest the wish-fulfillment fantasies of adolescent girls or powerless peasant women imagining themselves as witches. But a closer look reveals something else. Each of these powers in fact is a matter of the person coming into close connection with an "other"—whether a deep part of herself, another human being, a nonhuman animal, an object, or an elemental force such as the wind. It is this connection, this movement into interplay with the other, that allows the exercise of a nonphysical power. These powers, then, no matter how fantastic-seeming when read literally, can be seen as commenting on what we commonly call empathy.

In saying "what we commonly call empathy," as in enclosing "unusual mental powers" in quotation marks earlier, we wish to call into question assumptions held about this form of activity. The powers exercised by the women of the Wanderground are not "mental powers" as we most often think of "mental"—detached, "rational," superior, controlling. Instead, these powers are a matter of connection, of listening-and-speaking, of coming into harmony while asking that the other also come into harmony. Nor are these powers "unusual"; they are not regarded as setting their possessors apart (superior to the common run of humanity) in the way we might suppose. Rather than as unusual mental powers, the powers described in Gearhart's Wanderground might more usefully be thought of as the ability to receive and send information in other than language-based ways and the ability to focus one's energy to an extent, and to the achievement of ends, not commonly considered possible.

Our usual notions of empathy are no more helpful in understanding its actuality than are assumptions that the powers described by Gearhart are a form of magic or an indication of native superiority. In our culture, empathy is either doubted and disparaged, or it is glorified. Its glorification is particularly dangerous, for those who talk up empathy most often are those who wish to exploit (while denying) the empathy of others. Embedded in the glorifications of empathy is the misconception that empathy is a matter of *being nice*—warm, wonderful, soft, feminine, selfless. By contrast, those who are empathic are aware that empathy has a cost, and they are capable of learning that empathy does not stand in contradiction to sternness or even to considered rejection of the person or thing that is empathically understood.

Patriarchal culture has forced women to develop empathy through abusive relationships, so that this human capacity has been assigned to women and denied to men. But we simply fall for patriarchy's lie about the nature of empathy if we therefore reject it.

Feminist science fiction, in its exploration of "unusual mental powers," lets us see what it could be like to reject not empathy but empathy's false semblance—to reject the despised, demanded emotional labor of taking on the abuser's perspective while losing one's own. The treatment of unusual mental powers in feminist science fiction gives women a sense of what it could be like for our simply human empathy to be honored, seen as the skilled work it is, studied in ourselves with care, and provided with safeguards because it is understood and accepted rather than coveted. When women begin to imagine such a thing, we are better able to leave or to demand change in situations where our empathy is treated as a limitless natural resource to be mined by others.

From the first days of the contemporary women's movement, the coming-together of women in small groups to share and discuss our experiences has been a continual source of our collective energy. In large part, we would argue, women's groups have been (and continue to be) so important because they allow women to claim our empathy as our own and to begin to use it for our own well-being as well as others'. A woman talking in a respectful, supportive group environment about her daily, "trivial" interactions with others eventually can begin to see the reality of the emotional work she is doing in those interactions, can learn from other women's stories that they also are engaged in such work, and can receive empathic understanding from the other women and begin to believe that she, too, is worthy of care. As a result, women in such groups generally become more able to demand mutuality and respect in their relationships and to see that they are not obliged to offer others a boundless "understanding" that excuses others' aggression or that fails to demand self-understanding from others. Here, then, is one way in which women, both as individuals and as members of a group, begin to confront and challenge the daily forms of our victimization.

Language: Articulating Our Perspective

Language, like the affiliative qualities of women, is frequently disparaged in our culture. Language often is spoken of as "just words," as if it had no power or reality. But feminist science fiction (like literature generally) makes us aware of the true power language possesses to make or remake our worlds.

A language will reflect the dominant language-using group's view of reality. And the controversy generated when the existing structures of and assumptions about a language are challenged by a subordinate group shows that language is anything but trivial (cf. Martyna 1983).

Patriarchal language is hierarchical, controlling, objectifying, and alienating. Often, to express relational or feeling concepts that reflect women's values and experience, one must use lengthy descriptions or create new words. Recall Gearhart's verbal creations, employed in the previous section: "mind-stretch," "lonth," and "gather-stretch." Too often, women are silenced by lack of access to a language that represents our reality. This silencing is described in the theory of muted groups developed by two anthropologists, the Ardeners (Hunter College Women's Studies Collective 1983). Their theory explains how the dominant ideology of a society provides a vocabulary which reflects the image of reality held by the dominant group (men). Women appear inarticulate because we are forced to express ourselves through a vocabulary insufficient to convey our perceptions of reality. Male language is one of the barriers that keeps women, in Johnson's (1987) metaphor, "trapped in our patriarchal minds."

Because women's own language is needed for us to formulate an alternative ideology and a new reality, language figures significantly in several works of feminist science fiction. Language as a primary tool for affirming women's reality plays an important part in Elgin's *Native Tongue* (1984) and *The Judas Rose* (1987), Atwood's *The Handmaid's Tale* (1986), and Piercy's *Woman on the Edge of Time* (1976), each of which we will discuss here.

In Elgin's books, women succeed in creating and disseminating a new language, one which reflects women's experience and perspective. This new language, Láadan, allows women to express themselves precisely and compactly, without the fumbling and long-winded qualifications imposed by existing languages. The grammar as well as the vocabulary of Láadan recognizes women's experiences as real and worthy of report. For instance, Láadan contains seven "evidence morphemes," used at the ends of sentences to indicate speakers' bases for their statements. The evidence morpheme "wáa" is used to indicate that the information just transmitted is assumed by the speaker to be false, because the speaker distrusts the source. In Láadan, therefore, you can compactly say, "Bíi mehal withid izh mehal ra with waá," while to communicate this in English you would need to say, "Men work but women don't work—at least that's what I've been told, but, considering the source, I'm not really inclined to believe it" (Elgin 1988). Similarly, in Láadan you can use the evidence morpheme "wá" ("I myself have perceived this") in the sentence "Bíi mehal with izh mehal ra withid wá," and it is clear that your statement, "Women work but men don't work," is made on the basis of your own perceptions. Elgin (1988, p. 129) notes that this feature of Láadan works against a hearer's refusal to accept a speaker's statement as having any acceptable basis. Unfortunately, we are all too familiar with hearers' frequent refusal to credit what women say. In her novels, Elgin (1984, 1987) shows that women using Láadan, because they are no longer forced by inadequate languages to appear stupid or obsessed with the trivial, grow self-assured and capable of taking action which furthers their own ends.

In Atwood's dysutopian *Handmaid's Tale,* the power of language is equally evident. Women in the Republic of Gilead are not permitted to read. (Judd, one of the architects of the Republic, is credited with saying, "Our big mistake was teaching them to read. We won't do that again" [p. 307].) The shops are known by their pictorial signs alone, women are expected to keep silent or to utter only approved phrases, and playing Scrabble with a woman is indecent—titillating. Yet the rebels use a system of manual signs, a silent language, to communicate. And the Handmaid finds in her closet a message in Latin (the language once forbidden to women) scratched there by the previous, now dead, Handmaid: "Nolite te bastardes carborundum"—Don't let the bastards grind you down. And the Handmaid insists on telling her story, on speaking to us, even though she is not even sure we exist. Talking to themselves, to other women, and to a hoped-for future audience, the officially silent women of this story insist on language as their own, as a way of affirming their existence.

In Piercy's *Woman on the Edge of Time,* a work simultaneously utopian and dysutopian, language appears both as a tool of social control and as reflection of freedom. Connie, the protagonist, is labeled crazy by a patriarchal psychiatric system that attempts to control the speech, as well as action, of uncooperative inmates through chemical, electrical, and surgical means. She is silenced when her speech is ignored, when she is forbidden to "self-diagnose," and when she is described in the mechanical phrases of medical-chart notes. The communication-repressing, thought-repressing, feeling-repressing language of the mental hospital is echoed in the meaningless chatter and repetitions both of Dolly, Connie's pimp-controlled, drug-numbed niece, and of Gildina, the prostitute/housewife of the dysutopian future Connie stumbles into. By contrast, language bubbles over into song and reveals its essential fluidity in the utopian future of Mattapoisett, where Connie is taken by Luciente, a woman of that time. In Mattapoisett and the other settlements of this future time, our English has altered in ways that invite our thinking to alter. "Per" (for "person") has unobtrusively replaced both "he" and "she," and "com" (for "co-mother") has been introduced to describe those who have chosen to be parents—as one of a set of three adults, none biologically related to the child. The women and men of this future have engaged with language as the lovely toy and workaday friend it is, neither allowing themselves to be bullied by it nor employing it for domination.

Each of these books indicates the subversive potential of language, not only reminding us how language has been and is used to alienate women from our experience but also inviting us to consider the everyday audacity of private and public language use as a form of mental liberation. A woman who speaks to herself about the gap between the abuser's language and her reality has begun to create a chink in the wall of isolation that keeps her captive. A woman who speaks to other women about her reality and theirs has begun to move toward collective as well as individual action.

In her poem, "Käthe Kollwitz," Muriel Rukeyser (1968, p. 103) has written that if one woman spoke the truth about her life, the world would split open. We have witnessed this again and again in the women's movement. Women speaking out publicly on taboo topics of male violence against women (topics such as rape, sexual harassment and sexual discrimination in the workplace, wife battering, child physical abuse, and incest) has led to dramatic changes in the criminal-justice, the legal, and the mental-health systems. Even though most women do not believe these changes have gone far enough in protecting women from abuses of male power, and even though in some cases such changes are being misused against women, changes never would have occurred at all if women had kept quiet.[2] The patriarchal backlash against women is predictable and should be a signal that women are being effective.

Changes in our language also have occurred as a result of women telling our stories. For example, until recently, terms like "acquaintance rape" and "marital rape" would have been dismissed as linguistic nonsense. Also, after centuries of patiently trying to explain to, and convince, men that their behaviors toward us are damaging, women hit upon the phrase "Men just don't get it" during the Clarence Thomas–Anita Hill sexual harassment controversy. In coining this phrase, women turned the tables on men, who now are in the position of needing to prove that they can "get it." Being able to name an experience is a powerful force for change.[3]

Individual women, whether they are struggling with discrimination in the workplace, abuse in the home, everyday sexual harassment, the aftereffects of rape, or any of the other isolating conditions so common in patriarchy, can begin to reduce their resulting Societal Stockholm Syndrome by claiming language as their own. Keeping a journal or even a list or record of offensive events is one way to do this (assuming the written material can be kept out of others' hands). If private telephone conversations are possible, arranging to talk with another woman—one who will listen nonjudgmentally—on a regular basis can be very helpful. Subscribing to a feminist publication, particularly one with a vital "Letters" section, also can provide a way to share speaking with other women.[4] And women's support and consciousness-raising groups give them a chance to stay with their (often diffuse and inarticulate) concerns long enough to gain some clarity about the phenomena they are dealing with, to develop concise ways of describing those phenomena, and to develop confidence in themselves as having the right and ability to communicate their experiences. Since social change requires social recognition of that which needs to be changed, it is essential that women speak among each other in order to develop the language to describe our realities and to demand change.

Envisioning, Coming Together, and Prospering

Revolutionary Visions

Feminist science fiction is revolutionary in several respects. First, it makes women central actors in life's drama instead of relegating us to the peripheral roles in which patriarchy casts women (fictional and real alike). Frye (1983) discusses the importance of shifting our attention away from men in order to transform patriarchy into a new reality. Using an analogy from the stage, she points out that, for a play to be convincing, attention must be focused on the actors while props and the stagehands who manipulate the props must remain unobtrusive. If the audience shifts its attention so that scenery and stagehands become the foreground, the play cannot continue. In her analogy, the actors are, of course, men and the stagehands, women. Johnson (1987) makes a similar observation when she writes: "As soon as we change our feeling that the men and what they are doing is what is important in the world—that it is important *at all,* as soon as we take our eyes off the guys, and *only* when we do, we will see a new reality opening before us. Until then, we will be stuck fast in the patriarchal mind, wasting our energies, trapped and despairing" (p. 339). Feminist science fiction offers us a way to take our eyes off men as the important people, the visible actors, and instead turn the stagehands and props of patriarchy (women) into visible reality.

Feminist science fiction is revolutionary in presenting visions of matriarchal societies, which exist nowhere on our planet and may never have existed. Whereas patriarchy imagines matriarchy as a matter of reversal in the power relation between men and women, matriarchy requires a rejection of the dichotomous thinking on which this male fantasy is founded. Matriarchy is a completely different form of organization than patriarchy, emphasizing what Miller (1986) describes as *power with,* as distinct from *power over.* Love and Shanklin (1983) define matriarchy as a society in which all interpersonal relationships are modeled on the nurturant relationship between a mother and her child. According to these authors this nurturant mode would inform all social institutions. The goal of the nurturant relationship would be to strengthen "the unique will of each individual to form open, trusting, creative bonds with others" (p. 279).[5]

Women's Coming Together

Women existing in a patriarchal culture right now can nurture ourselves, and move toward the new society envisioned in feminist science fiction, by coming together in small groups that foster both reflection and action. Women's coming together is the reality underlying each of the four feminist science fiction themes we have discussed: in these stories, women teach one another the powers of connection and support their exercise in daily life. The stories show women who are determined to share with each other their individual experiences and to communicate clearly to the world their shared experience. The women learn from each other how to trust and mistrust appropriately and how to hold accountable those not deserving of their trust. And women in these stories are not isolated individual warriors, no matter what their achievements; instead, they stand as powerful individuals against supportive backgrounds that assume their right and ability to defend themselves and to fight for their values.

Women's coming together disrupts the four interlocking Stockholm Syndrome-producing conditions of threat to survival, isolation, inability to escape, and dependence on the oppressor's kindness. Clearly, women who come together, in a way that permits honest discussion of our lives, are breaking down the psychological isolation that keeps us imprisoned in Societal Stockholm Syndrome. As women, connecting with each other, receive from each other the nurturance, affirmation, and consideration each human being needs, we will grow less dependent on men's small kindnesses as our primary way of experiencing a sense of self-worth. In discussing our situations with one another and developing strategies of resistance, we decrease our inability to escape. And as we see our successes, no matter how temporary or small, and the successes of other women in sometimes moving outside patriarchy's control, the actual power of patriarchy is weakened. Our culture, though still woman hating, no longer possesses total power to dictate all aspects of women's lives. Women can thus press forward: patriarchy no longer poses the same absolute threat to our survival.

Like Steinem (1992, November/December), we see the need to restore to women everywhere the option of small groups that will nourish personal growth and political renewal. We are concerned that feminists notice and learn from the situations that have caused women to "forget" about such groups.

Women's self-hatred, associated with Societal Stockholm Syndrome, can cause us to dislike, mistrust, and disparage other women. We have come to see ourselves as our oppressors see us—as unimportant, silly, and conniving. This problem is compounded by patriarchally imposed divisions of women by class, race, ethnicity, religion, age, and sexual orientation. Pheterson (1986) notes that women as an oppressed group have internalized domination behaviors which we often display toward subgroups culturally labeled as especially inferior (for instance, women of color, lesbians, old women, or Jewish women). Healing what Starhawk (1982) calls the inner self-hater and building bridges between various groups of women are essential in a movement that sets women free.

We do not advocate a blithe, no-questions-asked approach to group involvement. Rather, we advocate groups that operate within clearly articulated guidelines that protect all members—guidelines that include confidentiality, speaking from one's own experience, no amateur psychotherapy, adherence to agreed-upon starting and ending times, and equal opportunity (not pressure) to speak (see Steinem 1992, November/December, pp. 27–29; National Organization for Women 1982; Allen 1970).

We believe that women so often fail to connect or stay connected with social action not because action strategies are difficult to develop but because we have not yet found a way to connect *as full people* with a collective struggle.[6] Small women's groups can provide the needed bridge between individual authenticity and collective action, for they provide a way for women to tell our stories, the stories that connect what we live and have lived with what we work for, so that it may come to be the story of all women.

Opposing Patriarchy and Prospering

We are aware that the very virtue of women's groups that we advocate here—their power as bridges into social action—is exactly what makes the idea of taking part in a group so frightening for many women: to come together with other women is to risk being seen as resisting patriarchy and therefore is to risk being punished. But this fear overlooks the facts that women are punished whether or not we resist and, most importantly, *women are already resisting patriarchy*.

Table 6.1, taken from Rawlings and Carter (1977), illustrates the different strategies of resistance adopted by women, reminding us that even the most docile and traditional women are resisting in their own way. Rawlings and Carter compared the ego defenses used by women with those Allport (1954) had documented for minority groups such as African-Americans and Jews. In table 6.1 the defenses described by Allport are in capital letters while the defenses seen in women are in lower case. Allport classified each defense as either intropunitive (anger turned inward) or extropunitive (anger turned outward). In table 6.1, the left-hand column shows the intropunitive defenses of traditional women and the middle column displays the extropunitive defenses of traditional women. The right-hand column lists the extropunitive defenses of feminist women.

In our interpretation of table 6.1, traditional intropunitive women show more Societal Stockholm Syndrome and do not openly dispute their second-class citizenship. However, the wife who has a headache to avoid sex and the housewife who becomes immobilized by depression and therefore cannot do her housework or perform other wifely duties are protesting patriarchal demands. The traditional intropunitive woman's resistance takes passive forms and often appears self-destructive. The traditional extrapunitive woman, by contrast, is viewed within patriarchy as the classic "bitch" or evil woman. She manipulates men and the male system for her own benefit and refuses to follow the patriarchal rules defining a "good woman." Women using both these traditional strategies are resisting, but their awareness of their protest usually is low and intermittent and they lack a conscious analysis of the oppression they are resisting. Feminism provides an analysis of that oppression, makes it clear that women are combatting a political reality as well as apparently isolated individual situations, and therefore makes it possible to direct protest to bring about personal and social change.

All women resist patriarchy, and all women are punished, whether or not we resist. The issue, then, is not *whether* we should resist but *how* we

TABLE 6.1
Types of Ego Defenses among Victims of Discrimination

Intropunitive Individuals	Extropunitive Individuals	Extropunitive Individuals
TRADITIONAL WOMEN	TRADITIONAL WOMEN	FEMINIST WOMEN
Denial of Membership in Own Group	*Slyness and Cunning*	*Obsessive Concern and Suspicion*
Deriving pleasure from "thinking like a man"	Manipulation of men	Hypersensitivity to sexist remarks
Preferring the company of men	*Neuroticism*	*Strengthening In-Group Ties*
Withdrawal and Passivity	Narcissism	Consciousness-raising groups
Indecision	*Competitiveness*	Support groups
Misdirected anger to persons of less power	Put men down, either directly or indirectly ("castrating female")	Campus and community women's centers
Difficulty in expressing anger	Derive satisfaction only from competing with men	Financial and professional self-help collectives
Avoidance of conflict		Cooperative political action
Clowning		*Prejudice against Other Groups*
Giggling		Anger toward men
Being coy and cute		*Aggression and Revolt*
Humerous self-deprecation		Divorce
Self-Hate		Individual and class action lawsuits against employers
Acceptance of own "natural inferiority"		Radical feminism
Building a man's ego, especially at a woman's own expense		*Competitiveness*
Assuming the doormat posture with men		Compete for the prize, not to put down men or other women
Chronic depression		*Enhanced Striving*
In-Group Aggression		Striving for better jobs, for better salaries, and for higher academic degrees
Competitive with other women		
Back-biting and gossiping		
Putting down other women		
Sympathy with All Victims		
Sentimentality		
Volunteer and charity work		

TABLE 6.1 *(Continued)*
Types of Ego Defenses among Victims of Discrimination

Intropunitive Individuals	Extropunitive Individuals	Extropunitive Individuals
TRADITIONAL WOMEN	TRADITIONAL WOMEN	FEMINIST WOMEN
Symbolic Status Striving Expensive house, beautiful clothes, professional husband and his financial success, well-behaved children and their accomplishments *Neuroticism* Helplessness, phobias, and hysteria		

From E. I. Rawlings and D. K. Carter, *Psychotherapy for women: Treatment toward equality* (1977). Courtesy of Charles C. Thomas, Publisher, Springfield, Illinois. (They adapted the table from Gordon Allport, *The Nature of Prejudice* [1954], p. 157.)

can resist most effectively. In advocating feminist action, then, we are not calling for a revolution but are pointing out that *the revolution is in progress* and *we're all in it*. So let's engage with it the best we can. As Lorde (1984, pp. 42, 44) reminds us, women's silence will not protect us:

> We can sit in our corners mute forever while our sisters and our selves are wasted, while our children are distorted and destroyed, while our earth is poisoned; we can sit in our safe corners mute as bottles, and we still will be no less afraid. . . . We have been socialized to respect fear more than our own needs for language and definition, and while we wait in silence for that final luxury of fearlessness, the weight of that silence will choke us.

A given woman may resist patriarchy as part of a small group or as an individual, and she may use one approach in one period or area of her life and the other in other periods or areas. Therefore we want to be clear that our advocacy of small groups does not suggest that social action cannot be taken by individuals as well. Each needs the other, just as social action needs to occur both in public and in one's private life. Walker (1992, pp. 213–214) illustrates this integration, telling us that to be a feminist "is to search for personal clarity in the midst of systematic destruction, to join in sisterhood with women when often we are divided, to understand power structures with the intention of challenging them." She also illustrates this integration in telling women to hold men accountable in all areas of life: "Do not vote for them unless they work for us. Do not have sex with them, do not break bread with them, do not nurture them if they don't prioritize our freedom to control our bodies and our lives."

In this spirit, we present here four methods of resistance that can be employed individually and collectively, to generate social action in both the private and the public spheres. The methods we present are the equivalent of folk wisdom—knowledge of how to prosper against the odds and without getting locked into an "each one for herself" mentality. These methods, recognizable as the property of all groups living in social adversity, are claiming space, keeping track, looking out for one's own, and getting savvy.

This focus on methods of generating social action, on the *principles* of resistance, arises both from our view of the problem (Societal Stockholm Syndrome) and from our view of our audience (women). First, *the* problem we are dealing with is too big for the development of a model program. *The* problem, pointed out in the preceding chapters, is patriarchy; *the* problem is the all-pervasiveness of the four conditions producing Societal Stockholm Syndrome. To weaken those conditions, women need to work simultaneously on a variety of fronts (educational, legal, religious, therapeutic, economic, and so forth), to work simultaneously on several levels (personal, interpersonal, and institutional), and to combat simultaneously a variety of manifestations of *the* problem (acquaintance rape, stranger rape, job discrimination, battering, child abuse, pornography, power inequalities in marriage, homophobia, prostitution, male-controlled governments, and so on). An entire chapter could be devoted to setting forth a model program for addressing just one of these many manifestations of patriarchy.[7]

Furthermore, if women are encouraged to use just one strategy or to pour all our energies into opposing a specific current manifestation of patriarchy, women will be taken off guard and exploited when patriarchy does a flip-flop, as it tends to do. ("OK, you can have the vote. Now disband and go away"; "Factory jobs aren't important now that the war's over. Child-rearing is what *really* matters.") By contrast, knowledge of the principles of resistance, the methods already at hand for combatting the four Societal Stockholm Syndrome-producing conditions, can give women the flexibility to make creative use of whatever opportunities open up for feminist action. The four methods of claiming space, keeping track, looking out for one's own, and getting savvy provide women with power that is wide-ranging, flexible, and women's own.

To look at this issue of the problem in another way, women don't need to come up with a model program for addressing the problem, because that model program exists—it is the feminist movement. And what women need to do is *to do feminism*—not justify, explain, or theorize in ways that distract us from doing feminism and from noticing that the theory is abundantly present in our practice.

Now, as to our view of our audience. We would like to point out that feminists are not at a loss for programs. Women are not dumb: we don't need to be told what to do to change abusive structures. And women are not lazy: we are already at work in a variety of effective ways.[8]

Claiming Space

Claiming space is a basic method for prospering used by oppressed groups. Individuals dream of owning their own houses or of owning land. Groups dream of building their own church or meeting hall. And these dreams sustain hope, lead to plans, guide actions, and sometimes become realities.

Women are like members of other oppressed groups in this regard, yet we also struggle with a unique set of constraints as the only oppressed group forced to live on intimate terms with the oppressor group. While the immigrant factory worker may dream of owning a house, a woman will dream of having a room of her own. Most women in the modern Western world have no space of our own in the home—no den, basement workshop, garage, outside domain, or special chair in the living room. Though the kitchen and bedroom often are thought of as "her" rooms, they are hers only as spaces in which she is expected to provide services to and for her man. Private space—space in which she can just be, space where she does not have to justify her presence by being engaged in work—is nonexistent unless she actively creates and maintains it. This also holds for women as a group within organizations. The women's church group rarely has its own room, though the male ushers may have their own headquarters, just as the priest has his vestry. And most forms of paid work outside the home that are readily available to women are performed in full view of managers or the public at all times. The ghetto and the barrio are instruments of oppression, yet ones that Jews, African-Americans, and Hispanics have learned to use to their own ends as well, creating a cultural space that keeps the oppressor group out as well as keeping themselves in. But in most parts of the modern world, women have lost even the gynaecum/harem/women's quarters. To see this clearly, though, is not to counsel despair—it is to understand that claiming space is a basic method of resistance.

A hallmark of the contemporary women's movement has been the establishment of battered women's shelters, university and community women's centers, and women's bookstores. We can maintain the revolutionary impulse behind these spaces by asking, "In what ways can I claim free space, women-space for myself? For my group of women?" Choosing to work in or use an existing women-only space such as a shelter, a women's center, or a women's bookshop is one way a woman can develop the resolve to create more free space for herself and for women as a group.

Individual women may begin claiming space by more consciously defining their physical personal zone (both at home and at work); by rearranging furniture; by claiming their own corner of the kitchen, bedroom, or basement or claiming their special chair—and establishing "do not interrupt" rules for the times they spend in that space. Any of these moves can embolden a woman to make still more, opposing the patriarchal constriction of women both within and beyond the family.

Women also can make such moves in conjunction with other women, either by publicly raising issues that rouse other women to the extent that a grassroots coalition takes shape, or by working within groups of which they already are members. We can claim space for women as a class by asking why one's town has no office where rape crisis counselors can meet with sexual assault survivors, asking why a room hasn't been set aside for the use of the women's church group, asking for commitment and financial support to establish a battered women's shelter.

Symbolic space also has been created within professional organizations by women members who have formed women's caucuses or divisions to ensure that women's issues are addressed within those organizations and to ensure that annual conventions include multiple meetings devoted to women's concerns in relation to the subject matters dealt with by the organizations. Women can join, support, and affirm the importance of these caucuses and divisions—or create them where they do not yet exist—as another way of finding *and enlarging* the space available to women in a currently patriarchal universe.

Our space can be space solely for women. It also can be space where women are recognized as real—by men as well as other women. Asking where there is space for us—in nonphysical as well as physical domains—therefore is always important. Where is there space for women in the curriculum? The judiciary? The media? Where is there space for women in the day and in the week? Where is there space for women in the museums? Where is there space for women in conversation? Is it a space or a corral? How can we enlarge it? These are the questions to ask if women want to combat the inescapability of patriarchal domination. Voicing our desire and need for safe places for women to be alone, to gather with other women, and to be recognized by men as a real force provides women a basic method for prospering despite adversity. It is a way not only to maintain the gains already made but to discover new ways of advancing the revolt against patriarchy. Women's own space gives us a way to establish our relation to the universe as our own human world, not an inescapable patriarchal prison.

Keeping Track

Like claiming space, keeping track (that is, writing our history as we live it) is a method by which women can give concrete form to our vision. It allows us to devise strategies and take advantage of opportunities to advance our safety and well-being, reducing the diffuse sense of inescapable terror that pervades women's lives under patriarchy. Keeping track has two components: women documenting reality/telling stories, and documenting the actions of men with whom women deal.

Telling Stories/Documenting Reality. Burstow (1992, p. 18) points out that "women's vision may be seen as an act of resistance in its own right. Seeing out of our eyes is itself disobeying the patriarchy." Having one's own perspective, distinct from that of one's oppressors, is essential for recovering one's sense of self. However, unless that perspective is preserved and shared, it is unlikely to lead to personal or social change.

Throughout time, literate women have recorded their thoughts and experiences in diaries and letters. But the privacy of these media, which made it possible for women to safely create records, also kept women's lives invisible. Women lack a history of our own; we have been handed a patriarchal, self-serving history by men that ignores women's achievements and heroisms. Feminist scholars are painstakingly attempting to reconstruct women's history, but much of it has been lost forever. This should make women all the more aware of the importance now of preserving and sharing our history as we create it each day and year.

The feminist movement has given women many public forums in which we can be "heard into being" (Johnson 1987): consciousness-raising groups, speakouts, women's international tribunals, candlelight vigils, and take-back-the-night marches. The feminist movement has provided women with a context that legitimates speaking of the previously hidden violence in our lives—the incest, rape, battering, and harassment that shape our days. And revealing the pervasiveness of this violence exposes the falsity of the patriarchal myths that such incidents are isolated; are committed only by a few deranged, aberrant men; are only fantasies of delusional, hysterical, or "crazy" women; or are fantasies originating in women's desires.

Television has helped disseminate women's stories of violence. Almost every weekday, at least one major talk show now addresses the topic of some type of violence in women's lives. The audience participation that is encouraged, as well as the story-telling format, ensures that more than the dominant patriarchal position is aired. Therefore, viewers' ideological isolation is reduced. In addition to the talk shows, television movies, "magazine" programs, and documentaries frequently tell women's personal stories of violence. (And, interestingly, these programs sometimes show both a woman's active attempts to fight back against violence and the unjust treatment she receives from the legal system when she does fight back—making it clear that the patriarchal justice system, rather than the woman, has failed.)[9] As a result, millions of people now are being exposed to such stories. Without forgetting that television producers for the most part are simply trying to exploit issues to draw audiences, we can be alert to the audiences' real engagement with the issues and we can work on promoting and nurturing that engagement.

It is important for women to press for change by continuing to tell and record our experiences publicly. In the past, public outrage at injustices directed at women has been a powerful lever for changing the justice system. During the past twenty years of the feminist movement, significant progress has been made in changing laws that failed to protect women from male violence and exploitation. For instance, laws in most states have been modified to keep a rape victim's prior sexual history from being brought up to discredit her. And, more recently, mandatory arrest laws have been adopted in some U.S. counties and stalking laws have been introduced in a few states. These changes did not come about because progress is automatic; they occurred only because women publicly raised their voices to register their experiences as part of history. Continuing to do this and to support other women who do so is a basic method whereby all women can push back patriarchy and begin to prosper.

The impact of courageous women risking their own security to give testimony against male perpetrators of violence cannot be overestimated. A compelling example is that of Professor Anita Hill, who came forward during the U.S. Senate confirmation hearings on the nomination of Judge Clarence Thomas for Supreme Court Justice to testify regarding Thomas's sexual harassment of her. Hill was subjected to vicious personal attacks on her motives, character, and mental stability. Yet her courageous testimony set into motion a chain of events that continues to produce dramatic changes.

In particular, Hill's testimony had a direct effect on bringing sexual harassment in the workplace out of the closet. Despite many dire predictions that U.S. senators' verbal abuse of Hill and the subsequent Senate confirmation of Thomas would frighten into silence victims of sexual harassment, the opposite happened. More women began speaking out about their experiences of being sexually harassed on the job, more lawsuits were filed, Equal Employment Opportunity Commission (EEOC) regulations were changed to make sexual harassment easier to report, and the percentage of Fortune 500 companies that provided sexual harassment sensitivity training rose from 35 to 81 percent in the year following Hill's testimony (DeAngelis 1992, December; Trost 1992, October 13).

We believe that the nation's collective consciousness is being enlarged to take in the reality of men's abuse and exploitation of women. We see this as being brought about by the combination of a visible feminist movement (which has openly discussed violence toward women and has provided an analysis of it in terms of men's socially programmed need to subordinate women) and television's insatiable need for programming that contains both human interest value and a fair amount of sensationalism. Though many may agree with this statement now, no one could have predicted that the 1990s would bring such widespread recognition of violence against women or such a far-reaching event as Hill's testimony. And without women's continued insistence on keeping track of their experiences and speaking the truth of those experiences, none of this would have occurred.

Nor is the impact of this basic method of keeping track confined to national events and powerful players remote from most women's everyday lives. For instance, a newspaper survey by the Cincinnati YWCA in 1976—a survey in which women reported the reality of their experiences—convinced the community that battering was a serious, widespread issue in the area and generated support for a women's shelter and related programs ("A Flawed Proposal," December 19, 1992). If we continue to keep track of our experiences, we will be in a position to speak out forcefully, both when we are asked and when we are not; we will be able to use and to create opportunities for change. The more voices are raised in testimony to male abuse of women, the less isolated and deviant the victims will feel, the harder it will be for patriarchy to minimize the problem, and the greater the societal pressure will become to end male violence.

Documenting Men's Actions. Keeping track of the behavior of others is essential in bringing about personal and social change regarding the violence in women's lives. Recording the details can help us see the pattern, which in turn can help us recognize what we're up against in specific situations.

Describing a situation on paper can serve as proof that certain events actually did take place. This is important, since it is not unusual for people to question their memories and even their sanity when they find themselves dealing with abuse. Documenting procedures developed by Dr. June Peters (in press) in her work with battered women may be useful to women in general and can be used by women individually or in groups. One of Peters's procedures is to have a woman write out— verbatim—the interactions and communications that leave her feeling confused or diminished. This often can quickly reveal how abusive the woman's ordinary, everyday interactions are.

Another procedure involves a woman's writing down all the abusive names her partner has called her. The woman then notes how frequently (how many times per day, week, month, or year) her partner has called her each of these names. She then multiplies each frequency by the length of time she has been with her partner. Finally, she sums these totals to obtain a grand total of the abusive verbalizations that have been directed at her for the duration of the relationship. (These grand totals sometimes run to five or six figures.) When this procedure is used in a group, the women can be asked to compare the names they have been called, and they invariably find that their partners tend to use the same epithets. As a result of this procedure, a woman in an abusive relationship can come to see both the extent to which the verbal abuse has eroded her self-esteem and the fact that the words directed at her have little to do with her as an individual. Rather, they are names that men call women—every woman.

This documenting procedure is useful for a woman who is not a victim of battering, rape, or incest. If a woman took the time to document all the verbal violence directed toward her over her lifetime—in the form of demeaning advertising, disparaging jokes and innuendos, exposure to pornography, street hassles, sexual remarks by male acquaintances and co-workers, and obscene phone calls—she would be astonished at the amount of "normal" male violence she has absorbed without even being physically touched. If any of us were to record all the verbal mini-abuses we encounter in just one week, we would be astonished, enraged, and more fully prepared to work against male violence in the situations we en-counter.

Women working in groups also can keep track of the behavior of employers and of elected and appointed officials. Organizations such as the National Organization for Women (NOW) and the Fund for the Feminist Majority do this with respect to politicians at the national level, but local monitoring is also possible and necessary. And it gets results. One example is the success of a Wisconsin women's group in petitioning for the removal of a judge who had ruled that a sexually abused minor girl was seductive and therefore responsible for her abuse ("Judge Faces Recall," 1983).

Keeping track of men's behaviors in relation to women personally and to other women can allow women to disentangle ourselves from bad personal situations and to put employers and officials on notice that women demand respect from them in their private as well as their public actions. We should never forget that the outcome of a grievance action or a legal dispute often hinges on the presence or absence of documentation, since memory about dates and specifics may be (or be regarded as) unreliable. As women continue to engage in keeping track, we should remember that documents can include letters, memos (to others or to oneself), diary entries, canceled checks, tapes, and medical or legal re-cords. It is worth keeping in mind, too, that personal documentation carries more weight when it is shared with someone else: you can show your documents, as you create and preserve them, to at least one other person and have that person sign and date the document as proof that it existed at that given time. This witnessing person may be either someone you know and trust or a notary. When in doubt, document. Even if, at the time a situation occurs, you do not plan to file a grievance or lawsuit, having the documentation gives the option of using it later in case there is a change of circumstances or of mind. And having documentation can also protect you and other women against unfair charges or allegations.

Each occasion on which women keep track of our experience and of the behavior of those around us allows us to affirm our reality (as individ-uals and as members of a group that exists in history), to claim language as our own, and to hold men accountable. Each exercise of this basic revolutionary method decreases the sense and the actuality of inescapability that makes male violence so damaging to all women.

Looking Out for Our Own

A third method women can use to oppose patriarchy is looking out for our own. This is a matter of looking at what women have to give—money, votes, and endorsements—and considering women first when we give it.

Though women have little discretionary income in comparison to men, we can consciously direct a portion of that income to individuals and groups that address rather than ignore women's needs. We can choose to give our five-dollar and two-dollar contributions (or more, if we happen to have the money) to the Ms. Foundation for Women, the National Women's Political Caucus, NOW's Legal, Defense, and Education Fund, EMILY's List, and other such organizations rather than to the mainstream charities, the Democrats, or the Republicans.[10] We can designate our United Appeal contributions to go to women's causes such as rape crisis programs and battered women's shelters. (And if no such agencies are funded by the local United Appeal, we can ask why.) When besieged by mailings and telephone calls from numerous organizations requesting money, we can say to those that do not specifically support women's needs and development, "Sorry. On my income I can afford to give only X dollars a month, total, to worthy organizations, and all that goes to feminist causes." (If men can say, "I gave at the office," so can women.)

Women can also choose where to direct our nondiscretionary income. We can purchase our goods and services from women, preferably feminist women, while holding them to the same standards of quality we hold other providers and being willing to pay them as much as we pay other providers. Even those of us who seem not to have a choice can do this: students can make it known to administrators that they want female, as well as male, physicians at their student health center; and women covered by managed health-care plans can do the same with regard to the pool of health-care providers with which they are presented. Women can give preference to women lawyers, women auto mechanics, women vets, and women-owned businesses that sell in their area or by mail order.

Women can also look out for our own by using our political votes and our votes of confidence. NOW, other women's organizations, and *Ms.* magazine frequently publish information on the stands taken by women candidates—so it is not difficult to determine whom we want to support with our votes. As Lewis (1992, September/October, p. 85) so clearly puts it, "Don't vote for women 'because of gender.' Vote for them because of what they stand for, and what they're going to fight for. Vote because our lives are at stake." Votes of confidence also have impact in women's everyday lives—we can tell our friends, neighbors, and co-workers about the women providers of goods and services with which we are pleased, helping to build female solidarity and maintain women's livelihood, so that we are not economically trapped as individuals and as a group within patriarchy.

Clearly, all of these ways of supporting our own can be pursued by individual women. And by speaking up in groups to which we belong, we can remind those groups—unions, clubs, churches, schools, and more—that they, too, can give their business to women and can endorse women's causes. In beginning to see "our own" as women, not just our individual families, races, religions, or classes, women significantly weaken the isolation that patriarchy imposes on us, and we will become far less dependent on men as a group for the small kindnesses that allow women to feel we can survive but that meanwhile trap us in Societal Stockholm Syndrome. The surge of pride and love we feel when seeing a feminist science fiction hero defend another woman (as the healer Snake does in *Dreamsnake* when she rescues the abused child Melissa) should remind women of our own capacities to look out for one another and our own right to receive such care.

Looking at what women have to give to our own even when we appear to have nothing is a way of remembering our power to combat patriarchy and prosper in the process. Thinking globally while acting locally is the habitual practice of many women all around the world. It is a habit we can preserve, revive, and practice consciously and articulately so that we and the women around us will take heart, develop pride in womanhood, and thrive.

Getting Savvy

To support and engage in action leading to social change, we need to be savvy about patriarchal thinking and the messages used to confuse, placate, or intimidate women trying to bring about change. The basic activity of getting savvy is summed up by Morgan as "feminist principle 101: *question everything*" (1992, September/October, p. 1). Getting savvy is a basic method for generating social action because it is ongoing—each new understanding about how patriarchy works nourishes women's anger, motivates action, and helps women anticipate and protect themselves from the established system's response. In this section we will give several examples of patriarchal ploys and tactics in order to communicate some of the content of feminist savvy. This content is not the process of getting savvy, though. Getting savvy itself has to do with paying close attention to proponents of patriarchy, keeping two things in mind: (1) since patriarchy is founded on a lie (the lie of women's natural inferiority), patriarchal logic usually is the reverse of the truth, and we therefore can get at the truth by reversing patriarchal messages (Johnson 1987, pp. 322, 339; 1989); and (2) when proponents of patriarchy get mad, we should get interested, not get afraid (for their anger indicates we've touched a hot button or in some way gotten too close to the truth for their comfort).

A common patriarchal tactic is to try to silence a woman who speaks up by calling her a man hater, a lesbian, or a feminist. To the patriarchal mind, these three names are interchangeable—all refer to women who are not dedicating their lives to the support of men.

Distraction, or the verbal bait-and-switch, is a common patriarchal maneuver. For instance, women who oppose pornography often are asked why they are so prudish. These sorts of accusations are based on implicit definitions unconnected in fact to the phenomenon defined. In this case, pornography is being implicitly defined as having to do with sex, when in fact it has to do with domination and violation. Ridicule of women who oppose patriarchal practices usually is based on this sort of false, concealed definition. For instance, when a woman complains about sexual harassment and men say that she could not have been harassed because "she just isn't that attractive," they are implicitly defining harassment as having to do with sexual attraction, when it actually has to do with domination.

Blame-the-victim responses, such as saying of a rape victim, "What does she expect—dressing that way?" also are attempts to impose false definitions on the terms of the discussion.

Appeals to "femininity" are designed to keep women from claiming greater power, and such gallant-sounding appeals often contain threats. For instance, men may say that political activity is "too dirty" for women or they may contend that women soldiers will be subjected to rape by the enemy if they are captured. What is ignored here is the fact that being "feminine" never has protected women from male violence: if women don't claim power, we still will be politically savaged; whether or not we go to war as soldiers, women have always been and still are subject to rape by our "own" men, as well as by enemy forces.

A common patriarchal tactic is to trivialize women's demands for freedom and equality. For instance, feminists have been referred to as "women's libbers," and women working in professional positions often are described as "doctors' wives" or "bored faculty wives." Similarly, feminist demands that standard language use be changed to be more inclusive of women are ridiculed as frivolous and picky.

Guilt-tripping is a perennial patriarchal ploy. Those who raise women's issues often are asked how they can be so concerned about these matters when Africans are starving or South Americans are being tortured. African-American women who advocate women's rights are routinely accused of draining energy from the cause of black advancement (Gillespie 1993, January/February). Conveniently overlooked here are the facts that at least half of all starving Africans, tortured South Americans, and discriminated-against blacks are women, and that it is only women, never men, who are expected to forsake their gender in order to prove their seriousness when working for social change.

Divide and conquer is a common patriarchal strategy. Feminists have learned that "you are not like those other women" or "I can talk to *you*" are not compliments, even though presented as such by men. These statements are subtle reminders to a woman to be a good subordinate—passive, compliant, and gullible. What's going on here is an attempt to separate these women from the support of other women. The same sort of maneuver is being used when men in power scapegoat an outspoken woman and do all they can to imply that "she just has a (personal) problem." The patriarchal hope here is that not only will the scapegoated woman be intimidated and silenced but that other women will also fall for this splitting and will strive to show that they aren't like her, in the hope that they'll be safe from attack.

Co-optation is a form of divide and conquer. When a woman is effective in advocating for women's rights, she may be offered a plum position that will make her part of the men's inner circle—with the implicit message that she needs to "tone it down" in order to stay in the power circle. Here, too, the other women around her, as well as the targeted women, should be wary, for they are being encouraged to sit back and let a leader do it all for them.

Acceding to some minor demands made by women is a time-honored patriarchal strategy. When men gallantly meet some demand that women are making, women should not be overly grateful for small kindnesses that we are due as human beings in any case. The implication often exists that because men already have done "so much," they shouldn't be asked to do more. Also, changes allegedly designed to increase fairness may be turned against women. This is especially true for changes that give women equal responsibilities while we still lack access to equal resources. For example, many states now require that the noncustodial parent pay child support when a couple divorces. As a result, women who must work for minimum wages (due to economic discrimination) can be required to pay child support to their former husbands, whose salaries are significantly higher. Women should be alert to setups such as these. We should notice, for instance, that when women complain about such inequities, men respond, "Well, you want equal treatment, but then you whine when we give it to you."

Patriarchal co-optation also can take the form of giving support to feminist-developed organizations serving women—but attaching sizable strings to their support. For instance, feminists started many rape crisis centers and battered women's shelters in the 1970s and ran them using feminist principles, including egalitarian decision-making and task-sharing. When the staffs of these organizations, desperate for money to keep them going, applied for governmental funding, they soon learned that the "gift" of funds came with requirements to change from a feminist nonhierarchical organization to a social-service-agency organization with a hierarchical chain of command and preset rules that the women in need of services had to follow in order to receive services (Ahrens 1981; Pride 1981; Schechter 1981, 1982).

All these patriarchal maneuvers, clearly, work to invoke or intensify the four conditions producing Societal Stockholm Syndrome: they cause women to feel afraid, trapped, cut off from the support of other women, and at men's mercy. They make women feel confused. Coming to understand how these maneuvers work, getting savvy to them, provides women with a sense of perspective and mastery, which encourages us to develop ways to expose, confront, and defy men's maneuvers.

Women can practice the ongoing art of becoming savvy to patriarchy by learning how to identify and defend ourselves against verbal abuse (see Elgin 1989)—and by sharing this knowledge with other women. Women can talk with other women, comparing notes and engaging in group analyses of the patterns of speech and behavior we encounter in the men around us. Women can familiarize ourselves with feminist analyses of patriarchal interactions—analyses available not only in feminist political and philosophical writings, but also in women's fiction (e.g., Cholmondeley 1899/1985) and feminist humor (e.g., Russ 1980b). Asking oneself—and other women—"What's going on here? What definitions are being slipped in on us unawares? How are we being set up to distrust or avoid each other? How are we being made to feel guilty or insignificant or inadequate? How are we being co-opted or bought off?" will always prove to be a fruitful source of understanding and action.

Conclusion

The four methods of resistance—claiming space, keeping track, looking out for our own, and getting savvy—are visible in feminist science fiction, are learned by women from women when we come together, and provide ways in which women can act not simply to survive but to thrive. Articulated, claimed as our own, and consciously practiced, these methods give women a flexible plan while affirming our native good sense.

These four methods are not exclusive of each other, for they do not represent some neat analytical scheme. They do not prescribe but, instead, describe women's successful actions in the continuing struggle against patriarchy. In fact, most successful feminist actions are shaped by more than one of these methods. For instance, an economic boycott of an organization or state that exploits or imposes unfair restrictions on women will likely have arisen out of women's efforts to keep track of the organization's or state's behavior and out of women's impulses to look out for our own, to claim space for ourselves within the decision-making process of the organization or state, and to succeed as a result of women's ongoing self-education about patriarchal ploys.

Any number of specific issues can be responded to and any number of tactics can be used in women's actions arising from these methods of opposing patriarchy, for these methods do not *dictate* women's revolutionary actions—they *generate* them. They are ways of creatively provoking women ourselves—mindsets that make it natural to respond to issues and develop tactics. Asking ourselves, "Where can we claim space? How can we claim space?" is likely to be more fruitful than asking, "What should we do about issue X?" We believe that women need to (as well as choose to) address a variety of issues and employ a variety of tactics in our shared opposition to patriarchy. The authors offer descriptions of these four methods in order to help women more readily create our own forms of action.

If women want to end, rather than reinforce, Societal Stockholm Syndrome, we need to nourish our sense of cause as one shared by all women. The more women are aware that some kind of action is called for, the more we act in ways that work best for us, the more we will reclaim our personal and collective power for action. Our own hope and belief is that at some point a critical mass of resistance and noncompliance will be achieved and, like the late Soviet Union, the patriarchy will one day cease to be. No army conquered it, no experts predicted its sudden demise. So may it be with patriarchy—if we all keep working in our various ways.

Both to women already working in groups and to individual women whose personal needs and situations make working alone more productive, we say, "You're already in a group—just look around you." The women's movement has created a context that makes it possible for women to speak the truth of our experiences and be heard—by other women and by some men. It has created a context women enlarge whenever we claim space for ourselves. It has created a context in which women can look out for each other. It has created a context in which women's individual and collective knowledge can accumulate. For all women at this point, the question of how to "join" the revolution is simply a question of how to be in a group more effectively. Remembering and honoring where we already are, connecting with the knowledge and strategies we already have, allows women to connect more fully with ourselves and more effectively with one another.

We began this chapter with several questions posed by Swift (1987, p. 20) about women's dilemma as captives in a battering culture. Here, now, are our brief answers as a summary of what we have said in this chapter:

"Where is that other world, that world outside the battering environment?" In our visions, our stories, and our dreams.

"Where are our safe houses?" Within an all-women space we create and maintain.

"How can we break [our] connection [to a patriarchal, battering culture]?" By connecting with other women in small groups that nourish mind and soul, and by coming together to form a mass movement opposing male violence.

We end this chapter with the belief that women someday will cease loving men simply in order to survive and, instead, will thrive with love—love of ourselves, of other women, and of men who choose to join with us in mutually empowering relationships. We end this book with a call to the shared reflection and action that will make the vision of a matriarchal system of shared power a reality.

Potential Aspects of Stockholm Syndrome

1. Captive dissociates from her/his body in order not to feel the pain created by the captor.[1]

2. Captive finds self needing captor's nurturance and protection.

3. Captive feels intensely grateful to captor for kindness, however small, shown to her/him.

4. Captive is hypervigilant to captor's needs to the neglect of her/his own needs.

5. Captive shows splitting (that is, dichotomous thinking).

6. Captive bonds to positive side of captor.

7. Captive dwells on kindness shown by captor while overlooking captor's violence against her/him.

8. Captive denies captor's violence against her/him and focuses on captor's positive side.

9. Captive denies own anger toward captor so that she or he may not even know that she or he is angry.

10. Captive sees captor as omnipotent.

11. Captive is "overcompliant."

12. Captive puts captor's needs before her/his own and often does not know what her/his own needs are.

13. Captive sees herself/himself as "special" to captor.

14. Captive demonstrates the "salvation ethic."

15. Captive tries to control everyone in her/his environment, besides captor, to protect herself/himself from captor's violence.

---

1. This list identifies characteristics observed in one or more "hostage" groups. As such, the characteristics are *potential* aspects of Stockholm Syndrome. Empirical research is needed to determine which are, in fact, aspects of Stockholm Syndrome and whether the composite of aspects observed in different "hostage" groups are similar. All characteristics listed are viewed as *responses* to, not causes of, interpersonal abuse.

16. Captive loves (cares for) captor even as she or he fears captor.

17. Captive feels closer to (and wants to be closer to) captor than to persons with whom she or he had or has a more mutually empowering relationship.

18. Captive takes captor's perspective, not her/his own. Captive may not even know what her/his perspective is.

19. Captive believes captor's violence toward her/him is deserved or caused by her/his own behavior. She or he rationalizes captor's abuse.

20. Captive feels hatred for that part of her/him that captor said led to captor's abuse of her/him.

21. Captive feels shame for abuse done to her/him by captor.

22. Captive sees herself/himself as captor sees her/him: less valuable, less capable, and to blame for captor's problems as well as own problems.

23. Captive shows low self-esteem.

24. Captive is supersensitive to rejection.

25. Captive is depressed.

26. Captive has feelings of helplessness and powerlessness.

27. Captive shows ritualistic behaviors.

28. Captive is unable to recognize own feelings.

29. Captive displays anxiety reactions.

30. Captive is unable to concentrate.

31. Captive feels she or he is losing touch with reality.

32. Captive has physical and psychophysiological problems.

33. Captive is distrustful of others.

34. Captive loses her/his own sense of self; sees herself/himself as captor sees her/him.

35. Captive feels she or he must have captor's favor or love to survive; appears emotionally dependent on captor.

36. Captive acts impulsively; loses internal control over own behavior.

37. Captive is unable to make decisions.

38. Captive has a chameleon personality.

39. Captive expresses an idealized picture of her/his relationship with captor and loses touch with the reality of the relationship.

40. Captive resents outsiders' attempts to free her/him from captor.

41. Captive resents outsiders who point out her/his oppression by captor.

42. Captive demonstrates unresolved feelings regarding captor.

43. Captive develops sexual dysfunction (if relationship with captor becomes sexual).

44. Captive expects the same exploitation from others as she or he receives from captor.

45. Captive begins to have difficulty forming close interpersonal relationships; shows psychological and physical withdrawal from others.

46. Captive finds it psychologically and emotionally difficult or impossible to physically leave or emotionally detach from captor, particularly if captor does not want her/him to leave.

47. Captive has difficulty maintaining boundaries between herself/himself and others.

48. Captive shows "push-pull" dynamics in relating with captor.

49. Captive shows "push-pull" dynamics in relating to others besides captor.

50. Captive has borderline personality characteristics.

51. Captive has difficulty keeping friends due to her/his "testing" them.

52. Captive feels her/his relationship with captor is the most compelling relationship she or he has had.

53. Captive seeks to re-create intense feelings of captive-captor relationship in relationships with other persons besides captor.

54. Captive fears that captor will come back to get her/him even if captor is dead or in prison.

55. Captive becomes involved in other abusive relationships (besides that with captor).[2]

56. Captive is unable to feel warmth toward herself/himself and what she or he has been through.

57. Captive begins to feel overly responsible for outcome of relationships.

58. Captive is emotionally bonded with captor.

59. Captive displaces her/his anger at captor onto self and persons other than captor.

60. Captive identifies with the victim in the captor, projecting own victim status onto captor.

61. To account for captor's abusive behavior, captive sees the captor as a victim and captor's abusive behavior as resulting from captor being victimized.

62. Captive seeks to end captor's need to abuse through love, caring, kindness,

2. While we do not believe that this characteristic will be shown empirically to be an aspect of Stockholm Syndrome, it is included in this list as one which should nonetheless be subjected to empirical test due to ongoing debate about the issue.

etc. These efforts enable the captive to feel in control while a victim of another's uncontrollable abuse.

63. Captive experiences herself/himself as a childlike figure in relation to captor; responds to captor as to a parent figure.

64. Captive develops symptoms of ongoing trauma or, following release, Post-Traumatic Stress Disorder (PTSD).

65. Captor-captive relationship is sado-masochistic.[3]

66. Small kindnesses by captor create hope in captive that relationship with captor will get better.

3. See n. 2.

Notes

ONE: *Love Thine Enemy*

1. In my opinion, hostages' perceiving they are unable to go home because the police, not the captors, are pointing guns at them is evidence that the syndrome has already developed.

2. I object to the pejorative term, "infantilism," here. Infants are completely incapable of the behaviors required of hostages, who, to survive, appease, submit, comply, cooperate, etc., on cue, in response to the whims of their captors.

3. I consider it demeaning to hostages, and other trauma victims, to explain their responses to captors as regression to an earlier development period. Rather than seeing regression, wherein hostages use the defenses associated with an earlier developmental period, as central to Stockholm Syndrome, I see the extreme power imbalance as central. Thus, the parent/infant analogy is useful, but only in the sense that the power imbalance between parent and infant is as extreme as the power imbalance characterizing the captor/hostage relationship. In many ways the hostage is unlike the infant: the hostage is competent to comply with the commands of the captor, to remain vigilant to the nuances in the captor's behavior and thus to reduce the likelihood of abuse and death, and to take care of herself or himself if permitted by the captor to do so.

As an aside, the infant/parent analogy raises an important question: If Stockholm Syndrome is the result of an extreme power imbalance—one that is extreme to the same degree as that found between parents and infants—to what extent is infants' and children's love for their parents a Stockholm Syndrome response?

4. By definition, all abductions are (at least psychologically) abusive. In addition, if one is chronically abused by another, one must in some sense be a captive of the other.

TWO: *Graham's Stockholm Syndrome Theory*

1. In addition, I use the words "abuse" and "captor," "victim" and "hostage," and "abuse" and "violence" interchangeably. This is because the subject I am addressing is *chronic* interpersonal abuse. Chronic abuse would not continue if the victim were not in some sense captive. Furthermore, all captives are, at a mini-

mum, psychologically abused, and frequently are physically abused as well. Captive status is maintained through either physical force or threat of physical force. "Psychological abuse" is used synonymously with "psychological violence" and "emotional violence." "Physical abuse" is used synonymously with "physical violence."

Physical abuse involves aggressive behavior directed at the victim's body. Psychological abuse involves aggressive behavior directed at and destructive to the victim's emotional state and/or psychology, such as degradation; threats of violence against the victim, the victim's possessions, or persons the victim cares about; verbal aggression such as calling someone names like "nigger," "pussy," "stupid," etc.; attacks on the self-esteem and sense of self of the victim; and communicating to the person that she or he is not as good as others or is a "second-class citizen." Sexual abuse can be both physically and psychologically abusive and usually is both.

2. Stanley Schachter (1959) found that, when subjected to conditions of high as opposed to low fear, people sought to be with others who were undergoing the same experience, even if not permitted to discuss the experience with the others. Furthermore, fearful people sought affiliation for the purposes both of reducing their fear and of evaluating their opinions and abilities relative to those of others. Schachter presumed that this preference to be with others undergoing the same experience occurred "when an objective nonsocial means (e.g., a reality check or reference to an authoritative source) of evaluation is not possible" (p. 113). In the situation being discussed here, the authoritative source is the captor/abuser. In hostage situations such as the bank takeover in Stockholm discussed in chapter 1, hostages bonded with their captors more than one another, and following release, sought further contact with their former captors, not one another. Thus it appears that, if given the opportunity to seek nurturance and protection from other hostages, the captor, or even the police, hostages look first to their captor—the person most immediately holding their lives in his or her hands. Such behavior is not limited to humans. There is abundant evidence that nonhuman, infant victims also seek close physical proximity to abusers when frightened (for example, see Harlow and Harlow 1971). Research findings provide equivocal support regarding the efficacy of companionship in actually reducing anxiety, however (Epley 1974).

3. One of the difficulties in our attempt to account for the phenomenon of bonding to an abuser in a wide range of abuse populations is that, because the phenomenon occurs in humans as well as nonhumans, the hypothesized underlying psychodynamics should be relevant to humans as well as nonhumans. Is the construct of hope relevant to nonhuman animals? Curt Richter (1959) found the construct of hopelessness useful in accounting for "unexplained sudden death" in healthy rats "when all avenues of escape appeared to be closed and the future [held] no hope" (p. 311). On the other hand, rats endured when they

were provided with inoculatory experiences that provided "hope" of future escape.

4. Persons who experience their sense of self through their abusers' eyes will answer the question, "Who are you?" in the language of their abusers. That is, they will report how their *abusers* perceive them. If asked how they feel about something, they will report how their abusers feel about it. If what they are doing is pointed out to them and they are once again asked these questions, they will answer *they* do not know.

5. There are a number of psychological processes that might explain the emotional bond that the captive develops with the captor. One possible process is described by Bem's (1965) "self-perception theory," which says that people interpret their own behavior just as they interpret that of others. Having denied the danger, victims don't see that they have any *external* reason for their compliance and even hypervigilance, save the small demonstration of kindness expressed by the captor, but certainly this small show of kindness is not sufficient to explain their behavior. To make sense of their behavior to themselves, they deduce that they must be doing these things for their captor because they *like, care about,* or *love* the captor. That is, having denied the real reason for their behavior, that is, terror, they interpret their own behavior—compliance and hypervigilance—as indicating that they have strong positive feelings for the captor. Festinger's (1957) "cognitive dissonance theory" leads to the same conclusions as Bem's theory but postulates an inner aversive state (caused by the contradictory feelings of love and hate, fear and gratitude) that victims would be motivated to reduce by attributing their behavior to love for the captor.

Strengthening this understanding of their own behavior is the anxiety (terror) that victims of captivity and abuse feel, but for which they have no explanation since they have denied the danger they are in and their own rage (to avoid retaliation). This *unexplained* high arousal level created by terror then gives rise to a third possible process that may account for bonding to an abuser in humans. How are victims to understand this anxiety? Schachter and Singer (1962) obtained empirical support for their "two-factor theory of emotion," which states that people use *environmental cues* to help them interpret (provide a label for) their own *unexplained* physiological states of arousal. Applied here, a victim who has denied the source of her or his high arousal state will look to the environment for cues about how to interpret it.

Consistent with the "two-factor theory of emotion," a number of investigations have found experimentally induced strong states of arousal, such as anxiety or fear, are likely to be misinterpreted as indicating attraction, even sexual attraction, toward another (see, for example, Brehm et al. 1967, cited by both Dutton and Aron 1974 and Kenrick and Cialdini 1977; Driscoll, Davis, and Lipetz 1972; Follingstad et al. 1988; Lo and Sporakowski 1989). This is known as the "misattribution view of romantic attraction" (Kenrick and Cialdini 1977; see also

Walster 1971 and Walster and Berscheid 1971). Both in laboratory and naturalistic studies, under conditions of high arousal, induced, for example, by anxiety, fear, violence, or frustration, people misattribute the increased arousal they feel, presuming it is due to attraction or love rather than the conditions actually producing the arousal. It is therefore likely that, under certain high arousal conditions, victims of chronic interpersonal abuse will interpret their extreme anxiety as evidence of strong sexual attraction toward their abuser, just as hostages do with their captors (cf. Moorehead 1980).

Another related phenomenon in studies of high arousal is that contact with the object of attraction reduced the subjects' arousal level. These observations led Kenrick and Cialdini (1977) to posit that the attraction develops in response to the lowered arousal provided by the contact, or what psychologists would call "negative reinforcement" (that is, the reduction of an unpleasant state is rewarding and will increase the behavior that led to the reduction). Negative reinforcement has been posited as accounting for bonding to an abuser in both humans and nonhumans when kindness follows the termination of abuse. Dutton and Painter (1981) have proposed a negative-reinforcement model to account for the bonding of women to abusive partners, a process they refer to as "traumatic bonding."

Any or all of the above psychological processes may account for bonding under conditions in which the actual source of arousal is denied, suggesting that bonding to an abuser in humans may be multidetermined, or even overdetermined.

6. Research on humans and nonhumans indicates that the *belief* that one has control improves one's ability to adapt to stressful circumstances (Glass, Reim, and Singer 1971; Glass, Singer, and Friedman 1969; Staub, Tursky, and Schwartz 1971), act to escape or avoid stressful circumstances (Overmier and Seligman 1967), or just survive (Richter 1959; Weiss 1971).

7. It is possible, though, that the bond is *not* created by the misattribution that arousal and hypervigilance (caused by terror) are due to love. A compelling argument that the bond would develop anyway is provided by the fact that nonhumans as well as humans, and infants as well as adults, bond to their abusers/ captors, and there is no evidence that nonhuman animals, much less nonhuman infants, either deny terror or interpret their behavior and arousal. The misattribution that the arousal and hypervigilance are caused by love, not terror, may be present only in humans and thus may represent only higher animals' cognitive need to understand their behavior and feelings. Alternatively, different processes or psychodynamics may be involved in human versus nonhuman, and infant versus noninfant human, bonding with an abuser. If cognitive distortions play a secondary role in both humans and nonhumans, one or more additional processes must be responsible for promoting bonding with an abuser. What might those processes be? One possibility is negative reinforcement, wherein the abuser's kindness signals escape from further abuse (Dutton and Painter 1981; Kenrick and

Cialdini 1977; Walker 1979). Another possibility is a highly prepared, or strongly instinctual, behavior pattern, little affected by learning in *any* species.

8. It is not clear whether such cognitive distortions arise prior to the fear-induced bond, after the fear-induced bond has arisen, or simultaneous with the fear-induced bond. (The phrase "fear-induced" is used to distinguish this bond from any bond that may have existed prior to victimization, as might have been the case with victims of acquaintance rape, marital rape, child abuse, and wife abuse, for example.) The direction of effect, if any exists between the cognitive distortions and the fear-induced bond, is also not clear. Do the cognitive distortions give rise to the bond, does the bond give rise to the cognitive distortions, or do the two arise independently of one another?

9. Battered women provide an example. They are more likely to be killed or severely beaten after leaving their abusive partners than at any other time (Browne 1987; Serum 1979, cited by Okun 1986). Probably as a consequence, they return to shelters an average of seven to eight times before finally leaving the abusive partners for good. Yet, until they figure out how they can leave their partners for good, a sizable proportion continues to profess love for their partners. The loss of sense of self resulting from chronic abuse makes finding a way to leave for good more difficult than it would otherwise be. Also, the fact that, as abuse victims, battered women are highly focused on surviving in the here-and-now makes their strategizing about future escape difficult. And, when the consequences for a failed escape attempt are great, battered women, like other abuse victims, are not likely to take chances. Their labeling their feelings as "love" may be, then, an attempt to interpret their behavior and high state of anxiety in a way that reduces their terror, otherwise they are forced to acknowledge they must live with a person who seeks to seriously harm and possibly even murder them. They stay with the partner, not because they love him (as they tell themselves and others), but because they as yet see no way to escape his violence except by staying. When the likelihood of being killed by the partner if they stay with him approaches the likelihood of their being killed if they leave him, they leave the partner.

10. Subsequently, after 13 1/2 years of abuse and after realizing there was no other way to escape her ex-husband's killing her, she killed him by setting him on fire as he slept after he got drunk, beat her, and raped her (McNulty 1980).

THREE: *"Here's My Weapon, Here's My Gun"*

1. Both males and females experience this fear, but the fear is likely to result in males' identifying with the aggressor and females' identifying with the victim.

2. The author thanks Andrea Dworkin and Catharine A. MacKinnon for their "seminal" work in this area. The conceptualization presented in this section is built upon, and thus is strongly influenced by, their work.

3. Interestingly, feminists have argued that this is the reason women are heterosexual. Recall that, in the view of feminists, daughters become heterosexual, despite their initial primary attachment to their mother, because men have power that women (including the mother and we ourselves) don't have. Females gain access to this male power, then, by attaching ourselves to males (for example, our father, a male partner, or sons). These attachments to males, not females, have the effect of isolating women from one another.

FOUR: *En-Gendered Terror*

1. The reader may want to compare our conceptualization with Schachter and Singer's (1962) "two-factor theory of emotion" described in note 5 of chapter 2.

2. Does women's hatred of gay men grow out of our fear that men will not permit women to live if men no longer need women's services (domestic, sexual, emotional, and reproductive; cf. Dworkin 1983)? Might women oppose the rights of gays to have and raise children because women know the only service women provide men which men cannot provide one another is reproductive? These questions suggest that misogyny in gay men may be very frightening to women—even lesbians. Identification with males (who as a group are opposed to gays having children because it threatens their right to dominate women) also strengthens women's opposition to gay men.

3. Males' greater aggression *may* be, in part, a biologically based sex difference. It also may not be. Some people might argue that a biological sex difference in aggression is the basis of patriarchy and therefore sets the stage for Societal Stockholm Syndrome in females. However, even if the sex difference was biologically determined, aggression can be acted out in prosocial ways; it need not be used to establish or maintain a dominance hierarchy. For example, one can aggressively pursue fairness, equality, or friendship.

4. Surprisingly, Canary, Cunningham, and Cody (1988) found that females reported more use of personal criticism and anger strategies in response to a recent personally experienced conflict than males. While these findings seem contradictory to the pattern we have been describing, buried in a footnote was the information that females used higher personal criticism and anger strategies in all situations except *relationship change*. In relational change situations involving partner conflicts about advancing the relationship, maintaining current level of intimacy, and de-escalating the relationship, males used more personal criticism and anger strategies than did women. This suggests that women *are* more anger inhibited than men in conflicts involving relationships.

5. Russell's study was based on a random sample of 930 females from the greater San Francisco area, and she used in-depth interviews by trained interviewers to obtain data. The Russell study does not report the sexual orientation of the self-acknowledged female rapists. Though Brand and Kidd also obtained their

sample from the greater San Francisco area, most of their participants were obtained from a women's college with other participants coming from an ongoing lesbian discussion group and advertisements placed in newspapers. Participants in this study completed a brief 24-item questionnaire.

6. A rather esoteric form of child abuse described by Robins and Sesan (1991), Munchausen Syndrome by Proxy (MSP), is unique in that it appears to be an exclusively female form of child abuse. As described by the authors, "Adult Munchausen syndrome is characterized by an adult's chronic and relentless pursuit of medical treatment, involving some combination of consciously self-inflicted injury and falsely reported symptomatology" (p. 285). MSP is the result of mothers creating and fabricating their children's symptoms, usually to obtain the care and attention of the medical profession for themselves.

7. The authors attributed infanticide to the immaturity and psychological stress of very young mothers who lack social support.

8. A major problem with research on nonverbal behavior carried out to date is that it is based primarily on studies carried out in a laboratory, not the real world. In the laboratory, the goal is to determine which sex can best "read" others' expressions *when both sexes are equally motivated to do so.* In the real world, the two sexes may not be equally motivated to read others' faces. In fact, we would argue that in current patriarchal culture, women, as subordinates, are motivated to read accurately men's emotions, and men, as dominants, are motivated to not recognize women's emotions. We know little about men's versus women's sensitivity to others' feelings under real-life, uncontrived circumstances.

9. It is clear that men come to expect women's hypervigilance to their moods. Many women complain that men expect women to know what the men want and need without the men telling them, and that the men get angry when women guess wrong. Sattel (1989) has argued that men's inexpressiveness is both a function of their dominance over women and a way of strengthening their dominance.

10. A caveat is that when AOO has been examined in relation to gender, findings have been mixed. Sometimes women are found to be more altruistic than men and sometimes the reverse is found (Grauerholz 1988). A similar measure— that of *agape,* or all-giving, selfless, love—has been found to be endorsed by males and females equally (Hendrick and Hendrick 1986). More research needs to be done to ascertain how these attitudes are expressed in men's versus women's *behavior* and how their expression might reflect men's and women's differential status. It is also important to separate out beliefs in myths (for example, about men's protection of women) from men's and women's actual behavior.

11. Findings suggest that both lower-class females and black females prefer a more feminine sex role than middle-class and white females, respectively (Rabben 1950; Ward 1973). One would think that groups that are more discriminated against (lower-class and black females) would show more ambivalence toward the feminine sex role than females who are less discriminated against (middle-class

and white females). The fact that this may not be the case suggests that the studies cited above may be measuring something other than sex-role preference, such as maleness and masculinity as norm. It may be, though, that, for one to feel ambivalent about one's gender and sex, one has to identify gender and sex as the *cause* of one's oppression. Lower-class and black females, as groups, may not perceive the sources of their oppression as having much to do with their sex or their gender. If not, their ambivalence may be directed elsewhere, for example, toward class or race, and may thus be expressed as a preference to be rich or white rather than male or masculine.

12. Even if this occurs because boys' toys are intrinsically more interesting, the fact that most girls eventually come to play with the less interesting "girls' toys" itself demonstrates adoption of a devalued status.

13. One study by Callahan-Levy and Messe (1979)—involving first through tenth graders—revealed that subjects' self-pay increased as the masculinity of their occupation preferences increased ($r = .66$). This finding suggests that the more a female internalized the notion that girls should be feminine, the less entitled she felt to the same pay as boys. However, Major, McFarlin, and Gagnon (1984, study 1) found that this relation between masculinity and self-pay existed only among their male subjects.

14. Although we are not necessarily proposing that women physically separate from men, it would be possible for women and men to live apart from one another and the human species continue by using artificial insemination or by having only brief physical contact with one another.

FIVE: *The Beauties and the Beasts*

1. This is so even if one is lesbian, for lesbianism is culturally defined as a rejection of these three characteristics.

2. Consistent with this notion, both Antill (1983) and Kurdek and Schmitt (1986) found that couples that had at least one member who was either feminine or androgynous reported higher relationship quality than couples in which neither member was feminine or androgynous.

3. Jane Elliot, in *The Eye of the Storm*, has demonstrated that people perform better on intellectual tasks when they are members of the dominant group. Zanna and Pack (1975) have shown that college-age females perform more poorly on an intellectual task when they believe they will be interacting with a man who endorses traditional, as compared with untraditional, sex-role values.

4. St. Claire (1989) defines "handicap" as "a socially constructed disadvantage which limits, prevents or devalues a given outcome in the handicapped person's life" and contrasts the term with "limitation caused by an objective, physical, mental or behavioural problem" (p. 130). Using this definition, St Claire argues that women as a group suffer three handicaps: limited access to roles, bias in

evaluation that is due to people's negative associations to the female sex role, and, as a consequence, negative self-expectations.

5. Gender differences are greatest in same-sex groups. Why would this be the case if dominance issues underlie gender differences in discourse style? If women's discourse style communicates that we are not vying for dominance, the struggle for dominance should be greatest in male-male interactions or in all-male groups, and it is. In female-female interactions or all-female groups, two things may be occurring: (1) females may be practicing their "warding off danger" and "bridge building" discourse skills within the safety of female company; (2) females may use these all-female interactions for *healing*. Therein women may do emotional work which helps us manage the psychological (and physical) violence associated with our subordinate role. This work may be accomplished by sharing our experiences and feelings with one another and by exchanging support and encouragement.

Recall that women—threatened with male violence—first turn to men, our captors or abusers, for support and promises of safety. Men, whose foremost goal is maintenance of male domination, cannot provide women complete safety, for they remain vigilant to, and posed to squelch, early signs of rebellion, resistance, or takeover by women, as well as by other men. Thus, despite the isolation created between women by our survival-based needs both to bond with men and to compete with one another for a favored position in men's hearts, women are the primary providers of emotional support for other women.

6. The attitudes of men that lead them to reject autonomy in women, including daughters, may be the same attitudes that foster male violence toward women (for instance, that women are not important, that women are not fully human). Threats of physical violence and actual physical violence are used by men to ensure that women do not think and act autonomously.

7. Another interpretation of this finding is that if anyone in this culture had anything approaching an egalitarian relationship, they would correctly perceive as slim their chances of finding anyone as good or better.

8. It is probably for this reason that women experience the greatest male violence from male intimates within the family.

9. We deliberately choose the phrase "other sex" rather than "opposite sex" because men and women are "opposites" only in terms of power arrangements.

10. Female masturbation is much rarer than male masturbation in our culture. Although less popular today, parents and the church encourage women to be virgins, to "save" ourselves for our future husbands. In some African cultures, young women are subjected to brutal mutilations called clitorectomies to keep them from enjoying sexual pleasure. Women often "fake orgasm" in order to please men rather than complain we have not received sexual satisfaction.

11. It's one thing for dominants to rule *resistant* subordinates. It's another thing for dominants to rule subordinates who say they *want* to be dominated. In the latter case, dominants can rule and still feel good about themselves.

12. In the absence of Societal Stockholm Syndrome theory, women's eroticization of male domination has been difficult to comprehend.

13. The author wishes to thank Dr. Roberta Rigsby for suggesting that this point be clarified.

s i x : *Moving from Surviving to Thriving*

1. For an elegant dissection of this male fantasy, see Joanna Russ (1980a).

2. Two examples of changes being used against women or of women being punished for having brought about such changes are the arrest (under the mandatory arrest laws in cases of domestic violence) of some women who fight back in self-defense against battering, and the loss of child custody by some women who complain to the courts that their children are being sexually abused by the fathers.

3. Resisting the patriarchal backlash involves being aware that the self-appointed arbiters of "correct" language often have no qualms about disguising as good linguistic taste their political opposition to certain words and phrases. An example appears in James J. Kilpatrick's (1992, December 5) autocratic assertion that "we ought to stomp on 'dysfunctional' before it spreads."

4. One such publication is *Ms.: The World of Women*. For subscription information, write to *Ms.*, P.O. Box 57132, Boulder, CO 80322-7132. Another such publication is *On the Issues: The Progressive Woman's Quarterly*; write to P.O. Box 3000, Dept. OTI, Denville, NJ 07834. Various grassroots feminist newsletters also provide information and opportunity for dialogue. Information on many such newsletters, focused on a wide range of topics, can be found in the Resources sections of *The New Our Bodies, Ourselves* (Boston Women's Health Book Collective, 1984). Two of the many newsletters that have appeared since *The New Our Bodies, Ourselves* was published are *Women's Recovery Network* (WebWords Press, Inc., P.O. Box 141554, Columbus, OH 43214), which is "a grassroots feminist forum for women who have known abuse and/or addiction, and who now seek political and spiritual solutions," and *Write to Heal* (P.O. Box 358, Fair Oaks, CA 95628-0358), a newsletter "both published and written by and for survivors of trauma, as well as their allies in healing."

5. In connection with the disruption of such child rearing for men under patriarchy, see Bergman (1991).

6. For those ready to move into action, resources on how to do so are readily available. See, for instance, *The New Our Bodies, Ourselves* (Boston Women's Health Book Collective 1984); *Freedom from Violence: Women's Strategies from around the World* (Schuler 1992); and the work of Best (1983) and Thorne (1986) on gender arrangements in schools.

7. For instance, see Grauerholz and Koralewski (1991, pp. 109–183) for strategic programs addressing structural barriers to women's safety from sexual coercion. Also, Delacoste· and Newman (1981) have documented numerous examples of

American women's creative resistance to male violence, and French (1992, pp. 200–207) has given many examples of inspiring and "richly varied" actions by women globally.

8. Again, see Grauerholz and Koralewski (1991, pp. 109–183) for just one example of current feminist energy in this direction.

9. Similarly, television and radio programs often are being aired locally and nationwide about women being unfairly denied custody of their children, the inequitable effects of divorce laws on women, and women who get AIDS from men.

10. For just one example of information about such organizations, see "EMILY's List: Supporting Women Political Candidates," *Woman of Power 22* (Summer 1992): 46–47. Our favorite sentence from that article is: "People see that they really are making a difference, and it gives them a sense of collective power" (p. 46). For additional information on EMILY's List, write to EMILY's List, 1112 16th St. N.W., Suite 750, Washington, D.C. 20036, or call (202) 877-1957.

References

Abbey, A. (1982). Sex differences in attributions for friendly behavior: Do males misperceive females' friendliness? *Journal of Personality and Social Psychology, 42*(5), 830–838.

———— (1987). Misperceptions of friendly behavior as sexual interest: A survey of naturally occurring incidents. *Psychology of Women Quarterly, 11*, 173–194.

Abbey, A., and Melby, C. (1986). The effects of nonverbal cues on gender differences in perceptions of sexual intent. *Sex Roles, 15*(5/6), 283–298.

Abramson, L. Y., and Andrews, D. E. (1982). Cognitive models of depression: Implications for sex differences in vulnerability to depression. *International Journal of Mental Health, 11*(1–2), 77–94.

Ahrens, L. (1981). Battered women's refuges: Feminist cooperatives vs. social service institutions. In F. Delacoste and F. Newman, eds., *Fight back! Feminist resistance to male violence,* pp. 104–109. Minneapolis: Cleis Press.

Alexander, S. (1979). *Anyone's daughter.* New York: Viking Press.

———— (1985). *Nut-cracker. Money, madness, murder: A family album.* New York: Dell.

Allen, G. (1991). Separation issues of battered women. Master's thesis, University of Cincinnati, Cincinnati, Ohio.

Allen, P. (1970). *Free space: A perspective on the small group in women's liberation.* New York: Times Change Press.

Allport, G. W. (1954). *The nature of prejudice.* Reading, Mass.: Addison-Wesley.

Amburgy, V. (1986, June). Letter to the Editor. *Life, 9*(6), 13.

American Psychiatric Association (1987). *Diagnostic and statistical manual of mental disorders.* 3d ed., rev. Washington, D.C.: The American Psychiatric Association.

Amnesty International (1975). *Report on torture.* New York: Farrar, Straus & Giroux.

Annin, P. (1985, July 8). Hostages: Living in the aftermath. *U.S. News and World Report, 99*, 34.

Antill, J. K. (1983). Sex role complementarity versus similarity in married couples. *Journal of Personality and Social Psychology, 45*, 145–155.

Aries, E. (1987). Gender and communication. In P. Shaver and C. Hendrick, eds.,

Sex and gender, pp. 149–176. Vol. 7, *Review of Personality and Social Psychology.* Beverly Hills, Calif.: Sage.

Atkins, S. (1977). *Child of Satan, child of God.* Plainfield, N.Y.: Logos International.

Atkinson, T.-G. (1974). *Amazon odyssey.* New York: Links Books.

Atwood, M. (1986). *The handmaid's tale.* Boston: Houghton Mifflin.

Bailey, W. C.; Hendrick, C.; and Hendrick, S. S. (1987). Relation of sex and gender role to love, sexual attitudes, and self-esteem. *Sex Roles, 16*(11/12), 637–648.

Barry, K. (1979). *Female sexual slavery.* Englewood Cliffs, N.J.: Prentice Hall.

Barry, K.; Bunch, C.; and Castley, S. (1984). *International feminism: Networking against female sexual slavery.* New York: International Women's Tribune Centre.

Bart, P. (1983, November/December). Women of the Right: Trading for safety, rules and love. Review of A. Dworkin, *Right Wing Women,* in *The New Women's Times Feminist Review,* pp. 9–11.

Bart, P., and O'Brien, P. H. (1985). *Stopping rape: Successful survival strategies.* New York: Pergamon.

Bar-Tal, D., and Saxe, L. (1976). Physical attractiveness and its relationship to sex-role stereotyping. *Sex Roles, 2*(2), 123–133.

Barthel, J. (1981). *A death in California.* New York: Dell.

Beck, M., with Glick, D., and Annin, P. (1993, June 21). A (quiet) uprising in the ranks. *Newsweek, 121*(25), 60.

Belenky, M. F.; Clinchy, B. M.; Goldberger, N. R.; and Tarule, J. M. (1986). *Women's ways of knowing: The development of self, voice, and mind.* New York: Basic Books.

Belle, D. (1990). Poverty and women's mental health. *American Psychologist, 45*(3), 385–389.

Bem, D. J. (1965). An experimental analysis of self-persuasion. *Journal of Experimental Social Psychology, 1,* 199–218.

——— (1972). Self-perception theory. In L. Berkowitz, ed., *Advances in Experimental Social Psychology, 6,* 2–62.

Bem, S. L. (1974). The measurement of psychological androgyny. *Journal of Consulting and Clinical Psychology, 42*(2), 155–162.

——— (1975). Sex role adaptability: One consequence of psychological androgyny. *Journal of Personality and Social Psychology, 31,* 634–643.

——— (1981). Gender schema theory: A cognitive account of sex typing. *Psychological Review, 88*(4), 354–364.

Bemis, K. M. (1978). Current approaches to the etiology and treatment of anorexia. *Psychological Bulletin, 85,* 593–617.

Benjamin, J. (1988). *The bonds of love.* New York: Pantheon Books.

Bergman, S. J. (1991). Men's psychological development: A relational perspective.

Work in Progress No. 48. Wellesley College, Mass.: Stone Center Working Papers Series.

Bernard, C., and Schlaffer, E. (1983). The man in the street: Why he harasses. In L. Richardson and V. Taylor, eds., *Feminist frontiers: Rethinking sex, gender, and society*, pp. 172–175. Reading, Mass.: Addison-Wesley.

Bernard, J. (1971). *Women and the public interest: An essay on policy and protest.* Chicago: Aldine Atherton.

Bernardez-Bonesatti, T. (1978). Women and anger: Conflicts with aggression in contemporary women. *Journal of the American Medical Association, 33*(5), 215–219.

Best, R. (1983). *We all have scars: What boys and girls learn in elementary school.* Bloomington: Indiana University Press.

Bettelheim, B. (1943). Individual and mass behavior in extreme situations. *Journal of Abnormal and Social Psychology, 38,* 417–452.

Biderman, A. D. (1964). Captivity lore and behavior in captivity. In G. H. Grosser, H. Wechsler, and M. Greenblat, eds., *The threat of impending disaster,* pp. 223–250. Cambridge, Mass.: MIT Press.

Blackwood, E. (1984). Sexuality and gender in certain Native American tribes: The case of cross-gender females. *Signs, 10*(1), 27–42.

Blinder, M. (1985). *Lovers, killers, husbands and wives.* New York: St. Martin's Press.

Block, J. H. (1976). Issues, problems, and pitfalls in assessing sex differences: A critical review of *The Psychology of Sex Differences. Merrill-Palmer Quarterly, 22*(4), 283–308.

Boston Women's Health Book Collective (1984). *The new our bodies, ourselves.* New York: Simon and Schuster.

Brand, P. A., and Kidd, A. H. (1986). Frequency of physical aggression in heterosexual and female homosexual dyads. *Psychological Reports, 59,* 1307–1313.

Brody, L. R.; Hay, D. H.; and Venditor, E. (1990). Gender, gender role identity, and children's reported feelings toward the same and opposite sex. *Sex Roles, 23*(7/8), 363–387.

Broverman, I. K.; Broverman, D. M.; Clarkson, F. E.; Rosenkrantz, P. S.; and Vogel, S. R. (1970). Sex role stereotypes and clinical judgments of mental health. *Journal of Consulting and Clinical Psychology, 34,* 1–7.

Brown, D. G. (1956). Sex-role preferences in young children. *Psychological Monograph, 70*(14, Whole No. 421).

——— (1957). Masculinity-femininity development in children. *Journal of Consulting Psychology, 21,* 197–202.

Brown, L. S. (1985). Women, weight, and power: Feminist theoretical and therapeutic issues. *Women and Therapy, 4*(1), 61–71.

Browne, A. (1987). *When battered women kill.* New York: Free Press.

Browning, D., and Boatman, B. (1977). Incest: Children at risk. *American Journal of Psychiatry, 134,* 69–72.

Brownmiller, S. (1975). *Against our will: Men, women and rape.* New York: Simon and Schuster.

Bugliosi, V., with Gentry, C. (1974). *Helter skelter: The true story of the Manson murders.* New York: W. W. Norton.

Bunch, C. (1983). Not for lesbians only. In L. Richardson and V. Taylor, eds., *Feminist frontiers: Rethinking sex, gender, and society,* pp. 366–368. Reading, Mass.: Addison-Wesley.

Bunster, N. (1984). The torture of women political prisoners: A case study in female sexual slavery. In K. Barry, C. Bunch, and S. Castley, eds., *International feminism: Networking against female sexual slavery,* pp. 94–102. New York: International Women's Tribune Center.

Burger, J. M. (1981). Motivational biases in the attribution of responsibility for an accident: A meta-analysis of the defensive-attribution hypothesis. *Psychological Bulletin, 90*(3), 496–512.

Burnett, R. C., Templer, D. I., and Barker, P. C. (1985). Personality variables and circumstances of sexual assault predictive of a woman's resistance. *Archives of Sexual Behavior, 14*(2), 183–188.

Burstow, B. (1992). *Radical feminist therapy: Working in the context of violence.* Newbury Park, Calif.: Sage.

Caignon, D., and Groves, G. (1987). *Her wits about her: Self-defense success stories by women.* New York: Harper and Row.

Callahan-Levy, C. M., and Messe, L. A. (1979). Sex differences in the allocation of pay. *Journal of Personality and Social Psychology, 37,* 433–446.

Calway-Fagen, N.; Wallston, B. S.; and Gabel, H. (1979). The relationship between attitudinal and behavioral measures of sex preference. *Psychology of Women Quarterly, 4,* 274–280.

Campbell, E. K. (1991). Sex preference for offspring among men in the western area of Sierra Leone. *Journal of Biosocial Science, 23*(3), 337–342.

Canary, D. J.; Cunningham, E. M.; and Cody, M. J. (1988). Goal types, gender, and locus of control in managing interpersonal conflict. *Communication Research, 15*(4), 426–446.

Cancian, F. M., and Gordon, S. L. (1988). Changing emotion norms in marriage: Love and anger in U.S. women's magazines since 1900. *Gender and Society, 2*(3), 308–342.

Caplan, N., and Nelson, S. D. (1973). On being useful: The nature and consequences of psychological research on social problems. *American Psychologist, 28,* 199–211.

Cecil, E. A.; Paul, R. J.; and Olins, R. A. (1973). Perceived importance of selected variables used to evaluate male and female job applicants. *Personnel Psychology, 26,* 397–404.

Chambless, D. L., and Goldstein, A. J. (1980). Anxieties: Agoraphobia and hysteria. In A. Brodsky and R. T. Hare-Mustin, eds., *Women and psychotherapy: An assessment of research and practice,* pp. 113–134. New York: Guilford.

Charnas, S. M. (1978). *Motherlines*. New York: Berkley Books.

Chodorow, N. (1978). *The reproduction of mothering: Psychoanalysis and the sociology of gender*. Berkeley: University of California Press.

Cholmondeley, M. (1985). *Red pottage*. Harmondsworth, England: Penguin/Virago Press. (Originally published 1899).

Clark, L., and Lewis, D. (1977). *Rape: The price of coercive sexuality*. Toronto, Canada: Women's Press.

Cochrane, R., and Stopes-Roe, M. (1981). Women, marriage, employment and mental health. *British Journal of Psychiatry, 139,* 373–381.

Cohen, S. L., and Bunker, K. A. (1975). Subtle effects of sex role stereotypes in recruiter's hiring decisions. *Journal of Applied Psychology, 60,* 566–572.

Coleman, J. (1985). *At mother's request*. New York: Pocket Books.

Collins, G. (1986, July 10). Women murderers share pattern. *The Cincinnati Enquirer,* p. E-4.

Crelinsten, R. D. (1977, June 3–5). Analysis and conclusions. In R. D. Crelinsten, ed., *Dimensions of victimization in the context of terroristic acts,* pp. 187–211. Final report of proceedings, Evian, France.

Crittenden, P. M., and Craig, S. E. (1990). Developmental trends in the nature of child homicide. *Journal of Interpersonal Violence, 5*(2), 202–216.

Crocker, J., and McGraw, K. M. (1984). What's good for the goose is not good for the gander. *American Behavioral Scientist, 27,* 357–369.

Daly, M. (1978). *Gyn/ecology: The metaethics of radical feminism*. Boston: Beacon.

Davis, M. A.; LaRosa, P. A.; and Foshee, D. P. (1992). Emotion work in supervisor-subordinate relations: Gender differences in the perception of angry display. *Sex Roles, 26*(11/12), 513–531.

DeAngelis, T. (1992, December). Hill-Thomas face-off brought harassment issues out in open. *APA Monitor,* p. 32.

Deaux, K., and Emswiller, T. (1974). Explanations of successful performance on sex-linked tasks: What's skill for the male is luck for the female. *Journal of Personality and Social Psychology, 29,* 80–85.

Deaux, K., and Farris, E. (1977). Attributing causes for one's own performance: The effects of sex, norms, and outcome. *Journal of Research in Personality, 11,* 59–72.

Delacoste, F., and Newman, F. (1981). *Fight back! Feminist resistance to male violence*. Minneapolis: Cleis Press.

Devor, H. (1989). *Gender blending: Confronting the limits of duality*. Bloomington: Indiana University Press.

Diiorio, J. A. (1989). Sex, glorious sex: The social construction of masculine sexuality in a youth group. In L. Richardson and V. Taylor, eds., *Feminist frontiers II,* pp. 261–269. New York: Random House.

Dinitz, S.; Dynes, R. R.; and Clarke, A. C. (1954). Preference for male or female children: Traditional or affectional? *Marriage and Family Living, 16,* 128–130.

Dinnerstein, D. (1976). *The mermaid and the minotaur: Sexual arrangements and human malaise*. New York: Harper Colophon.

Dion, K. L., and Dion, K. K. (1973). Correlates of romantic love. *Journal of Consulting and Clinical Psychology*, 41(1), 51–56.

Dipboye, R. L.; Fromkin, H. L.; and Wiback, K. (1975). Relative importance of applicant sex, attractiveness and scholastic standing in evaluation of job applicant resumes. *Journal of Applied Psychology, 60,* 39–43.

Dobash, R. E., and Dobash, R. (1977/78). Wives: The "appropriate" victims of marital violence. *Victimology,* 2(3–4), 426–442.

Domash, L., and Balter, L. (1976). Sex and psychological differentiation in preschoolers. *The Journal of Genetic Psychology, 128,* 77–84.

Donnerstein, E. (1984). Pornography: Its effect on violence against women. In N. M. Malamuth and E. Donnerstein, eds., *Pornography and sexual aggression*, pp. 53–81. New York: Academic Press.

Dortzbach, K., and Dortzbach, D. (1975). *Kidnapped*. New York: Harper and Row.

Doyle, J. A. (1976). Attitudes toward feminism—forty years later. *Sex Roles, 2*(4), 399–405.

Driscoll, R.; Davis, K.; and Lipetz, M. (1972). Parental interference and romantic love: The Romeo and Juliet effect. *Journal of Personality and Social Psychology, 24,* 1–10.

Druss, V., and Henifin, M. S. (1979). Why are so many anorexics women? In R. Hubbard and M. S. Henifin, eds., *Women looking at biology looking at women: A collection of feminist critiques*. Cambridge, Mass.: Schenkman.

Duley, M. I. (1986). Toward a theory of gender stratification: Selected issues. In M. I. Duley and M. I. Edwards, eds., *The cross-cultural study of women*, pp. 78–106. New York: Feminist Press at The City University of New York.

Dutton, D. G. (1989). The victimhood of battered women: Psychological and criminal justice perspectives. In E. A. Fattah, ed., *The plight of crime victims in modern society*, 161–176. New York: St. Martin's Press.

Dutton, D. G., and Aron, A. P. (1974). Some evidence for heightened sexual attraction under conditions of high anxiety. *Journal of Personality and Social Psychology, 30*(4), 510–517.

Dutton, D. G., and Painter, S. L. (1981). Traumatic bonding: The development of emotional attachments in battered women and other relationships of intermittent abuse. *Victimology: An International Journal, 6,* 139–155.

Dworkin, A. (1974). *Woman-hating*. New York: E. P. Dutton.

——— (1983). *Right-wing women*. New York: Perigee.

——— (1987). *Intercourse*. New York: Free Press.

Eagly, A. H., and Steffen, V. J. (1986). Gender and aggressive behavior: A meta-analytic review of the social psychological literature. *Psychological Bulletin, 100*(3), 309–330.

Efron, R. C. (1985). Women's responses to recalled sexually-explicit material and sexually-suggestive advertisements and their association with attitudinal, personal, and demographic variables. Ph.D. diss., University of Cincinnati, Cincinnati, Ohio.

Egerton, M. (1988). Passionate women and passionate men: Sex differences in accounting for angry and weeping episodes. *Journal of Social Psychology, 27,* 51–66.

Ehrenreich, B., and Piven, F. F. (1984). The feminization of poverty: When the family wage system breaks down. *Dissent, 31,* 162–170.

Ehrlich, S. (1989). *Lisa, Hedda, and Joel: The Steinberg murder case.* New York: St. Martin's Press.

Eisner, J. (1980). *The survivor.* New York: William Morrow.

Elgin, S. H. (1984). *Native tongue.* New York: DAW Books.

——— (1987). *Native tongue II: The Judas rose.* New York: DAW Books.

——— (1988). *A first dictionary and grammar of Láadan.* 2d ed. Madison, Wisc.: Society for the Furtherance and Study of Fantasy and Science Fiction.

——— (1989). *Success with the gentle art of verbal self-defense.* Englewood Cliffs, N.J.: Prentice Hall.

Elshtain, J. B. (1985, September). Reflections on the Stockholm Syndrome. *Christianity and Crisis, 45,* 354–356.

Epley, S. (1974). Reduction of the behavioral effects of aversive stimulation by the presence of companions. *Psychological Bulletin, 81*(5), 271–283.

Erdwins, C.; Small, A.; and Gross, R. (1980). The relationship of sex role to self-concept. *Journal of Clinical Psychology, 36,* 111–115.

Ewing, C. P. (1987). *Battered women who kill: Psychological self-defense as legal justification.* Lexington, Mass.: Lexington Books.

Fallon, A. E., and Rozin, P. (1985). Sex differences in perceptions of desirable body shape. *Journal of Abnormal Psychology, 94*(1), 102–105.

Farley, L. (1978). *Sexual shakedown.* New York: McGraw-Hill.

Feinblatt, J. A., and Gold, A. R. (1976). Sex roles and the psychiatric referral process. *Sex Roles, 2,* 109–122.

Ferber, M., and Lowry, H. (1976). Women: The new reserve army of labor. In M. Blaxall and B. Reagan, eds., *Women and the Workplace,* pp. 213–233. Chicago: University of Chicago Press.

Ferraro, K. J. (1983). Rationalizing violence: How battered women stay. *Victimology, 8,* 203–212.

Festinger, L. (1957). *A theory of cognitive dissonance.* Stanford, Calif.: Stanford University Press.

Fidell, L. S. (1970). Empirical verification of sex discrimination in hiring practices in psychology. *American Psychologist, 25,* 1094–1098.

Fidell, L.; Hoffman, D.; and Keith-Spiegel, P. (1979). Some social implications of sex-choice technology. *Psychology of Women Quarterly, 4,* 232–246.

Finkelhor, D. (1979). *Sexually victimized children*. New York: Macmillan.

———— (1980). Risk factors in the sexual victimization of children. *Child Abuse and Neglect, 4,* 265–273.

———— (1983). Common features of family abuse. In D. Finkelhor, R. J. Gelles, G. T. Hotaling, and M. A. Straus, eds., *The dark side of families: Current family violence research,* pp. 17–28. Beverly Hills, Calif.: Sage.

Finkelhor, D.; Gelles, R. J.; Hotaling, G. T.; and Straus, M. A., eds. (1983). *The dark side of families: Current family violence research,* pp. 17–28. Beverly Hills, Calif.: Sage.

Finkelhor, D., and Yllo, K. (1985). *License to rape: Sexual abuse of wives.* New York: Holt, Rinehart & Winston.

Fischer, D. G.; Kelm, H.; and Rose, A. (1969). Knives as aggression-eliciting stimuli. *Psychological Reports, 24,* 755–760.

A flawed proposal (1992, December 19). *The Cincinnati Post,* p. 10A.

Fly, C. (1973). *No hope but God.* New York: Hawthorn Books.

Flynn, C. P. (1990). Sex roles and women's response to courtship violence. *Journal of Family Violence, 5*(1), 83–94.

Flynn, E. E. (1990). Victims of terrorism: Dimensions of the victim experience. In E. Viano, ed., *The victimology handbook: Research findings, treatment, and public policy,* pp. 93–117. New York: Garland Publishing.

Follingstad, D. R.; Rutledge, L. L.; Polek, D. S.; NcNeill-Hawkins, K. (1988). Factors associated with patterns of dating violence toward college women. *Journal of Family Violence, 3*(3), 169–182.

Foucault, M. (1976/78). *The history of sexuality.* Vol. 1., *An Introduction.* New York: Pantheon. (Original work published 1976.)

Franzblau, S. H. (1979). Effects of observed violence on females. A critical review. In C. B. Kopp and M. Kirkpatrick, eds., *Becoming female: Perspectives on development,* pp. 259–287. New York: Plenum Press.

French, M. (1992). *The war against women.* New York: Summit Books.

Freud, S. (1925). Some psychological consequences of the anatomical distinction between the sexes. Trans. J. Strachey. Vol. 5 of *Collected Papers,* pp. 186–197. New York: Basic Books, 1959.

———— (1931). Female sexuality. Trans. J. Strachey. Vol. 5 of *Collected papers.* New York: Basic Books, 1959.

Frieze, I. (1983). Investigating the causes and consequences of marital rape. *Signs, 8*(3), 532–553.

Frieze, I. H.; Parsons, J. E.; Johnson, P. B.; Ruble, D. N.; and Zellman, G. L. (1978). *Women and sex roles: A social psychological perspective.* New York: W. W. Norton.

Frodi, A.; Macaulay, J.; and Thome, P. R. (1977). Are women always less aggressive than men? A review of the experimental literature. *Psychological Bulletin, 84*(4), 634–660.

Frye, M. (1983). *The politics of reality: Essays in feminist theory.* Trumansburg, N.Y.: Crossing Press.

Garner, D. M.; Garfinkel, P. E.; Schwartz, D.; and Thompson, M. (1980). Cultural expectations of thinness in women. *Psychological Reports, 47,* 483–491.

Garner, D. M.; Olmstead, M. P.; and Polivy, J. (1983). Development and validation of a multidimensional eating disorder inventory for anorexia nervosa and bulimia. *International Journal of Eating Disorders, 2*(2), 15–34.

Gayford, J. (1975). Wife battering: A preliminary survey of 100 cases. *British Medical Journal, 1,* 194–197.

Gearhart, S. M. (1979). *The wanderground: Stories of the hill women.* Boston: Alyson Publications.

Gelles, R. J. (1989). Child abuse and violence in single-parent families: Parent absence and economic deprivation. *American Journal of Orthopsychiatry, 59*(4), 492–501.

Giarretto, H. (1976). The treatment of father-daughter incest. *Children Today, 4,* 2–5.

Gillespie, M. A. (1993, January/February). What's good for the race?: Solidarity speak still revolves around racism's impact on men. *Ms.,* pp. 80–81.

Gilligan, C. (1982). *In a different voice: Psychological theory and women's development.* Cambridge, Mass.: Harvard University Press.

Gilman, C. P. (1979). *Herland.* New York: Pantheon Books.

Gilroy, F., and Steinbacher, R. (1983). Preselection of child's sex: Technological utilization and feminism. *Psychological Reports, 53,* 671–676.

Glass, D. C.; Reim, B.; and Singer, J. E. (1971). Behavioral consequences of adaptation to controllable and uncontrollable noise. *Journal of Experimental Social Psychology, 7,* 244–257.

Glass, D. C.; Singer, J. E.; and Friedman, L. N. (1969). Psychic cost of adaptation to an environmental stressor. *Journal of Personality and Social Psychology, 12,* 200–210.

Goldberg, S. (1974). *The inevitability of patriarchy.* New York: William Morrow.

Goldman, J. A.; Smith, J.; and Keller, E. D. (1982). Sex-role preference in young children: What are we measuring? *The Journal of Genetic Psychology, 141,* 83–92.

Goodman, E. (1993, January 26). Gays and the military: What men fear. *The Cincinnati Post,* p. 7A.

Gordon, M. T., and Riger, S. (1989). *The female fear.* New York: Free Press.

Gough, K. (1975). The origin of the family. In R. Reiter, ed., *Toward an anthropology of women,* pp. 51–76. New York: Monthly Review Press.

Gould, L. (1972). X: A fabulous child's story. *Ms.,* pp. 74–76, 105–106.

Gove, W. R. (1973). Sex, marital status, and mortality. *American Journal of Sociology, 79*(1), 45–67.

Graham, D. L. R. (1987). Loving to survive: Men and women as hostages. Unpublished manuscript, University of Cincinnati, Cincinnati, Ohio.

Graham, D. L. R.; Foliano, J.; Latimer, D.; and Rawlings, E. I. (1990). Stockholm Syndrome in young women's dating relationships: A test of the validity of Stockholm Syndrome theory. Unpublished manuscript, University of Cincinnati, Cincinnati, Ohio.

Graham, D. L. R.; Ott, B.; and Rawlings, E. I. (1990). Stockholm Syndrome and battered women: A test of the validity of Graham's Stockholm Syndrome theory. Unpublished manuscript, University of Cincinnati, Cincinnati, Ohio.

Graham, D. L. R., and Rawlings, E. I. (1991). Bonding with abusive dating partners: Dynamics of Stockholm Syndrome. In B. Levy, ed., *Dating violence: Young women in danger*, pp. 119–135. Seattle: Seal Press.

Graham, D. L. R.; Rawlings, E. I.; Ihms, K.; Latimer, D.; Foliano, J., Thompson, A.; Suttman, K.; Farrington, M.; and Hacker, R. (1993). A scale for identifying Stockholm Syndrome in young women's dating relationships: Factor structure, reliability, and validity. Submitted manuscript.

Graham, D. L. R.; Rawlings, E. I.; and Rimini, N. (1988). Survivors of terror: Battered women, hostages, and the Stockholm Syndrome. In K. Yllo and M. Bograd, eds., *Feminist perspectives on wife abuse*, pp. 217–233. Beverly Hills, Calif.: Sage.

Grauerholz, E. (1987). Balancing the power in dating relationships. *Sex Roles, 17*(9/10), 563–571.

——— (1988). Altruistic other-orientation in intimate relationships. *Social Behavior and Personality, 16*(2), 127–131.

Grauerholz. E., and Koralewski, M. A. (1991). *Sexual coercion: A sourcebook on its nature, causes, and prevention*. Lexington, Mass.: Lexington Books.

Griffin, S. (1979). *Rape: The power of consciousness*. New York: Harper and Row.

Hacker, F. J. (1976). *Crusaders, criminals, crazies: Terror and terrorism in our time*. New York: Bantam.

Hacker, H. M. (1981). Women as a minority group. In S. Cox, ed., *Female psychology: The emerging self*, pp. 164–178. 2d ed. New York: St. Martin's Press. (Originally published in *Social Forces*, 1951, *30*, 6–69.)

Hall, J. A. (1987). On explaining gender differences: The case of nonverbal communication. In P. Shaver and C. Hendrick, eds., *Sex and gender*. Vol. 7, *Review of personality and social psychology*, pp. 177–200. Beverly Hills, Calif.: Sage.

Halmi, K. A.; Falk, J. R.; and Schwartz, E. (1981). Binge-eating and vomiting: A survey of a college population. *Psychological Medicine, 11*, 697–706.

Hampden-Turner, C. (1971). *The radical man*. Garden City, New York: Anchor Books.

Harlow, H., and Harlow, M. (1971). Psychopathology in monkeys. In H. D. Kimmel, ed., *Experimental psychopathology*, pp. 302–329. New York: Academic Press.

Harris, M. B. (1991). Effects of sex of aggressor, sex of target, and relationship on evaluations of physical aggression. *Journal of Interpersonal Violence, 6*(2), 174–186.

Hartmann, H. I. (1987). The family as the locus of gender, class, and political struggle: The example of housework. In S. Harding, ed., *Feminism and methodology*, pp. 109–134. Bloomington: Indiana University Press.

Hartup, W. W., and Zook, E. A. (1960). Sex-role preferences in three- and four-year-old children. *Journal of Consulting Psychology, 24*(5), 420–426.

Hawkins, R. C., and Clement, P. F. (1980). Development and construct validation of a self-report measure of binge eating tendencies. *Addictive Behaviors, 5*, 219–226.

Hearst, P. C., with Moscow, A. (1982). *Every secret thing*. New York: Pinnacle Books.

Heinrich, P., and Triebe, J. K. (1972). Sex preferences in children's human figure drawings. *Journal of Personality Assessment, 36*, 263–267.

Hendrick, C., and Hendrick, S. (1986). A theory and method of love. *Journal of Personality and Social Psychology, 50*(2), 392–402.

Hendrick, S. S.; Hendrick, C.; and Adler, N. L. (1988). Romantic relationships: Love, satisfaction, and staying together. *Journal of Personality and Social Psychology, 54*(6), 980–988.

Henley, N. M., and LaFrance, M. (1984). Gender as culture: Difference and dominance in nonverbal behavior. In A. Wolfgang, ed., *Nonverbal behavior: Perspectives, applications, intercultural insights*, pp. 351–371. Lewiston, New York: C. J. Hogrefe.

Herman, J. L. (1992). *Trauma and recovery: The aftermath of violence—from domestic abuse to political terror*. New York: Basic Books.

Herman, J., with Hirschman, L. (1977). Father-daughter incest. *Signs, 2*(4), 735–756.

——— (1981). *Father-daughter incest*. Cambridge, Mass.: Harvard University Press.

Herman, J. L., and van der Kolk, B. A. (1987). Traumatic antecedents of borderline personality disorder. In B. A. van der Kolk, ed., *Psychological trauma*, pp. 111–126. Washington, D.C.: American Psychiatric Press.

Hilberman, E., and Munson, K. (1977/78). Sixty battered women. *Victimology: An International Journal, 2*, 545–552.

Hill, E. (1985). *The family secret: A personal account of incest*. Santa Barbara, Calif.: Capra Press.

Hill, P., with Friend, D. (1986, April). The angriest hostage: Hijacked, he couldn't get even, so he got mad. *Life, 9*(4), 50–52, 54–55, 59, 61, 64.

Hite, S. (1987). *The Hite report: Women and love, a cultural revolution in progress*. New York: Knopf.

Hoagland, S. L. (1989). *Lesbian ethics*. 2d printing. Palo Alto, Calif.: Institute of Lesbian Studies.

Hochschild, A. R. (1983). *The managed heart: Commercialization of human feeling*. Berkeley: University of California Press.

Hodge, J. L. (1975). Domination and the will in Western thought and culture. In

J. L. Hodge, D. K. Struckmann, and L. D. Trost, eds., *Cultural bases of racism and group oppression*, pp. 8–48. Berkeley, Calif.: Two Riders Press.

Hodge, R., and Hodge, P. (1965). Occupational assimilation as a competitive process. *American Journal of Sociology, 71*, 249–264.

Horney, K. (1967). *Feminine psychology*. New York: W. W. Norton.

Howard, J. A.; Blumstein, P.; and Schwartz, P. (1986). Sex, power, and influence tactics in intimate relationships. *Journal of Personality and Social Psychology, 51*(1), 102–109.

Hudson, D. (1987). You can't commit violence against an object: Women, psychiatry and psychosurgery. In J. Hanmer and M. Maynard, eds., *Women, violence and social control*, 110–121. Atlantic Highlands, N.J.: Humanities Press International.

Hunter College Women's Studies Collective (1983). *Women's realities, women's choices: An introduction to women's stuudies*. New York: Oxford University Press.

Jack, D. C. (1991). *Silencing the self*. Cambridge, Mass.: Harvard University Press.

Jacobson, M. B. (1979). A rose by any other name: Attitudes toward feminism as a function of its label. *Sex Roles, 5*(3), 365–371.

Jaggar, A. (1983). *Feminist politics and human nature*. Totowa, N.J.: Rowman and Allanheld.

Janeway, E. (1980). *Powers of the weak*. New York: Knopf.

Janoff-Bulman, R. (1979). Characterological versus behavioral self-blame: Inquiries into depression and rape. *Journal of Personality and Social Psychology, 37*(10), 1798–1809.

Janoff-Bulman, R., and Frieze, I. H. (1983). A theoretical perspective for understanding reactions to victimization. *Journal of Social Issues, 39*(2), 1–17.

Jimenez, J., as told to Berkman, T. (1977). *My prisoner*. Kansas City: Sheed Andrews and McMeel.

Johnson, A. G. (1980). On the prevalence of rape in the United States. *Signs, 6*, 136–146.

Johnson, S. (1983). *From housewife to heretic*. Garden City, N.Y.: Anchor Books.

——— (1987). *Going out of our minds: The metaphysics of liberation*. Freedom, Calif.: Crossing Press.

——— (1989). *Wildfire: Igniting the she/volution*. Albuquerque, N.M.: Wildfire Books.

Jones, A. (1980). *Women who kill*. New York: Holt, Rinehart & Winston.

Jones, C., and Aronson, E. (1973). Attribution of fault to a rape victim as a function of respectability of the victim. *Journal of Personality and Social Psychology, 26*(3), 415–419.

Jordan, J. V.; Kaplan, A. G.; Miller, J. B.; Stiver, I. P.; and Surrey, J. L. (1991). *Women's growth in connection: Writings from the Stone Center*. New York: Guilford Press.

Judge faces recall (1983). In L. Richardson and V. Taylor, eds., *Feminist fron-*

tiers: Rethinking sex, gender, and society, p. 171. Reading, Mass.: Addison-Wesley. (Originally published in *Columbus-Citizen-Journal*, January 20, 1982.)

Kaschak, E. (1992). *Engendered lives: A new psychology of women's experience*. New York: Basic Books.

Katz, S., and Mazur, M. A. (1979). *Understanding the rape victim: A synthesis of research findings*. New York: John Wiley.

Ka-Tzetnik 135633 (1981). *House of dolls*. Granada: Mayflower.

Kelly, L. (1987). The continuum of sexual violence. In J. Hanmer and M. Maynard, eds., *Women, violence and social control*, 46–60. Atlantic Highlands, N.J.: Humanities Press International.

Kemp, R. S., and Kemp, C. H. (1978). *Child abuse*. Cambridge, Mass.: Harvard University Press.

Kenrick, D. T., and Cialdini, R. B. (1977). Romantic attraction: Misattribution versus reinforcement explanations. *Journal of Personality and Social Psychology, 35*(6), 381–391.

Kephart, W. M. (1967). Some correlates of romantic love. *Journal of Marriage and the Family, 29,* 470–474.

Kercher, G., and McShane, M. (1984). Characterizing child sexual abuse on the basis of a multi-agency sample. *Victimology: An International Journal, 9*(3/4), 364–382.

Kidder, L. H.; Boell, J. I.; and Moyer, M. M. (1983). Rights consciousness and victimization prevention: Personal defense and assertiveness training. *Journal of Social Issues, 39*(2), 155–170.

Kilpatrick, J. J. (1992, December 5). Whether to use "whether or not." *Cincinnati Enquirer*, p. A-10.

Kinsey, A. C.; Pomeroy, W. B.; Martin, C. E.; and Gebhard, P. H. (1953). *Sexual behavior in the human female*. Philadelphia: W. B. Saunders.

Kite, M. E. (1984). Sex differences in attitudes toward homosexuals: A meta-analytic review. *Journal of Homosexuality, 10,* 69–81.

Koff, E.; Rierdan, J.; and Stubbs, M. L. (1990). Gender, body image, and self-concept in early adolescence. *Journal of Early Adolescence, 10*(1), 56–68.

Korman, S. K. (1983). The feminist: Familial influences on adherence to ideology and commitment to a self-perception. *Family Relations, 32,* 431–439.

Kors, A. C., and Peters, E. (1972). *Witchcraft in Europe, 1100–1700: A Documentary History*. Philadelphia: University of Pennsylvania Press.

Koss, M. P.; Gidycz, C. A.; and Wisniewski, N. (1987). The scope of rape: Incidence and prevalence of sexual aggression and victimization in a national sample of higher education students. *Journal of Consulting and Clinical Psychology, 55*(2), 162–170.

Krishnan, V. (1987). Preferences for sex of children: A multivariate analysis. *Journal of Biosocial Science, 19*(3), 367–376.

Kuleshnyk, I. (1984). The Stockholm syndrome: Toward an understanding. *Social Action and the Law, 10*(2), 37–42.

Kurdek, L. A., and Schmitt, J. P. (1986). Interaction of sex role self-concept with relationship quality and relationship beliefs in married, heterosexual cohabiting, gay, and lesbian couples. *Journal of Personality and Social Psychology, 51*(2), 365–370.

Lang, D. (1974, November 25). A reporter at large: The bank drama. *The New Yorker*, pp. 56–126.

Largey, G. (1972). Sex control, sex preferences, and the future of the family. *Social Biology, 19,* 379–392.

Lefcourt, H. M. (1973). The function and the illusions of control and freedom. *American Psychologist, 28,* 417–425.

Leghorn, L., and Parker, K. (1981). *Women's worth: Sexual economics and the world of women.* Boston: Routledge and Kegan Paul.

Leidig, M. W. (1981). Violence against women: A feminist-psychological analysis. In S. Cox, ed., *Female psychology: The emerging self,* pp. 190–205. 2d ed. New York: St. Martin's Press.

Levin, J., and Fox, J. A. (1985). *Mass murder: America's growing menace.* New York: Plenum Press.

Levinson, R. M. (1975). Sex discrimination and employment practices: An experiment with unconventional job inquiries. *Social Problems, 22,* 533–542.

Lewis, A. F. (1992, September/October). Why winning won't be easy. *Ms.,* p. 85.

Lifton, R. J. (1961). *Thought reform and the psychology of totalism: A study of "brainwashing" in China.* New York: W. W. Norton.

Lipari, J. A. (1993). Borderline personality characteristics and parent-child relationships: A study of Stockholm Syndrome theory of Borderline Personality etiology. Ph.D. diss., University of Cincinnati, Cincinnati, Ohio.

Lipman-Blumen, J. (1984). *Gender roles and power.* Englewood Cliffs, N.J.: Prentice Hall.

Lo, W. A., and Sporakowski, M. J. (1989). The continuation of violent dating relationships among college students. *Journal of College Student Development, 30,* 432–439.

Lobel, K. (1986). *Naming the violence: Speaking out about lesbian battering.* Seattle: Seal Press.

Lorde, A. (1984). *Sister outsider: Essays and speeches.* New York: Crossing Press.

Love, B., and Shanklin, E. (1983). The answer is matriarchy. In J. Trebilcot, ed., *Mothering: Essays in feminist theory,* pp. 275–286. Totowa, N.J.: Rowman and Allanheld.

Lovelace, L., with McGrady, M. (1980). *Ordeal.* New York: Berkley Books.

Lucca, N., and Pacheco, A. M. (1986). Children's graffiti: Visual communication from a developmental perspective. *Journal of Genetic Psychology, 147*(4), 465–479.

McCann, B. S.; Woolfolk, R. L.; Lehrer, P. M.; and Schwarcz, L. (1987). Gender differences in the relationship between hostility and the Type A behavior pattern. *Journal of Personality Assessment, 51*(3), 355–366.

McCann, I. L.; Sakheim, D. K.; and Abrahamson, D. J. (1988). Trauma and victimization: A model of psychological adaptation. *The Counseling Psychologist, 16*(4), 531–594.

McClure, B. (1978). Hostage survival. *Conflict, 1*(1 and 2), 21–48.

Maccoby, E. E., and Jacklin, C. N. (1974). *The psychology of sex differences.* Stanford, Calif.: Stanford University Press.

McGoldrick, M.; Anderson, C. M.; and Walsh, F. (1989). Women in families and in family therapy. In M. McGoldrick, C. M. Anderson, and F. Walsh, eds., *Women in families: A framework for family therapy,* pp. 3–15. New York: W. W. Norton.

McIntyre, V. (1978). *Dreamsnake.* New York: Dell.

MacKinnon, C. A. (1979). *Sexual harassment of working women.* New Haven: Yale University Press.

——— (1983). Feminism, Marxism, method, and the state: Toward feminist jurisprudence. *Signs, 8*(4), 635–658.

——— (1987). *Feminism unmodified: Discourses on life and law.* Cambridge, Mass.: Harvard University Press.

McNeill, W. M. (1983). *The pursuit of power.* Oxford: Basil Blackwell.

McNulty, F. (1980). *The burning bed.* New York: Bantam.

Maisch, H. (1972). *Incest.* Trans. C. Bearne. New York: Stein and Day.

Major, B. (1987). Gender, justice, and the psychology of entitlement. In P. Shaver and C. Hendrick, eds., *Sex and gender.* Vol. 7, *Review of Personality and Social Psychology,* pp. 124–148. Beverly Hills, Calif.: Sage.

Major, B.; McFarlin, D. B.; and Gagnon, D. (1984). Overworked and underpaid: On the nature of gender differences in personal entitlement. *Journal of Personality and Social Psychology, 47*(6), 1399–1412.

Mann, C. R. (1990). Black female homicide in the United States. *Journal of International Violence, 5*(2), 176–201.

Mansbridge, J. J. (1985). Myth and reality: The ERA and the gender gap in the 1980 election. *Public Opinion Quarterly, 49,* 164–178.

Markle, G. E. (1974). Sex ratio at birth: Values, variance and some determinants. *Demography, 11,* 131–142.

Markle, G. E., and Nam, C. B. (1971). Sex predetermination: Its impact on fertility. *Social Biology, 18,* 73–82.

Martin, D. (1977). *Battered wives.* New York: Pocket Books.

Martin, P. Y., and Shanahan, K. A. (1983). Transcending the effects of sex composition in small groups. *Social Work with Groups, 6*(3–4), 19–32.

Martyna, W. (1983). Beyond the "He/Man" approach: The case for nonsexist language. In L. Richardson and V. Taylor, eds., *Feminist frontiers: Rethinking sex, gender, and society,* pp. 10–16. Reading, Mass.: Addison-Wesley.

Maslow, A. H. (1966). *The psychology of science*. South Bend, Ind.: Gateway Editions.

—— (1970). *Motivation and personality*. Rev. ed. New York: Harper and Row.

Matteson, R. L., and Terranova, G. (1977). Social acceptance of new techniques of child conception. *Journal of Social Psychology, 101,* 225–229.

Mayes, S. S. (1979). Women in positions of authority: A case study of changing sex roles. *Signs, 4,* 556–568.

Medea, A., and Thompson, K. (1974). *Against rape*. New York: Farrar, Straus & Giroux.

Merit Systems Protection Board (1981). *Sexual harassment in the federal workplace: Is it a problem?* Office of Merit Systems Review and Studies, Washington, D.C.: U.S. Government Printing Office.

Milgram, S. (1977, June 3–5). Comments. In R. D. Crelinsten, ed., *Dimensions of victimization in the context of terroristic acts,* pp. 61–66. Final report of proceedings, Evian, France.

Miller, D. T., and Porter, C. A. (1983). Self-blame in victims of violence. *Journal of Social Issues, 39*(2), 139–152.

Miller, J. B. (1976). *Toward a new psychology of women*. Boston: Beacon Press.

—— (1983). The construction of anger in women and men. *Work in Progress No. 4*. Wellesley College, Mass.: Stone Center Working Papers Series.

—— (1986). *Toward a new psychology of women*. 2d ed. Boston: Beacon Press.

—— (1991). The development of women's sense of self. In J. V. Jordan, A. G. Kaplan, J. B. Miller, I. P. Stiver, and J. L. Surrey, eds., *Women's growth in connection: Writings from the Stone Center,* pp. 11–26. New York: Guilford Press.

Mills, J. (1979). *Six years with God: Life inside Reverend Jim Jones's Peoples Temple*. New York: A & W Publishers.

Mills, T.; Rieker, P. P.; and Carmen, E. H. (1984). Hospitalization experiences of victims of abuse. *Victimology: An International Journal, 8*(3/4), 436–449.

Milner, J. S., and Robertson, K. R. (1990). Comparison of physical child abusers, intrafamilial sexual child abusers, and child neglecters. *Journal of Interpersonal Violence, 5*(1), 37–48.

Minnigerode, F. A. (1976). Attitudes toward homosexuality: Feminist attitudes and sexual conservatism. *Sex Roles, 2*(4), 347–352.

Mintz, L. B., and Betz, N. E. (1986). Sex differences in the nature, realism, and correlates of body image. *Sex Roles, 15*(3/4), 185–195.

Mitchell, J. (1974). *Psychoanalysis and feminism: Freud, Reich, Laing and women*. New York: Vintage Books.

Modleski, T. (1980). The disappearing act: A study of Harlequin Romances. *Signs, 5* (3), 435–448.

Monter, E. W. (1969). *European Witchcraft*. New York: John Wiley.

Moorehead, C. (1980). *Hostages to fortune: A study of kidnapping in the world today*. New York: Atheneum.

Morgan, R. (1989). The demon lover. *Ms.*, *17*(9), 68–72.

—— (1992, September/October). Take back the choice. *Ms.*, p. 1.

Naber-Morris, A. (1990). Stockholm Syndrome in adult abused children: A scale validation project. Ph.D. diss., University of Cincinnati, Cincinnati, Ohio.

Nadler, E. B., and Morrow, W. R. (1959). Authoritarian attitudes toward women, and their correlates. *The Journal of Social Psychology*, *49*, 113–123.

National Organization for Women (1982). *NOW guidelines for feminist consciousness-raising*. Washington, D.C.: National Organization for Women.

Nguyen, D. Q. (1993). Authoritarianism and sex-role identification: Their implications for the conceptualization of emotion and cognition. Master's thesis, University of Cincinnati, Cincinnati, Ohio.

Nolen-Hoeksema, S. (1987). Sex differences in unipolar depression: Evidence and theory. *Psychological Bulletin*, *101*(2), 259–282.

Norwood, R. (1985). *Women who love too much: When you keep wishing and hoping he'll change*. New York: Pocket Books.

Oakley, A. (1974). *Woman's work: The housewife, past and present*. New York: Vintage Books.

Ochberg, F. (1977, June 3–5). The victim of terrorism—Psychiatric considerations. In R. D. Crelinsten, ed., *Dimensions of victimization in the context of terroristic acts*, pp. 3–35. Final report of proceedings, Evian, France.

—— (1982). A case study: Gerard Vaders. In F. M. Ochberg and D. A. Soskis, eds., *Victims of terrorism*, pp. 9–35. Boulder, Colo.: Westview Press.

O'Keeffe, N. K.; Brockopp, K.; and Chew, E. (1986, November–December). Teen dating violence. *Social Work*, *31*, 465–468.

Okun, L. (1986). *Woman abuse: Facts replacing myths*. New York: State University of New York Press.

Oskamp, S. (1989). The editor's page. *Journal of Social Issues*, *45*(4), iii–iv.

Overmier, J. B., and Seligman, M.E.P. (1967). Effects of inescapable shock upon subsequent escape and avoidance responding. *Journal of Comparative and Physiological Psychology*, *63*, 28–33.

Pagelow, M. (1981). *Woman battering: Victims and their experience*. Beverly Hills, Calif.: Sage.

Parlee, M. B. (1983). Conversational politics. In L. Richardson and V. Taylor, eds., *Feminist frontiers: Rethinking sex, gender, and society*, pp. 7–10. Reading, Mass.: Addison-Wesley.

Peters, J. (in press). *Treatment for abused women*. Columbus, Ind.: Quinco Behavioral Health Systems.

Pheterson, G. (1986). Alliances between women: Overcoming internalized oppression and internalized domination. *Signs*, *12*, 146–161.

Philbrick, J. L.; Thomas, F. F.; Cretser, G. A.; and Leon, J. J. (1988). Sex differences in love attitudes of black university students. *Psychological Reports*, *62*, 414.

Piercy, M. (1976). *Woman on the edge of time.* New York: Fawcett Crest.

——— (1982). A just anger. In *Circles on the water: Selected poems,* p. 88. New York: Knopf.

Polk, B. (1976). Male power and the women's movement. In S. Cox, ed., *Female psychology: The emerging self,* pp. 400–413. 2d ed. New York: St. Martin's Press.

Pride, A. (1981). To respectability and back: A ten year view of the anti-rape movement. In F. Delacoste and F. Newman, eds., *Fight back! Feminist resistance to male violence,* pp. 114–119. Minneapolis: Cleis Press.

Rabban, M. (1950). Sex-role identification in young children in two diverse social groups. *Genetic Psychology Monographs, 42*(1), 81–158.

Rabinowitz, D. (1977, June). The hostage mentality. *Commentary, 63,* 70–72.

Rajecki, D. W.; Lamb, M. E.; and Obmascher, P. (1978). Toward a general theory of infantile attachment: A comparative review of aspects of the social bond. *The Behavioral and Brain Sciences, 3,* 417–464.

Rawlings, E. I., and Carter, D. K. (1977). *Psychotherapy for women: Treatment toward equality.* Springfield, Ill.: Charles C. Thomas.

Reingold, A. (1987, April). Penthouse interview: Andrea Dworkin. *Penthouse, 18*(8), 50–52, 56, 70, 72.

Rent, C. S., and Rent, G. S. (1977). More on offspring sex-preference: A comment on Nancy E. Williamson's "Sex preference, sex control, and the status of women." *Signs: Journal of Women in Culture and Society, 3,* 505–515.

Renzetti, C. M. (1992). *Violent betrayal: Partner abuse in lesbian relationships.* Newbury Park, Calif.: Sage.

Rich, A. (1980). Compulsory heterosexuality and lesbian existence. *Signs, 5*(4), 631–660.

Richardson, L. (1983). No, thank you! A discourse on etiquette. In L. Richardson and V. Taylor, eds., *Feminist frontiers: Rethinking sex, gender, and society,* pp. 5–7. Reading, Mass.: Addison-Wesley.

Richter, C. P. (1959). The phenomenon of unexplained sudden death in animals and man. In H. Feifel, ed., *The meaning of death,* pp. 302–313. New York: McGraw-Hill.

Rickett, A., and Rickett, A. (1973). *Prisoners of liberation: Four years in a Chinese Communist prison.* Garden City, N.Y.: Anchor Books.

Rigney, Father H. (1956). *Four years in a Red hell: The story of Father Rigney.* Chicago: Henry Regnery Co.

Robins, L. N.; Helzer, J. E.; Weissman, M. M.; Orvaschel, H.; Gruenberg, E.; Burke, J. D.; and Regier, D. A. (1984). Lifetime prevalence of specific psychiatric disorders in three sites. *Archives of General Psychiatry, 41,* 949–958.

Robins, P. M., and Sesan, R. (1991). Munchausen syndrome by proxy: Another women's disorder? *Professional Psychology: Research and Practice, 22*(4), 285–290.

Rogers, T. (1993, February 27). Men organizing to fight male violence against women. *The Cincinnati Post,* p. 1C.

Rose, S. (1985). Is romance dysfunctional? *International Journal of Women's Studies*, 8(3), 250–265.

Rosen, B., and Jerdee, T. H. (1974a). Effects of applicants' sex and difficulty of job on evaluations of candidates for managerial positions. *Journal of Applied Psychology, 59,* 511–512.

—— (1974b). Influence of sex role stereotypes in personnel decisions. *Journal of Applied Psychology, 59,* 9–14.

Rosen, B.; Jerdee, T. H.; and Prestwich, T. L. (1975). Dual-career marital adjustment: Potential effects of discriminatory managerial attitudes. *Journal of Marriage and the Family, 37,* 565–572.

Rossi, P. H. (1990). The old homeless and the new homelessness in historical perspective. *American Psychologist, 45*(8), 954–959.

Rotella, E. J. (1990). Women and the American Economy. In S. Ruth, ed., *Issues in Feminism: An Introduction to Women's Studies*, pp. 298–311. Mountain View, Calif.: Mayfield.

Rounsaville, B., and Weissman, M. (1977). Battered women: A medical problem requiring detection. *International Journal of Psychology, 8,* 191–202.

Rowland, R. (1984). *Women who do and women who don't join the women's movement.* Boston: Routledge and Kegan Paul.

—— (1986). Women who do and women who don't, join the women's movement: Issues for conflict and collaboration. *Sex Roles, 14*(11/12), 679–692.

Rubin, Z. (1970). Measurement of romantic love. *Journal of Personality and Social Psychology, 16,* 265–273.

Ruggiero, J. A., and Weston, L. C. (1983). Conflicting images of women in romance novels. *International Journal of Women's Studies, 6*(3), 18–25.

Rukeyser, M. (1968). Käthe Kollwitz. In *The speed of darkness*, pp. 99–105. New York: Random House.

Rule, A. (1980). *The stranger beside me.* New York: Signet.

Russ, J. (1980a). Amor vincit foeminam: The battle of the sexes in science fiction. *Science-Fiction Studies, 7,* 2–15.

—— (1980b). Dear colleague: I am not an honorary male. In G. Kaufman and M. K. Blakely, eds., *Pulling our own strings: Feminist humor and satire*, pp. 179–183. Bloomington: Indiana Univeristy Press.

Russell, D.E.H. (1982). *Rape in Marriage.* New York: Macmillan.

—— (1984). *Sexual exploitation: Rape, child sexual abuse, and workplace harassment.* Beverly Hills, Calif.: Sage.

—— (1986). *The secret trauma: Incest in the lives of girls and women.* New York: Basic Books.

Russo, N. F. (1990). Overview: Forging research priorities for women's mental health. *American Psychologist, 45*(3), 368–373.

Sackett, G.; Griffin, G. A.; Pratt, C.; Joslyn, W. D.; and Ruppenthal, G. (1967). Mother-infant and adult female choice behavior in Rhesus monkeys after various rearing experiences. *Journal of Comparative and Physiological Psychology, 63*(3), 376–381.

St. Claire, L. (1989). When is gender a handicap? Towards conceptualizing the socially constructed disadvantages experienced by women. In S. Skevington and D. Baker, eds., *The social identity of women,* pp. 130–151. Newbury Park, Calif.: Sage.

Sattel, J. W. (1989). Men, inexpressiveness, and power. In L. Richardson and V. Taylor, eds., *Feminist frontiers II: Rethinking sex, gender, and society,* pp. 270–274. New York: Random House.

Schachter, S. (1959). *The psychology of affiliation: Experimental studies of the sources of gregariousness.* Stanford, Calif.: Stanford University Press.

Schachter, S., and Singer, J. E. (1962). Cognitive, social and physiological components of the emotional state. *Psychological Review, 69,* 379–399.

Schechter, S. (1981). The future of the battered women's movement. In F. Delacoste and F. Newman, eds., *Fight back! Feminist resistance to male violence.,* 93–103. Minneapolis: Cleis Press.

——— (1982). *Women and male violence: The visions and struggles of the battered women's movement.* Boston: South End Press.

Schein, E. H., with Schneier, I., and Barker, C. H. (1961). *Coercive persuasion: A socio-psychological analysis of the "brainwashing" of American civilian prisoners by the Chinese Communists.* New York: W. W. Norton.

Scheppele, K. L., and Bart, P. B. (1983). Through women's eyes: Defining danger in the wake of sexual assault. *Journal of Social Issues, 39*(2), 63–81.

Schlafly, P. (1977). *The power of the Positive Woman.* New York: Arlington House Press.

Schlesinger, R. A. (1988). Grannybashing. In B. Schlesinger and R. Schlesinger, eds., *Abuse of the elderly: Issues and annotated bibliography,* pp. 3–11. Buffalo, N.Y.: University of Toronto Press.

Schuler, M. (1992). *Freedom from violence: Women's strategies from around the world.* New York: O.E.F. International, U.N. Development Fund for Women.

Schulman, R. G.; Kinder, B. N.; Powers, P. S.; Prange, M.; and Gleghorn, A. (1986). The development of a scale to measure cognitive distortions in bulimia. *Journal of Personality Assessment, 50*(4), 630–639.

Scott, J. P. (1963). The process of primary socialization in canine and human infants. *Monographs of the Society for Research in Child Development, 28*(1), 1–47.

Seay, B.; Alexander, B. K.; and Harlow, H. F. (1964). Maternal behavior of socially deprived Rhesus monkeys. *Journal of Abnormal and Social Psychology, 69*(4), 345–354.

Shapiro, R. Y., and Mahajan, H. (1986). Gender differences in policy preferences: A summary of trends from the 1960s to the 1980s. *Public Opinion Quarterly, 50,* 42–61.

Shaver, K. G. (1970). Defensive attribution: Effects of severity and relevance on the responsibility assigned for an accident. *Journal of Personality and Social Psychology, 14*(2), 101–113.

Shuntich, R. J., and Shapiro, R. M. (1991). Explorations of verbal affection and aggression. *Journal of Social Behavior and Personality, 6*(2), 283–300.

Silver, R. L.; Boon, C.; and Stones, M. H. (1983). Searching for meaning in misfortune: Making sense of incest. *Journal of Social Issues, 39*(2), 81–101.

Silverman, R. A., and Kennedy, L. W. (1988). Women who kill their children. *Violence and Victims, 3*(2), 113–127.

Silverstein, B.; Perdue, L.; Peterson, B.; and Kelly, E. (1986). The role of the mass media in promoting a thin standard of bodily attractiveness for women. *Sex Roles, 14*(9/10), 519–532.

Smith, K. C.; Ulch, E. E.; Cameron, J. A.; Musgrave, M. A.; and Tremblay, N. (1989). Gender-related effects in the perception of anger expression. *Sex Roles, 20*(9/10), 487–499.

Smith, M. D. (1988). Women's fear of violent crime: An exploratory test of a feminist hypothesis. *Journal of Family Violence, 3*(1), 29–38.

Smith, M. D., and Self, G. D. (1981). Feminists and traditionalists: An attitudinal comparison. *Sex Roles, 7*(2), 183–188.

Smith, T. W. (1984). The polls: Gender and attitudes toward violence. *Public Opinion Quarterly, 48,* 384–396.

Smith, W. E. (1985, December 9). Massacre in Malta. *Time,* pp. 42–44.

Smolowe, J. (1993, April 5). Sex with a scorecard. *Time,* p. 41.

Snodgrass, S. E. (1985). Women's intuition: The effect of subordinate role on interpersonal sensitivity. *Journal of Personality and Social Psychology, 49*(1), 146–155.

Snyder, D., and Hudis, P. (1976). Occupational income and the effects of minority competition and segregation. *American Sociological Review, 41,* 209–234.

Soskis, D. A., and Ochberg, F. M. (1982). Concepts of terrorist victimization. In F. M. Ochberg and D. A. Soskis, eds., *Victims of terrorism,* pp. 105–135. Boulder, Colo.: Westview Press.

Spender, D. (1982). *Women of ideas and what men have done to them: From Aphra Behn to Adrienne Rich.* Boston: Routledge and Kegan Paul.

Sprecher, S. (1985). Sex differences in bases of power in dating relationships. *Sex Roles, 12*(3/4), 449–462.

Starhawk (1982). *Dreaming the dark: Magic, sex and politics.* Boston: Beacon Press.

Stark, L. P. (1991). Traditional gender role beliefs and individual outcomes: An exploratory analysis. *Sex Roles, 24*(9/10), 639–650.

Starkey, J. L. (1991). Wives' earnings and marital instability: Another look at the independence effect. *The Social Science Journal, 28*(4), 501–521.

Staub, E.; Tursky, B.; and Schwartz, G. E. (1971). Self-control and predictability: Their effects on reactions to aversive stimulation. *Journal of Personality and Social Psychology, 18,* 157–162.

Steinem, G. (1992, November/December). Helping ourselves to revolution. *Ms.*, pp. 24–29.

Stiver, I. P. (1991). Beyond the Oedipal Complex: Mothers and daughters. In J. V. Jordan, A. G. Kaplan, J. B. Miller, I. P. Stiver, and J. L. Surrey, *Women's growth in connection: Writings from the Stone Center,* 97–121. New York: Guilford Press.

Straus, M. A.; Gelles, R. J.; and Steinmetz, S. K. (1980). *Behind closed doors: Violence in the American family.* New York: Doubleday/Anchor.

Strentz, T. (1980). The Stockholm Syndrome: Law enforcement policy and ego defenses of the hostage. *Annals of the New York Academy of Sciences, 347,* 137–150.

——— (1982). The Stockholm Syndrome: Law enforcement policy and hostage behavior. In F. M. Ochberg and D. A. Soskis, eds., *Victims of terrorism,* pp. 149–163. Boulder, Colo.: Westview Press.

Stringer, D. M. (1986, March 9). The Brownmiller legacy: A 10-year evaluation of unexplored issues in women and violence. A model for understanding male response to female efforts to change violence against women. Annual Conference of the Association for Women in Psychology, Oakland, Calif.

Sugarman, D. B., and Hotaling, G. T. (1989). Dating violence: Prevalence, context, and risk markers. In M. A. Pirog-Good and J. E. Stets, eds., *Violence in Dating Relationships: Emerging Social Issues,* pp. 3–32. New York: Praeger.

Swift, C. F. (1987). Women and violence: Breaking the connection. *Work in Progress No. 27.* Wellesley College, Mass.: Stone Center Working Papers Series.

Symonds, M. (1982). Victim responses to terror: Understanding and treatment. In F. M. Ochberg and D. A. Soskis, eds., *Victims of terrorism,* pp. 95–103. Boulder, Colo.: Westview Press.

Tannen, D. (1990). Gender differences in topical coherence: Creating involvement in best friends' talk. *Discourse Processes, 13,* 73–90.

Taylor, S. E.; Wood, J. V.; and Lichtman, R. R. (1983). It could be worse: Selective evaluation as a response to victimization. *Journal of Social Issues, 37*(2), 19–40.

Teitelbaum, M. S. (1970). Factors affecting the sex ratios in large populations. *Journal of Biosocial Science,* supp. 2, 61–71.

Thorne, B. (1986). Girls and boys together . . . but mostly apart: Gender arrangements in elementary schools. In W. Hartup and Z. Rubin, eds., *Relationships and development,* pp. 167–184. Hillsdale, N.J.: Lawrence Erlbaum.

Thornton, B.; Ryckman, R. M.; Kirchner, G.; Jacobs, J.; et al. (1988). Reaction to self-attributed victim responsibility: A comparative analysis of rape crisis counselors and lay observers. *Journal of Applied Social Psychology, 18*(5), 409–422.

Times Mirror Center for the People and the Press (1990, September 19). *The people, the press, and politics 1990: A Times Mirror political typology.* Washington, D.C.: Times Mirror Center for the People and the Press.

Tiptree, J. (1975). The women men don't see. In *Warm worlds and otherwise,* pp. 131–164. New York: Ballantine.

—— (1978). Houston, Houston, do you read? In *Star songs of an old primate,* pp. 164–226. New York: Ballantine.

Tormes, Y. (1968). *Child victims of incest.* Denver, Colo.: American Humane Society.

Trost, C. (1992, October 13). Checkoff. *Wall Street Journal,* p. A-1 (Midwest edition).

Turner, J. T. (1985). Factors influencing the development of the Hostage Identification Syndrome. *Political Psychology, 6*(4), 705–711.

—— (1990). Preparing individuals at risk for victimization as hostages. In E. Viano, ed., *The victimology handbook: Research findings, treatment and public policy,* pp. 217–226. New York: Garland Publishing.

Ventimiglia, J. C. (1982). Sex roles and chivalry: Some conditions of gratitude to altruism. *Sex Roles 8*(11), 1107–1122.

von Baeyer, C. L.; Sherk, D. L.; and Zanna, M. P. (1981). Impression management in the job interview: When the female applicant meets the male (chauvinist) interviewer. *Personality and Social Psychology Bulletin, 7*(1), 45–51.

Waisberg, J., and Page, S. (1988). Gender role nonconformity and perception of mental illness. *Women and Health, 14*(1), 3–16.

Walker, L. (1979). *The battered woman.* New York: Harper and Row.

—— (1984). *The battered woman syndrome.* New York: Springer.

Walker, R. (1992). Becoming the third wave. In R. Chrisman and R. L. Allen, eds., *Court of appeal: The Black community speaks out on the racial and sexual politics of Thomas vs. Hill,* pp. 211–214. New York: Ballantine.

Walstedt, J. J. (1977). The altruistic other orientation: An exploration of female powerlessness. *Psychology of Women Quarterly, 2*(2), 162–176.

Walster, E. (1966). Assignment of responsibility for an accident. *Journal of Personality and Social Psychology, 3*(1), 73–79.

—— (1971). Passionate love. In B. I. Murstein, ed., *Theories of Attraction and Love,* pp. 85–99. New York: Springer.

Walster, E., and Berscheid, E. (1971, June). Adrenaline makes the heart grow fonder. *Psychology Today, 5,* 46–50, 62.

Ward, W. D. (1973). Patterns of culturally defined sex-role preference and parental imitation. *The Journal of Genetic Psychology, 122,* 337–343.

Watson, R., with Nordland, R.; Stanger, T.; Walcott, J.; Warner, M. G.; and Kubic, M. J. (1985, July 8). The hard road to freedom. *Newsweek,* pp. 17–20.

Weiss, J. M. (1971). Effects of coping behavior in different warning signal conditions on stress pathology in rats. *Journal of Comparative and Physiological Psychology, 1,* 1–14.

Weissman, M. M., and Klerman, G. L. (1977). Sex differences and the epidemiology of depression. *Archives of General Psychiatry, 34,* 98–111.

Weitz, S. (1976). Sex differences in nonverbal communication. *Sex Roles, 2,* 175–184.

Weitzman, L. J. (1985). *The divorce revolution: The unexpected social and economic consequences for women and children in America.* New York: Free Press.

Wesselius, C. L., and DeSarno, J. V. (1983). The anatomy of a hostage situation. *Behavioral Sciences and the Law, 1*(2), 33–45.

Westen, D.; Ludolph, P.; Misle, B.; Ruffins, S.; and Block, J. (1990). Physical and sexual abuse in adolescent girls with borderline personality disorder. *American Journal of Orthopsychiatry, 60*(1), 55–66.

Westoff, C. F., and Rindfuss, R. R. (1974). Sex selection in the United States: Some implications. *Science, 184*(4137), 633–636.

Wheeler, L.; Reis, H.; and Nezlek, J. (1983). Loneliness, social interaction, and sex roles. *Journal of Personality and Social Psychology, 45*(4), 943–953.

Williams, S. R., and Williams, P. J. (1978). *Riding the nightmare.* New York: McClelland and Stewart, Ltd.

Williamson, N. E. (1976). *Sons or daughters: A cross-cultural survey of parental preferences.* Beverly Hills, Calif.: Sage.

Wittig, M. (1971). *Les guérillères.* Trans. D. Le Vay. Boston: Beacon Press.

Woll, S. B. (1989). Personality and relationship correlates of loving styles. *Journal of Research in Personality, 23,* 480–505.

Wood, C. H., and Bean, F. D. (1977). Offspring gender and family size: Implications from a comparison of Mexican and Anglo-Americans. *Journal of Marriage and the Family, 39,* 129–139.

Woods, W. (1974). *A casebook of witchcraft.* New York: G. P. Putnam's Sons.

Wortman, C. B. (1976). Causal attributions and personal control. In J. H. Harvey, W. J. Ickes, and R. F. Kidd, eds., *New directions in attribution research,* pp. 23–52, Vol. 1. Hillsdale, N.J.: Lawrence Erlbaum.

Yee, M. S., and Layton, T. N. (1981). *In my father's house: The story of the Layton family and the Reverend Jim Jones.* New York: Berkley Books.

Young, G. H., and Gerson, S. (1991). New psychoanalytic perspectives on masochism and spouse abuse. *Psychotherapy, 28*(1), 30–38.

Young, V. D. (1979). Victims of female offenders. In W. H. Parsonage, eds., *Perspectives on victimology,* 72–87. Beverly Hills, Calif.: Sage.

Zanna, M. P., and Pack, S. J. (1975). On the self-fulfilling nature of apparent sex differences in behavior. *Journal of Experimental Social Psychology, 11,* 583–591.

Zipp, J. F., and Plutzer, E. (1985). Gender differences in voting for female candidates: Evidence from the 1982 election. *Public Opinion Quarterly, 49,* 179–197.

Index